PSYCHOLOGY AT IOWA:
Centennial Essays

PSYCHOLOGY AT IOWA:
Centennial Essays

Edited by
JOAN H. CANTOR
University of Iowa

LAWRENCE ERLBAUM ASSOCIATES, PUBLISHERS
1991   Hillsdale, New Jersey   Hove and London

Lawrence Erlbaum Associates, Inc., Publishers
365 Broadway
Hillsdale, New Jersey 07642

Library of Congress Cataloging in Publication Data

Psychology at Iowa : centennial essays / edited by Joan H. Cantor.
p.   cm.
Includes bibliographical references and indexes.
ISBN 0-8058-0761-6
1. University of Iowa. Dept. of Psychology—History.
2. Psychology—Study and teaching (Higher)—Iowa—History.
3. Psychology—Iowa—History.   I. Cantor, Joan H.
BF80.7.U62I685   1991
150′.71′1777655—dc20   91-7920
                                                                          CIP

Printed in the United States of America
10 9 8 7 6 5 4 3 2 1

Contents

Preface

This volume is an outgrowth of and indeed the final chapter of the Centennial Celebration of the birth of psychology at the University of Iowa. On October 20–22 in 1988, the Department of Psychology hosted a grand event in celebration of the teaching of the first psychology courses at Iowa in the Fall of 1887 by George T. W. Patrick, newly arrived Professor of Mental and Moral Science and Didactics. Professor Patrick immediately began teaching Elementary Psychology and Experimental Psychology (with laboratory) among the seven (!) different courses he offered during his first year. He also began the development of one of the very earliest psychological laboratories in the United States.

The Centennial Celebration was attended by several hundred alumni and former faculty members of the Department of Psychology and the Institute of Child Behavior and Development (formerly the Iowa Child Welfare Research Station), regional and local faculty members and students, members of the Iowa Psychological Association and the Iowa School Psychologists Association, and many friends. The celebration was a joyous 3-day affair consisting of a mixture of serious scholarship, thought-provoking discussions, reminiscences, renewal of old friendships, and lots of laughter. Many of our distinguished alumni and former faculty members gave talks and participated in discussion panels. The speakers presented their views of the history of Iowa psychology in the context of retrospective and prospective views of their own areas. The discussion panels, representing each of the more recent decades in our history, described the major issues of their day and recounted unforgettable happenings and personalities.

It will be evident to the reader that many of the papers presented herein are based on the talks given at the celebration. I hope that the reader will not only learn the facts about Iowa's long and distinguished history of contributions to psychology, child development, and speech pathology, but will also acquire a strong sense of the "Iowa Tradition," so eloquently described in Howard Kendler's chapter. Because there is bound to be a strong historical perspective in such occasions and thus also in this volume, it is especially important to point out that this tradition is alive and well. Although the current Iowa faculty did not participate in the Centennial program, except in their role as hosts, they are vigorously continuing the Iowa tradition and providing leadership in many diverse areas, indeed in all the nooks and crannies of our field. Thus, it is my hope that in these pages, we have not only captured the spirit of the celebration itself, but also the spirit of a long and proud tradition of Iowa psychology that will continue to flourish long into the future.

Joan H. Cantor

All royalty rights of the authors and editor of this volume have been contributed to the Department of Psychology through the University of Iowa Foundation.

PSYCHOLOGY AT IOWA:
Centennial Essays

1 The Iowa Tradition

Howard H. Kendler
University of California, Santa Barbara

The Psychology Laboratory of the University of Iowa was started in 1887 and dedicated in 1890. Like the six American laboratories that preceded it and those that followed, the Iowa laboratory was an expression of a specific historical event and a general philosophical idea. The event, of course, was the founding by Wilhelm Wundt of the Psychology Laboratory at the University of Leipzig, which has been assigned the date of 1879. The philosophical idea, expressed in a variety of ways by numerous philosophers and scientists, was that if the methods of natural science could be applied to psychology, a level of understanding of the human mind and human action would be achieved that would approach our comprehension of physical, chemical, and biological phenomena. Such an achievement, it was widely thought, would work to the betterment of humankind.

Although all the early American laboratories share this common ancestry, they, like siblings of common parents, differ and assume distinctive personalities, in spite of obvious family resemblances. University policies, faculty appointments, social and intellectual atmospheres, and sometimes unanticipated events, all shape the character of a particular department of psychology. To understand the fundamental character of the Department of Psychology at the University of Iowa, it will prove necessary to first survey its history, then attempt to abstract the ideas that guided its development, and finally to critically evaluate its tradition in light of the historical growth of psychology.

A HISTORICAL SURVEY

The First Stage: The Founding
of the Psychology Laboratory

The psychology laboratory at the University of Iowa owes its birth to the efforts of George T. W. Patrick (1857–1949), a graduate of the University of Iowa, who received his doctorate at John Hopkins University under G. Stanley Hall, who had previously studied both with Wundt and William James. Professor Patrick bore little resemblance to modern day psychologists; his academic title was Professor of Mental and Moral Sciences and Didactics, and his annual salary was $1,800. On the most basic level, Patrick was a philosopher who had a side interest in psychology, including a desire to establish a psychology laboratory at Iowa similar to the one created at John Hopkins University in 1883. He was successful in this project, and by so doing he completed the first stage of development of psychology at the University of Iowa—the establishment of psychology as an independent scientific discipline. But Patrick, to his credit, realized that by interest and training he was ill-equipped to guide Iowa psychology beyond its creation. A real psychologist was needed, and to his great credit Patrick chose Carl E. Seashore (1866–1949) to lead Iowa psychology into the future.

The Second Stage: The Establishment of a Vigorous
Department of Psychology

Carl Seashore had obtained his doctorate at Yale in 1895. His subsequent distinguished career reflected two important ideas to which he was exposed at Yale: a functionalist approach to psychology and a tough-minded natural science conception of psychology. The functionalist attitude was acquired from George Trumball Ladd (1842–1921), a graduate of a theological seminary and an active minister for a decade before embarking on an academic career. He was the author of the influential book *Elements of Physiological Psychology* (Ladd, 1887) and several other texts that expounded on the relationship between the nervous system and mental phenomena. Ladd, who started an "informal laboratory" (Boring, 1950) conceptualized the mind as a useful organ. One does not hear much of Ladd these days because his prose was dreary, especially when compared with that of William James, and his systematic enunciation of a functionalist position failed to match the clarity of the Chicago School of Functionalism (Kendler, 1987). One reason for this lack of clarity was that Ladd, because of his theological commitments, assigned teleology a central role in his brand of functionalism.

More important to Seashore's career was the influence of his PhD mentor, Edward W. Scripture (1864–1945), a student of Wundt, who was responsible for establishing a well-equipped laboratory at Yale in 1892. Scripture, an opponent of "armchair psychology," a term he coined (Scripture, 1897), advocated a tough-minded view of psychology that used rigorous experimental methods and advanced technological equipment, with the goal of making psychology as accurate as physics. Facts, facts, and more facts were his primary concern, even those that fell beyond the boundaries of traditional experimental psychology such as the reaction times of different clinical diagnostic groups (Scripture, 1916).

Carl Seashore came to Iowa with ambitions that reflected the empirical rigorousness of Scripture and the aspirations of Patrick to develop a topnotch department of psychology. Seashore succeeded. Although the laboratory was devoted "primarily to fundamental research, contributing directly or indirectly to psychology as a pure science" (Seashore, 1930, p. 14), Seashore also held the view that psychology should offer solutions to society's problems. This ideal was met by training programs and research in the psychology of speech and hearing, child psychology, clinical psychology, psychological testing, and last, but not least, in various aspects of Seashore's passion, the psychology of music. Seashore's efforts were instrumental in establishing in 1917 the Child Welfare Research Station, which was formed with the social goal of providing the people of Iowa with information that would assist them in developing their greatest resource: their children.

Seashore, both as a scientist and administrator, was responsible for executing the transition of psychology from the first stage of development—an independent discipline—to the second stage—an experimental science that would generate a body of knowledge that would both dignify psychology and yield information and techniques that would be socially useful. The essence of Iowa during its second stage of development is reflected in the dedication in 1930 of the Psychology Laboratory in its new location in East Hall, a remodeled hospital that previously had been part of the College of Medicine:

> Insight into the Nature of Mental Life, Appreciation of its Beauty, and Wisdom in its Control.
> Development of Personality, Scientific Integrity, and the Art of Deliberate and Adequate Statement of Fact.
> Center for Fundamental Science and Service of Mankind. Memorial to the Pioneers in Psychology. Hearth for Comrades in Research.
> To These Ends this Laboratory is Solemnly Dedicated for the Commonwealth of Iowa.

Carl Seashore retired as Head of the Department of Psychology, as well as from the Deanship of the Graduate School in 1936 and a year later Lee E. Travis (1896–1987), an important researcher and clinician in the field of speech pathology, was officially appointed the Head of the Department of Psychology. A sequence of unanticipated events followed that altered the course of psychology at Iowa. A scandal, not matching the magnitude and impact of the one involving John B. Watson, but nevertheless occurring in the same ballpark, led to the appointment of the distinguished developmental psychologist and later university administrator, George D. Stoddard (1897–1981), as Acting Head of the Department of Psychology (1938–1939), in addition to his duties as Director of the Child Welfare Research Station and Dean of the Graduate School. Stoddard was also an active participant, with several of his colleagues (most notably Beth Wellman), in the famous controversy with Stanford psychologists Lewis Terman and Quinn McNemar about environmental and genetic influences on IQ scores, a debate that is still worthy of careful examination (e.g, Stoddard & Wellman, 1940).

During Stoddard's brief tenure, Dewey B. Stuit (born 1909), a specialist in aptitude testing, who later played the role of guardian of psychology as the Dean of the College of Liberal Arts, James B. Stroud (born 1897), an educational psychologist, and Kenneth W. Spence (1907–1967), who did much to create the Iowa tradition, were appointed as associate professors.

The Third Stage: Ambitious Theorizing

The appointment of John A. McGeoch as Head of the Department of Psychology in 1939 laid the foundation for the third stage of psychology at Iowa, in which the dream to emulate the natural sciences in terms of a body of reliable knowledge as well as theoretical sophistication flourished. Although McGeoch never expressed such an optimistic vision, he represented a tradition in psychology that was oriented in that direction. McGeoch took his doctorate with Harvey Carr, the most experimentally productive of the Dewey–Angell–Carr trinity that played a primary role in directing American psychology toward Functionalism. Carr, whose important ideas are frequently overlooked, was concerned with theory as an instrument of research: "Theories represent partial solutions of scientific problems and thus constitute a point of departure for further investigations" (Carr, 1925, p. 204). McGeoch shared this instrumental viewpoint and encouraged a debate at Iowa about the appropriate strategy for theory construction. Opposed to McGeoch's conservative instrumental stance was the view expressed by Kenneth Spence that theory was not merely a means by which some research goal could be achieved but instead was the ultimate goal of the entire scientific enterprise. The untimely death of McGeoch in 1942, at age 45, plus Spence's rapid development as a theoretical psychologist and appointments as Head of the Department of Psychology, essentially shifted Iowa from the slow lane of theorizing to the fast lane.

This shift to ambitious theorizing to satisfy the craving for a comprehensive theory was encouraged also by the presence, in the Iowa Child Welfare Station, of Kurt Lewin (1890–1947), whose psychological views and interests contrasted sharply with those of Kenneth Spence: holism versus atomism, experiential versus mechanistic models, personality–social versus conditioning and learning, and socially involved versus socially detached conceptions of scientists. Lewin has been a member of the Berlin Society for Empirical Philosophy, which was both contemporaneous with and similar in views to the Vienna Circle. Lewin was responsible for bringing Gustav Bergmann (1906–1987), a mathematician by training and a member of the Vienna Circle, to assist in the development of Lewin's topological psychology. For a variety of reasons, their joint effort failed, but this failure paved the way for the successful collaborations of Spence and Bergmann in their methodological analyses of fundamental psychological problems (e.g., Bergmann & Spence, 1941, 1944). This was the only case in which a close, personal, and intimate interaction occurred between a behaviorist and a logical positivist (Smith, 1986).

In addition to having a catalytic effect on Spence's talents as a methodologist, Bergmann assumed a central role in Iowa psychology with his course in the philosophy of science and later in the history of psychology. All in all, an atmosphere was created at Iowa in the early 1940s that placed psychology at the cutting edge of theoretical advances that would, it was hoped, transform psychology into a sophisticated natural science.

Thus, Iowa psychology in the early 1940s, despite the diversity of fields— learning, social, audition, personality, psychometrics, speech pathology, clinical, and intelligence—possessed a unity of purpose: to produce a reliable body of knowledge that could be theoretically integrated. An easy optimism reigned that the expected progress would be inevitable, and some even encouraged the dream that psychology would enter a new stage of development that would allow this discipline to take its rightful place among the hard sciences.

The key dream merchant for graduate psychology students at Iowa was Kenneth Spence. These dreams emerged from his collaborative efforts with his mentor at Yale, Clark L. Hull (1884–1952), to create the Hull–Spence theory of conditioning and learning (Hull, 1943, 1952; Spence, 1956). Spence's dreams were less optimistic than those of Hull, who equated his own role in psychology with that of Newton in physics. Although Spence acknowledged that psychology was in a "primitive state of development" (Spence, 1956, p. v), he nevertheless thought it to be at about the same point that physics was "at the time of Kepler and Galileo" (Spence, 1956, p. v).

Interestingly, Spence's views were congruent with Kurt Lewin's judgments, expressed more than a decade earlier, that psychology could profitably be viewed within a Galilean framework (Lewin, 1935). It is important to note that this shared opinion about a Galilean-type psychology was based on different interpretations: According to Spence, the empirical laws of conditioning had advanced us to a Galilean stage of science, whereas Lewin saw a similarity between his methodological commitment to an ahistorical topological analysis of a psychological field known as *life space* and Galileo's achievements in physics. Spence and Lewin agreed that great scientific progress was being made without agreeing on what constitutes progress—a problem that still plagues psychology.

The third stage of psychology, ambitious theorizing, underwent a change following World War II. Kurt Lewin's move to the Massachusetts Institute of Technology in 1944 removed the major theoretical counterweight to Kenneth Spence's neobehaviorist research program, leaving it to dominate the theoretical landscape at Iowa. However, Spence's theoretical orientation failed to penetrate the entire breadth and depth of Iowa psychology, simply because of the inability of any paradigm to serve the needs of all of psychology. Although Iowa psychology was recognized as the center of research for the Hull–Spence paradigm, such a description was incomplete. As a result of Carl Seashore's legacy, Iowa had a broad-based psychology program that provided opportunities for both ivory tower theorizing as well as real-world applications, a consequence of Seashore's talent for linking basic and applied research without compromising the needs or integrity of either.

The postwar boom in education found Iowa prepared for expansion of traditional graduate programs in experimental psychology as well as programs in applied psychology that had proved successful in the military. The surging interest in clinical psychology was met by the appointment of Arthur L. Benton, who was committed to a research-oriented clinical program. Benton's interest in biological psychology and collaboration with neurologists in Iowa's Medical School ultimately led to the development of a clinical program in health psychology that sought to integrate biological and behavioral knowledge. The program in clinical and counseling psychology was strengthened by the appointment of Leonard D. Goodstein in 1951 and Leonard D. Eron 11 years later. While new clinical directions were being explored, the old cultivated fields of speech pathology and related problems were being maintained by Wendell Johnson and Charles R. Strother, both of whom arrived in Iowa in the 1930s.

In areas other than clinical psychology, it seemed that at Iowa, the new merged with the old fairly smoothly considering the sensitivities of academic personalities. E. F. Lindquist, who played a major role in America in introducing R. A. Fisher's statistical techniques, continued to educate graduate psychology students in the mysteries of analysis of variance, while Don Lewis sought to promote their mathematical sophistication. Their efforts were continued by the appointment of Harold P. Bechtoldt in 1947 and later by the replacement of Lindquist by his student Dee W. Norton. A program in industrial psychology was initiated with the appointment of J. Richard Simon, and Milton E. Rosenbaum contributed to the expansion of the social psychology program. In the early 1960s a program in biopsychology began with the appointment of Stephen Fox, Walter Randall, and John A. Harvey. While the size of the psychology department was increasing, the close and intimate relation between it and the Child Welfare Research Station, which later became the Institute of Child Behavior and

Development, continued under the successive leadership of Robert R. Sears, Boyd R. McCandless, and Charles C. Spiker.

Acknowledging the need to enlarge the psychology offerings did not allow Spence to ignore his own neobehaviorist research program. He had no qualms about adding strength to strength. Individually and together, Judson S. Brown and I. E. Farber, both appointed during the middle 1940s, enlarged the Hull–Spence paradigm to include motivation (Brown, 1961), emotion and frustration (Brown & Farber, 1951), and experimental psychopathology (e.g., Farber, 1948), and to relate it to the clinical psychology program, while Charles Spiker (1970) expanded the Hull–Spence model to include children's learning.

The third stage of psychology at Iowa ended when Kenneth Spence left for the University of Texas in 1964. This stage, in which the fast lane of theorizing was being traveled, generated many fruitful hypotheses, interesting data, and a more realistic understanding of the methodological problems of psychological theorizing, plus a considerable number of Iowa PhDs who were to assume leading roles in American psychology. The list is too long to report and the danger of omitting someone is too great, but for the record it should be noted that during his nine-year tenure at Iowa, Kurt Lewin sponsored 10 doctoral students. Kenneth Spence, over a 26-year span, directed an amazing total of 72 doctoral theses, in a singular style: "All of his doctoral students carry with them some of Spence's ideas and commitments and a desire to achieve a level of quality in their own work that would be acceptable to their professor" (Kendler, 1967, p. 341).

The Fourth Stage: A Period of Reorientation

The fourth stage of Iowa psychology, a period of reorientation, was ushered in by Spence's departure. His general ideas persisted in his absence. The emphasis on the methodological underpinnings of psychology served as the binding force in Bergmann's history of psychology. Judson Brown, who chaired the psychology department from 1965 to 1972, carried the neobehavioristic torch that had been lit by Clark Hull, Kenneth Spence, and Neal Miller. Developmental psychology, always a topic of central concern at Iowa as a consequence of the Child Welfare Research Station, became a subject matter of even greater concern when a variety of attempts were made to expand Spence's (1936) theory of discrimination learning to include ontogenetic development. Furthermore, the importance of developmental psychology was later enhanced when major elements of the Institute of Child Behavior and Development merged with the Department of Psychology.

The area of conditioning retained a dominant research position at Iowa with the appointment of I. Gormezano in 1966. His research was greatly assisted by the substantial contribution Spence bequeathed to Iowa psychology in the form of a large modern research building, for which Spence was successful in obtaining matching funds from the National Science Foundation. The design of the building was assisted by the efforts of Judson Brown and Rudolph Schulz, the latter arriving in Iowa in 1960 to revitalize research in verbal learning that had been initiated by John McGeoch back in 1939. The building was dedicated as the Spence Laboratories of Psychology in 1969 and represented another sign of the favored position of psychology at Iowa, as well as a commitment to its future strength.

Spence's impact on the department gradually declined, most notably in the shift of attitude away from the ambitious theorizing that characterized his as well as Lewin's approach toward the instrumental orientation of the Functionalists. Some Iowans would describe this change of direction as a retreat, whereas others would suggest that it reflected a more realistic appraisal of the intrinsic nature of psychology at its present stage of historical development. Regardless of the interpretation, Iowa psychology has swerved toward the center of the road that American psychology is presently traveling. The research areas that have recently flourished are biopsychology, social psychology, health psychology, and cognitive psychology. Programs in child and developmental psychology have continued as well as those in animal learning, but the emphasis in the latter has been with the physiological substrate instead of its implications for learning theory.

THE IOWA TRADITION: CORE BELIEFS

Now that I have reviewed the history of Iowa psychology, I will try to highlight the dominant features of the Iowa tradition. The post-Spence fourth stage is too recent and incomplete for anyone to accurately discern its underlying character and assess its relationship to the previous history of psychology at Iowa.

Abstracting the Iowa tradition from the first three stages of its history must be done with the clear realization that any interpretation cannot claim validity, or even authority. Some clarification is needed, however, not only to understand the past but also to give direction to the future. From one vantage point, it can be suggested that the Iowa tradition represents the strivings for a mutually beneficial relationship between experimental and applied psychology, a close and intimate bond between research and comprehensive theorizing, and a constant concern with the methodological foundations of psychology. This tradition has been shaped by many psychologists, most notably by Carl Seashore and Kenneth Spence. By the force of the scientific standards he set and the scientific goals he achieved, Carl Seashore was able to earn psychology a privileged status at the University of Iowa, no mean achievement considering the suspicion, if not outright antagonism, with which the new science of psychology was viewed by traditional academics. By creating a supportive environment for psychology, Seashore offered his successors the opportunity to imprint their own special seal on Iowa psychology. Kenneth Spence seized this opportunity with his research ingenuity, theoretical creativity, and wizardry in transforming graduate students into productive researchers.

A Methodological–Historical Examination of the Iowa Tradition

Some appraisal of past efforts and an evaluation of their implications for the future is demanded if the Iowa tradition, with its emphasis on a constant methodological surveillance of psychology, is to preserve its vitality. An assessment of all the ideas and achievements that have emerged since the beginnings of psychology at Iowa demand at least a book. For the present purpose, an examination of some of the basic notions that appeared during the third stage of Iowa psychology, perhaps its most distinctive, will satisfy traditional obligations.

An exciting period in the history of Iowa psychology took place when Spence and Lewin, along with their students, sought a general theory of behavior. Their initial efforts were judged to be promising and earned them the support of sizable segments of the psychological community, who chose to operate within their theoretical orientation in the belief that ultimate success would be forthcoming. Their achievements, in retrospect, fell far short of the goal of a comprehensive theory to which they aspired, although their fruitful interpretations of limited empirical phenomena should be acknowledged. The historical conclusion that must be drawn is that their initial successes in general theorizing turned into delayed failures, an event that has repeated itself throughout psychology's past. However, failed experiments in theorizing, when scrupulously evaluated, offer constructive guidelines for future efforts.

One explanation, obviously true but pragmatically useless, for the failure of Spence's and Lewin's ambitious dreams is that psychological phenomena are overwhelmingly complex. Unless an effort is made to understand both the potential and limits of psychological theory, the acknowledgment of the complexity of the task merely serves as an excuse to pardon failures without offering a program for future success.

Theoretical Strategies

A return to the Iowa of the 1940s will prove helpful in understanding the theoretical failures. A good starting point is an examination of the Hull–Spence approach and that of Lewin. A core assumption of the Hull–Spence strategy was that principles of behavior would be mirrored by a thorough analysis of conditioning phenomena. Lewin, although not committed to the belief that fundamental psychological principles are contained in one particular research area, was nevertheless influenced, as were other Gestalt psychologists, by the capacity of perceptual phenomena to reflect the holistic principles that govern all psychological phenomena. Perceptual research was not the sole source of general psychological principles, but it was an extremely convenient one.

The dream that the secrets of psychology reside in a specific research area has not stood the test of time. Areas such as experimental introspection, the psychoanalysis couch, perception, conditioning (classical, instrumental, or operant), discrimination learning, or memory may reveal some truths but not the whole truth about psychology. History suggests that psychologists should not naively become hostage to any optimistic conviction that all, or even most, problems of psychology will succumb to systematic research in any given behavioral area.

Another basic issue confronting Iowa students was the role of conscious experience in psychology. To know what one is talking about when dealing with this slippery issue, the following quote from William James should prove helpful: "Introspective observation is what the [psychologists] have to rely on first and foremost and always. The word introspection need hardly be defined—it means, of course, looking into our own minds and reporting what we there discover" (James, 1890, 1, p. 185).

For Gestalt psychologists, conscious experience represented the sole foundation on which a psychological theory could be erected. Solomon Asch (1968) put it this way: "The phenomenal is the scene that humans inhabit, and it is the sole starting point for psychology. . . . To describe the nature of phenomenal events as such, uncontaminated by theoretical notions, is therefore a first requirement in [psychology]" (p. 116).

For Hull, self-observation was an anathema, to be avoided at all costs in psychological theorizing. To protect one against the pseudo explanations that self-observation encourages, one should, according to Hull, view a behaving organism, human or subhuman, "as a completely self-maintaining robot, constructed of materials as unlike ourselves as may be" (Hull, 1943, p. 27).

Psychology since the 1940s has apparently shifted away from Hull's antimentalism to the Gestalt position of embracing naive pheneomenology—"the unbiased scrutiny of experience" (MacLeod, 1968, p. 68). Although one cannot deny this simple historical conclusion, one can easily misinterpret its significance. It does not mean that a model of the mind is a sine qua non for psychological theorizing. In actual fact, the cognitive revolution does not send a clear signal regarding the role of phenomenology. There is no doubt that phenomenology has offered suggestive notions for cognitive theorizing. At the same time, the idea can be proposed that within cognitive psychology, the approach that seeks to stimulate cognitive processes with computer programming represents a strategy that has evolved from the mechanistic orientation of Clark Hull. Technological advances have converted Hull's robots into digital computers. Regardless of the program employed, the argument can be advanced that the computer imposes a mechanistic organization on the simulation of human cognition that is antithetical to the essence of pure phenomenology. The speculation can be offered that if Hull had been born 50 years later, he would have become a computer simulator without abandoning his disdain for a phenomenological strategy for theory construction.

The conflict between phenomenological and mechanistic strategies can be viewed within a perspective that can be described as *pragmatic* behaviorism, which essentially states that any kind of analogy—phenomenological, mechanistic, algebraic, or any other metaphor—is acceptable if it encourages effective natural-science theorizing. By accepting the distinction between the *context of discovery* and the *context of justification* (Reichenbach, 1938) and acknowledging the significant status of Tolman's (1932) cognitive learning theory, even though he did not favor it, Spence, contrary to the strategies of Lewin and Hull, judged theories purely in terms of their deductive consequences, not in terms of the thinking processes that created them.

The historical conclusion that can be drawn is that the role of strategies, phenomenological, mechanistic, or some other, has yet to be determined, and may never be. Only when compelling theories of thinking are available can we ever possibly understand the psychological processes that are responsible for fruitful strategies. But for the present, as a result of the past, theoretical psychologists would be well advised not to delude themselves and others that methodological recipes are available that guarantee theoretical success.

Behavioral Determinism Versus Neurophysiological Causality

The next step in our search to understand why the dreams of the 1940s failed to materialize is to examine the attitudes that prevailed about the meaning of theoretical constructs in behavior theory. These theoretical constructs, or what then were more commonly labeled intervening variables, served the function of bridging the gap between independent and dependent variables. The litmus test to determine their worth was their capacity to explain, in a deductive sense, a wide range of empirical phenomena. In a very fundamental way, they were conceptualized as fictions (Frank, 1941), in the sense that they were a product of pure imagination. This point of view is essentially correct because theorizing is an imaginative process. No rules of inductive logic exist that when applied to raw data can automatically create successful theories such as Darwin's theory of evolution. At the same time, characterizing theoretical constructs as fictions implies a degree of freedom comparable to that of a novelist creating a character with no holds barred. In retrospect, this fiction metaphor may suffer from a lack of restraint because theoretical speculations are bounded by the realities of biological and physical processes.

Although not as much confidence can be placed in historical conclusions as experimental data, a reasonable hypothesis can be offered that the dream of constructing a general behavior theory of the sort that Hull and Spence, and also Tolman and Lewin, envisioned was frustrated by an optimistic view known as behavioral determinism; behavior is a self-contained system that can be understood by reference only to environmental–behavioral relationships in the absence of neurophysiological processes. When theoretical controversies, such as latent learning (Kendler, 1987), could not be neatly resolved, we psychologists automatically assumed that the difficulty resulted from theoretical ambiguities, which if eliminated, would result in the theoretical resolutions by empirical means. In retrospect, perhaps another possibility should have been considered: Environmental–behavioral research is an open system in which many constant and fluctuating variables operate that are beyond the knowledge and the control of the researcher. In essence, precise theories that have general implications cannot be formulated if based only on environmental–behavioral relationships. Three kinds of historical evidence can be marshaled to support this conclusion. First, a long list of unresolved controversies—latent learning, cognitive dissonance, the number of memory stores, language acquisition, and many, many others—support the contention that intrinsic properties of black box theories preclude them from achieving a level of precision characteristic of theories in the hard sciences. The second bit of evidence stems from efforts that were initiated and encouraged by black box theorists to elevate the deductive precision of their conceptions by casting them into mathematical models. These mathematical learning theories proved to be formally elegant but empirically trivial. The third historical suggestion stems from a comparison between the theoretical progress made by genetics as compared to psychology, both disciplines being slightly more than 100 years of age. The relative theoretical maturity of genetics in comparison to psychology can reasonably be attributed to the realistic foundations of genetics as compared to the fictitious intervening variables of general psychological theories. One might question this conclusion by noting that the concept of the gene, prior to the discovery of its DNA core, was as imaginary as the Hullian theoretical concepts. I think not. The simply denoted physical characteristics of phenotypes that justified the concept of the gene appear far more substantial than the elaborate fabrications that rationalize environmental–behavioral theoretical construct. Admittedly, my argument is beyond logical proof, but at this point in time, history supports it. Although the concept of the gene has found its biochemical moorings, the intervening variables of the past are still floating in imaginary space. Thus, it would seem that if psychology aspires to a sophisticated natural science status (and it should be noted that a significant segment of the psychological community does not share this goal), a biopsychological strategy must replace the empty organism orientation.

Such a view did not prevail at Iowa in the 1940s although it was not rejected in principle. Spence and Hull did not favor a complete severance between psychology and physiology as Tolman and Skinner did. Hull, in fact, resisted conceptualizing his theoretical constructs as fictions or purely as mathematical representations, believing that they should reflect the internal biological mechanisms of the organism. His speculations were so naive and superficial, however, that they encouraged Spence to fear that the Hull–Spence theory would be mistakenly evaluated by the truth value of Hull's neurophysiological conjectures instead of the deductive capacity of the theory. Consequently, Spence essentially spurned a biopsychological approach in favor of a purely mathematical interpretation of environmental–behavioral relationships. With technological breakthroughs in neurophysiology, Spence later became more sympathetic to a biopsychological strategy although he himself never attempted to operate within such an orientation, as did his theoretical ally, Neal Miller.

Psychology: Descriptive or Prescriptive Science?

To offer a complete picture of Iowa in the early 1940s, reference must be made to an issue that appeared to be far removed from the daily concern of both faculty and students, the role of psychology in a democratic society. Yet the issue was beginning to simmer in anticipation of the boiling cauldron it has become in American psychology. The ethical implications of the science of psychology were hidden from view at Iowa in the 1940s because of the legacy of Seashore's pragmatic orientation to apply psychological knowledge to noncontroversial social goals (e.g., educational improvement or the treatment of stuttering) and the unity of purpose that dominated American society on the eve of, and during, World War II. But a basic difference was beginning to appear, and again that difference was highlighted by competing views of Spence and Lewin. Spence seemed to inhabit a world containing nothing but facts and theories. He equated his role as a citizen with that of being a hard-working, hard-nosed psychologist with a consuming passion for theoretical analysis of simple learning phenomena. This role expanded during World War II to include his involvement in applied research associated with the war effort. Spence never got deeply involved with the methodological issues of the relationship between facts and values, but he did share the views of Hull. Hull (1952) was resolute in insisting on a dichotomy between facts and values; facts do not logically generate ethical principles or social policies. Maintaining this position does not, however, as Hull pointed out, isolate psychology from problems of morality. Moral development and moral training are susceptible to empirical analysis and theoretical clarification. In addition, social policies, based on different ethical commitments, can be empirically analyzed to determine their consequences so that educated judgments can be made about their social utility (Kendler, 1981). In other words, psychology cannot validate moral principles but can, nevertheless, understand moral behavior and its consequences.

Kurt Lewin approached the relationship between psychology and ethics from a different perspective. The tragedy of Nazism and the trauma of his failed attempt to save his mother from extermination in a concentration camp made Lewin more involved with the problem of *practical ethics,* the planning of a moral society, than with *critical ethics,* the analysis of the nature of moral arguments. This concern with practical ethics finally encouraged Lewin to initiate a program known as *action research,* the purpose of which was to effectuate desirable social change. Lewin had reached a point in his career when explanations of behavior were no longer sufficient: "We must be equally concerned with discovering how people can change their ways so that they learn to behave better" (quoted in Marrow, 1969, p. 158).

Although the competing views of the neobehaviorists and Lewin were not diametrically opposed, the manner in which they were conceptualized encouraged an incompatibility. For the neobehaviorist, operating within the framework of critical ethics, the preference for a given social policy involves two independent components, empirical and evaluative. Supporting a law to restrict TV violence, for example, would be justified by (a) empirical evidence that indicates that such programming decreases social violence and (b) the value judgment that the good resulting from the reduced violence outweighs the bad resulting from the imposed censorship. The dichotomous relationship between "is" and "ought"—empirical data and value judgment—can be overlooked easily when practical ethics dominate one's concerns. For example, one can question whether Lewin was clearly aware of, or even accepting of, the factual-evaluative distinction when he encouraged Jewish parents to emphasize the Jewishness of their children, stating that "such an early build-up of a clear and positive feeling of belongingness to the Jewish group is one of the few effective things that Jewish parents can do for the later happiness of their children" (Lewin 1940/1948, p. 183).[1] Such a recommendation, when analyzed from the perspective of critical ethics, implies that empirical evidence demonstrates that ethnic training for Jewish children results in greater "later happiness," plus the independent value judgments that happiness is an ethical imperative and/or the goal of preserving the Jewish tradition is better than that of assimilation. Another interpretation of Lewin's recommendation is possible when considered in light of his active devotion to the ideals of Zionism. Bergmann, from the perspective of critical ethics, could argue that Lewin's opinion could be judged to be an "ideological statement":

> The motive power of a value judgment is often greatly increased when it appears within the rationale of those who hold it, not under its proper logical flag as a value judgment, but in the disguise of a statement of fact. (Bergmann, 1951, p. 210)

The point of airing the controversy about the relationship between facts and values that was beginning to brew at Iowa is neither to propose a resolution nor to offer an official Iowa position in regard to whether psychology should be a

---

[1]I agree with Lewin's counsel to Jewish parents, not because of any conviction that the evidence he reported could stand up to critical examination, but simply because of the value judgment that the Jewish tradition, which prizes intelligence and morality, is worth preserving.

descriptive or prescriptive science, that is, whether psychology should limit itself to facts or whether psychology has the capacity to validate ethical principles and social policies. The reason for referring to this overwhelmingly complex issue, which is infested with subtle distinctions, is merely to identify an important component of the Iowa tradition—grappling with problems at the heart of psychology.

A PERSONAL NOTE

A personal note may be in order to conclude this overview of 100 years of Iowa psychology by reference to the atmosphere that pervaded Iowa psychology when I was a graduate student (1940–1943). We students at Iowa were encouraged to have our feet on the ground and our heads in the sky, a posture designed to stretch our reach to the limits, even at the risk of suffering possible dislocations. A reverence for empirical facts was instilled in us but also a discontent for facts alone. Facts could become exciting and useful only when embedded in a theoretical structure capable of predicting future events. In essence, we were infused with the challenging and romantic dream that the methods of natural science could be successfully applied to psychology.

As noted, the dreams have not been realized. How can we cope with the discrepancy between our past dreams and present reality? One way is to change the rules of the game. Psychology can retain its honorific status as a science by redefining science. Stripping the word science of its distinctive meaning has been accomplished in two different ways. One is to exploit the fact that science involves subjective processes and that the dividing line between science and nonscience is not precise and probably never can be. As a consequence, natural science methodology can be perceived as being completely infiltrated with subjective bias and personal conviction, thus making a mockery of the ideals of reliable knowledge and predictive accuracy. Within such a framework, psychological principles are conveniently invented, not strictly demonstrated. The second method, which avoids the rigors of natural science methodology and is one that deserves more respect than the first alternative, is to insist that psychology should not be conceptualized as a natural science, but instead, as a human science that can offer a persuasive, but not necessarily a veridical, interpretation of human experience and existence. This phenomenological orientation—understanding the mind as it appears in human experience—has an honored position in the history of philosophy, but unfortunately it has been borrowed at time by some psychologists in a superficial and distorted manner (Kendler, 1987). In spite of the persistent and fascinating appeal of phenomenology, the Iowa tradition is devoted to the reliable knowledge and the compelling nature of theoretical explanations that are offered by natural science methodology.

In addition, a preference for natural science psychology is expressed because it can serve the needs of a political democracy. It can inform citizens about the likely consequences of competing social policies and political goals so that educated decisions can be made at the polls and, one hopes, implemented by government. Such benefits cannot be forthcoming, however, if psychologists contaminate so-called scientific knowledge with their own political bias or ethical preference, an action that will inevitably teach society to distrust psychology, to the mutual disadvantage of both.

My conclusion is that the Iowa tradition initiated by Patrick, expanded by Seashore, refined by Spence, and nourished by other Iowa psychologists, including 813 doctoral recipients, is worth preserving in spite of the obstacles it has failed to surmount. The goals are too important to be abandoned. We psychologists must profit from the lessons of the past so that future research and theoretical efforts can be improved. We have to make clear to society our scientific goals and social role. Eventual success at creating a comprehensive theory of psychology, a synergistic relationship between experimental and applied psychology, and a continuing methodological clarification of psychology can only be achieved by intellectual creativity and dedication to the ideals of natural science.

ACKNOWLEDGMENTS

This chapter is an expansion of a talk given at the Centennial Celebration of Iowa Psychology at the University of Iowa, October 20–22, 1988. The assistance of Joan H. Cantor and Dewey B. Stuit in providing essential information and advice for this chapter is acknowledged.

REFERENCES

Asch, S. E. (1968). Wolfgang Köhler: 1887–1967. *The American Journal of Psychology, 81,* 110–119.

Bergmann, G. (1951). Ideology. *Ethics, 61,* 205–218.

Bergmann, G., & Spence, K. W. (1941). Operationism and theory construction. *Psychological Review, 48,* 1–14.

Bergmann, G., & Spence, K. W. (1944). The logic of psychological measurement. *Psychological Review, 51,* 1–24.

Boring, E. G. (1950). *A history of experimental psychology* (2nd ed.). Englewood Cliffs, NJ: Prentice-Hall.

Brown, J. S. (1961). *The motivation of behavior.* New York: McGraw-Hill.

Brown, J. S., & Farber, I. E. (1951). Emotions conceptualized as intervening variables—with suggestions toward a theory of frustration. *Psychological Bulletin, 48,* 465–495.

Carr, H. (1925). *Psychology.* New York: Longmans, Green.

Farber, I. E. (1948). Response fixation under anxiety and non-anxiety conditions. *Journal of Experimental Psychology, 38,* 111–131.

Frank, P. (1941). *Between physics and philosophy.* Cambridge, MA: Harvard University Press.

Hull, C. L. (1943). *Principles of behavior*. New York: Appleton Century.

Hull, C. L. (1952). *A behavior system*. New Haven, CT: Yale University Press.

James, W. (1890). *Principles of psychology* (Vol. 1). London: Macmillan.

Kendler, H. H. (1967). Kenneth W. Spence: 1907–1967. *Psychological Review, 74*, 335–341.

Kendler, H. H. (1981). *Psychology: A science in conflict*. New York: Oxford.

Kendler, H. H. (1987). *Historical foundations of modern psychology*. Pacific Grove, CA: Brooks/Cole.

Ladd, G. T. (1887). *Elements of psysiological psychology*. New York: Scribner's.

Lewin, K. (1935). *A dynamic theory of personality: Selected papers*. New York: McGraw-Hill.

Lewin, K. (1940/1948). Bringing up the Jewish child. In G. W. Lewin (Ed.), *Resolving social conflict: Selected papers on group dynamics by Kurt Lewin* (pp. 169–185). New York: Harper & Row.

MacLeod, R. B. (1968). Phenomenology. In D. L. Sills (Ed.) *International encyclopedia of the social sciences* (Vol. 12, pp. 68–72). New York: Macmillan & Free Press.

Marrow, A. J. (1969). *The practical theorist*. New York: Basic Books.

Reichenbach, H. (1938). *Experience and prediction*. Chicago: University of Chicago Press.

Scripture, E. W. (1897). *Thinking, feeling, and doing*. New York: Flood & Vincent.

Scripture, E. W. (1916). Reaction time in nervous and mental diseases. *Journal of Mental Sciences, 62*, 698–719.

Seashore, C. E. (1930). The psychological laboratory in the State University of Iowa. In *Program of Dedicatory Exercises, December 30, 1930*. Iowa City: University of Iowa.

Smith, L. D. (1986). *Behaviorism and logical positivism*. Stanford, CA: Stanford University Press.

Spence, K. W. (1936). The nature of discrimination learning in animals. *Psychological Review, 43*, 427–449.

Spence, K. W. (1956). *Behavior theory and conditioning*. New Haven: Yale University Press.

Spiker, C. C. (1970). An extension of Hull-Spence discrimination learning theory. *Psychological Review, 77*, 496–515.

Stoddard, G. D., & Wellman, B. L. (1940). Environmental and the IQ. In *Thirty-ninth Yearbook of the National Society of Education* (pp. 405–442). Bloomington, IL: Public School Publishing.

Tolman, E. C. (1932). *Purposive behavior in animals and men*. New York: Appleton-Century-Crofts.

2 Bergmann's "History and Systems of Psychology" With Penultimate Reflections on Behaviorism

I. E. Farber
University of Illinois at Chicago

PERSONAL HISTORY AND BACKGROUND

Born in Vienna in 1906, Gustav Bergmann received his doctorate in mathematics at the University of Vienna in 1928. At about this time, he began attending the meetings of the famous Vienna Circle, along with two other young mathematicians, Kurt Gödel and Karl Menger. In a chapter on the Wiener Kreis in America, Herbert Feigl (1969) noted that the Circle was greatly enriched by their participation. Sometime during the next 7 years, Bergmann worked for a period in Berlin, as assistant to Albert Einstein in the mathematical development of his theories. He returned to Vienna where he took a juris doctor degree in 1935. He practiced corporation law for a while before the Nazi threat forced his departure to the United States in 1938. He was then 32.

Herbert Feigl had already arrived in this country 8 years earlier, having been awarded a fellowship at Harvard for research in the logic of scientific theories. According to Boring (1950), the preeminent historian of psychology, Feigl introduced Harvard psychologists to the ideas of their own colleague, Bridgman (1927), who had recently published *The Logic of Modern Physics*, to the perspectives of the Vienna Circle, and to operational concepts. Feigl himself (1969) wrote that he was the first "propagandist" in America of the outlook of the

---

*The first portion of this paper is comprised of the Bergmann Commemorative Lecture presented at the Centennial Celebration of the Department of Psychology, University of Iowa. The second portion, beginning with the section on Methodological Behaviorism, is taken from an address entitled "What has become of Behaviorism: Penultimate reflections" presented to the Southern Society for Philosophy and Psychology at Fort Worth, Texas, 1982.

Vienna Circle and, with a colleague, provided their philosophical movement its international trade name, *logical positivism,* later changed to *logical empiricism* or *scientific empiricism.*

By the end of the 1930s, the tenets of operationism and kindred perspectives of the logical positivists were eagerly seized upon by psychologists at Harvard and elsewhere. Skinner (1931) wrote about the need for operational definitions of psychological concepts in the publication of his doctoral dissertation and soon thereafter the latter-day structuralists, Boring (1936) and Stevens (1935), had used the term in the titles of influential papers. "They were looking for rigor of definition in laboratory situations where introspection had once ruled" (Boring, 1950, p. 657). Other psychologists with such diverse interests as Tolman (1936) and McGeoch (1935) had adopted operationist positions, and Pratt (1939) was soon to publish *The Logic of Modern Psychology,* as counterpart to Bridgman.

I have dwelt on this background at some length because Bergmann's influence on psychology and, indeed, his academic career, were shaped by these early trends and their protagonists. Thus, after a year at Harvard, Feigl came to the Philosophy Department of the State University of Iowa in 1931, in the position of Lecturer. Kurt Lewin, the eminent Gestalt psychologist, joined the Iowa Child Welfare Research Station in 1935 and, on Feigl's recommendation, in 1939 appointed Bergmann as his assistant.

Just a year later, when Feigl was called to a professorship at the University of Minnesota, Bergmann was appointed as his successor to the faculty of the Department of Philosophy. Kenneth Spence had come to Iowa in 1938, the year before John McGeoch assumed the headship of the Department. Spence's notions about the nature and methods of scientific psychology and, in particular, his views concerning the relations between the empirical and theoretical components of psychology meshed in detail with Bergmann's logical and epistemological perspectives. I don't know whether they already knew something about their intellectual concordance, from Feigl or other sources (the academic community was smaller and more intimate in those days), but they must have established their personal and professional relationships almost from the moment of Bergmann's arrival because they jointly presented two papers in a symposium at the meeting of the Midwestern Psychological Association in the Spring of 1940. An elaboration of these papers by Bergmann and Spence (1941), entitled "Operationism and Theory in Psychology," appeared in the *Psychological Review* the following year. So began a long association that, in Laird Addis' words, "proved eventually to be the keystone of a significant constituent of our recent intellectual culture—the alliance between logical positivism and behaviorism . . ." (Epitaph, 1987).

Following McGeoch's death in 1942, Spence became head of the Department of Psychology and, as a direct result, in the following year Bergmann received a joint appointment in Psychology. He noted, in an oral history interview about 13 years ago, that, so far as he knew, he was at the time the only joint member of a philosophy and a psychology department in an American graduate school. He stated that, until the end of the first decade of the century, the combination was quite common, but I think that wasn't quite the case. In the early days, philosophy and psychology were typically in a single administrative unit. At Iowa, the two were not separated until 1927. So, in those days, you couldn't find many, if any, professional philosophers in autonomous departments of psychology because you couldn't find autonomous departments of psychology. In any event, as Bergmann went on to observe, he wasn't your usual professional philosopher, inasmuch as his graduate degrees were in mathematics and law.

I have not taken a census, but rather suspect that, partly as a result of Bergmann's own demonstration of the conceptual relations between philosophy of science, philosophy of mind and psychological theorizing, his kind of administrative status is no longer unique.

McGeoch had taught a required graduate course, "History and Systems of Psychology," during his brief 3-year tenure at Iowa, and now, probably in 1943, but certainly by 1944, Bergmann took it over and, for over 30 years, put on it an impress of ebulliance, scholarliness, analytic skill, and philosophical sophistication rarely if ever matched in any classroom.

Professor Laird Addis (Bergmann's student and now his successor in philosophy at Iowa) has noted that Bergmann had more than a bit of the showman in him. I dare say it would have been considered flamboyance in anyone of less powerful and incisive intellect. For instance, who can forget his lying down on the seminar table, solemnly flicking ashes in the European manner, to signal the need for a moment's silent reflection? Or what I remember most vividly, the characteristic way in which he would, at one and the same time, accentuate an important point, express satisfaction with the form of its delivery, and seek signs of appreciative recognition from his audience: A sharply inflected "Hm-m?"

All these mannerisms, and they were attention-getting, were expressions of his conviction that intellectual argument is at once a very serious and very delightful business. For many of us, that made him, as Professor Addis has said, simply the best teacher we ever had.

Gustav's own intellectual exuberance affected and was affected by a feeling of mission that permeated psychological enterprises throughout East Hall (which then housed Education, Speech Pathology, and Child Welfare, as well as Psychology and Philosophy). When I came to Iowa as a graduate student in 1939, McGeoch, Spence, Lewin, Stoddard, Feigl, Wendell Johnson, and Lindquist, among others, were clearly convinced that they were engaged, in their very different ways, in matters of salient import to psychology. By the time I returned after the war for my final student year in 1945, Sears was director of Child Welfare, Spence was head of Psychology, Jud Brown was about to arrive, and Bergmann was in full swing. They shared a more-or-less common perspective and believed even more strongly that what they were writing and teaching was of major significance. I thought then and think now that they were right.

A final word should be said about Bergmann's general approach. He was, of course, a philosopher, not a psychologist. Psychologists know him almost exclusively as a philosopher of science, and it is in that field that his reputation was first established. But as Charles Spiker (1976) has put it, he dealt with philosophy of science with his left hand, as it were, while his right hand, especially after the first decade of his academic life, dealt with more classical areas of philosophy—metaphysics, philosophy of mind, and philosophy of logic.

His philosophy of science informed his view of theoretical psychology, which is not the same as psychological theory. The former is philosophy and deals with the logical and epistemological problems of psychology, not its empirical or theoretical statements. His views of theoretical psychology, as everyone has noted, accorded well with the theoretical approaches of the advocates of *methodological behaviorism* (his term) or *neo-behaviorism* (their term) among whom Hull, Spence, and many of their students figure prominently.

I was rather startled to read in Gustav's epitaph by Laird Addis that Bergmann eventually moved farther from the doctrine of logical positivism than any other member of the movement. Professor Addis has since reassured me by stating that Gustav's shifts did not at all implicate his view of strictly scientific and especially psychological metatheory. I find that credible. Engrossed as he was with philosophical issues, he would nevertheless dismiss some preoccupations of scientists in general and of psychologists in particular with a shrugged "that's purely philosophical puzzlement," without, he would add, disparagement of either discipline.

SUBSTANTIVE MATTERS

The foregoing commentary on personal history and background reflects what Gustav used to call "the Hedda Hopper approach to History" (a dated expression). It's fun, and may even be somewhat illuminating, but it is only talk about the setting of his course in History and Systems. It's time to turn to substantive matters. Still, some prefatory qualifications. First, no one expects these relatively brief remarks to do justice to the multifarious and complicated contents of the course. I won't disappoint that negative expectation. Second, my presentation of the few highlights time and space permit would probably dismay a competent philosopher. I console myself by recalling Gustav's apothegm, stated in his accustomed nonpejorative style, "There are some philosophical distinctions that are too nice for psychologists." And finally, not everything that follows comes directly and explicitly from Gustav's course. After 37 years of teaching Theories of Personality, and 20 years of teaching History and Systems (unabashedly copied after Gustav's course), countless discussions with Kenneth Spence, Jud Brown and Gustav himself, and studying their writings and those of Kendler, Amsel, Kimble, and Brodbeck, among others, affirm that Gustav's course is only the core of a larger contextual framework whose origins are diffuse and, by now, somewhat uncertain. So much for preface.

British Associationists/Empiricists

Of all areas of historical and systematic psychology, I believe the issues uniting and dividing the British Associationists/Empiricists were closest to Gustav's heart. They were his springboard for the analyses of differences between Aristotle and Descartes, and for the contrasting of both with the Galilean–Newtonian science adopted by the British philosophers as their model for the mind.

Although he was thoroughly aware of its inadequacies, this model, or at least its metaphorical implications, engaged in one way or another most of Gustav's analyses and evaluations of the major historical and systematic views of psychology.

You'll be happy to note that I'm not going to say much about them. But I will repeat one of his exemplifying demonstrations (one that Gustav's students are familiar with and that I have repeated every time I have taught the course—about 20 times in 20 years).

What do you see in my hands? A sheet of paper, an eraser—and something else. The eraser is on top of the paper, it is thicker, it is darker in color, and so on. You see, in brief, certain relations between the two things.

These are our conscious contents. What are they due to? Some British Empiricists, the Sensationalists, traced them to the external world—the eraser, paper, and the relations between them are all "out there"—part of the physical world. Other British Empiricists traced the perception of only the eraser and paper to the external world. These are impressed from without, but the discriminable relations between them are not. Perception of the relations may be phenomenologically pure in the sense that they are elementary givens, but they are nevertheless contributions of the organism, not things that happen to the organism. Here we find Locke, among others, providing an entering wedge for Act Psychology. Thus, said Bergmann, relational content supplied by the organism is an act, and an act implies an agent, and the name of the agent is the Self. He noted, rather sympathetically, I believe, that many of the Empiricists viewed the notion of the self with such distaste that they had a hard time dealing with the problem of relations altogether. Here, of course, we find James Mill, not an easy fellow to explain to students.

Finally, there emerged the possibility, not admitted by British Empiricists, that not only are relations due to acts of the mind, but the eraser and the paper as well. It is all inside story.

This is an egregiously abbreviated and oversimplified account of the delightful nuances of these views and to some may be more confusing than clarifying, but I can testify that, with the help of Bergmann's further elaborations, they afforded some important insights for me. For one, I finally, after courses in History and Systems with Melton and with McGeoch, began to get a glimmer of where classical Gestalt Psychology was coming from. They were thoroughgoing sensationalists, but of a special kind, neither empiricist nor associationist. For them, what is most evidently and mainly out there are relations-relevant structures. If our phenomenological world changes—is reorganized—it is because of structural reorganization of the physical world. By extension, if behavior changes, it is because physical stimulus events have changed. Indeed, the change in the world out there is certified and in some sense identified by the change in behavior.

Structuralism

For the Structuralists, following Wundt, there are indeed things out there, apprehended by the mediation of the mind. The natural sciences are concerned with those things, but not psychology, whose subject matter is, instead, the study of the contents of *immediate* experience, including relations as content, not act. Their task, as exemplified by Titchener, was to complete the work of the British Associationists, by filling out the inventory of mental contents. What are the irreducible elements, what is their number, how are they combined? They didn't succeed ultimately, because they couldn't achieve an adequate level of intersubjective agreement. Nevertheless, Gustav accorded them a degree of ungrudging admiration. For one thing, a good deal of what we know about sensory psychology originated in or was aided by the meticulous controls and sophisticated application of the psychophysical methods that characterized structuralist experimental psychology. A very substantial portion of the first semester of Gustav's course was given over to a detailed examination of research and theory concerning the interrelations among physical, physiological, and phenomenal variables in sensation and perception. This was rather unexpected, although it should not have been. He was, after all, a product of classical European education. For some of us, it was not the most exciting part of the course. But it was solid stuff. Much of it still is, over 40 years later.

I have often wished that the descriptions of the so-called mind-expanding, consciousness-raising, sensation-enhancing effects or accompaniments of mystical rituals or the psychotropic drugs could be produced under the kinds of precise measurement conditions and formulated in the disciplined language that typified classical introspective psychology. At least, if there is anything worth studying, such reports would be far more illuminating than phenomenological descriptions limited to a phrase such as "Man, it's the most!" But I suppose that people who are too dumb to stay out of situations of that sort are too dumb to do it right.

Still, the structuralist enterprise raised legitimate questions about the nature of classical introspectionists' reports. Were they veridical reports of what was observed or just reports of what observers had been carefully instructed to look for? It is certainly the case that introspectionists' training was rigorous and prescriptive, perhaps because, as Gestalt psychologists insisted, they had to learn to ignore the almost irresistible demands of their actual immediate experience.

Gestalt

I have mentioned that, according to Gestalt psychologists, the phenomenological world corresponds to—is "isomorphic", as they used to say—with the physical world. To understand behavior, then, we need only to know how the world is perceived. Our behavior is a function of our psychological environment rather than the external physical environment, i.e., distal cues. The term *psychological environment* owes to Koffka (e.g., 1935), who depicted its importance by recalling an old legend about the traveler who arrived at an inn one winter evening in a driving snowstorm that covered all paths and landmarks. When asked where he had come from, he pointed behind him. Told that he had ridden across Lake Constance, he dropped dead of fright. Gustav always liked that story because it so well demonstrates the ad hoc nature of explanations of behavior in terms of the psychological environment when our inferences about the psychological environment are based on the very behavior it purports to explain. "Is it not the business of science to ascertain which objective factors in the past and present states of the organism and its environment account for the differences in response . . ." (Bergmann, 1943, p. 133) and, for that matter, the psychological environment itself?

Howard Kendler (1987) surmised that Koffka's unfortunate traveler might have died of a heart attack that could have occurred whether or not he learned where he had been. At various times, I have told my classes that I thought he died of an excess of exhilaration, or of anger at being wrongly directed, or of half-a-dozen other phenomenal states, for none of which I have any more evidence than did Koffka. What is most clearly suggested by the story is the significance of the objective cues available to that legendary traveler. Had he plunged into a watery grave? No, his horse's footing was apparently firm. The proximal cues were those of dry land. What changed his state of mind to fear or whatever it was? No one familiar with the emotion-arousing potential of verbal cues should be surprised by their occasional deleterious effects (although, in this sort of case, it would be reasonable to investigate Kendler's hunch about a predisposing heart condition). In short, the objective situational cues are in principle, at least, quite adequate to an explanation of the consequent behaviors. The concept of "psychological environment" is gratuitous.

Dewey

Gustav's criticisms of Gestalt, as of other systematic views, were frequently indirect and allusive. An expert at unpacking complex issues, he would point to inadequacies in a given formulation by dissecting an ostensibly different one. In the case of Gestalt, his surrogate target was John Dewey. Uneasy as he was with the underlying philosophical tenets of the classical gestalters, he shared and respected their intellectual origins. He thought Dewey really should have known better.

Not that Dewey was all bad. He was one of the founders of the American tradition of intellectual history, and, of course, with Angell, was a founder of the Functionalist School of Psychology. On the whole, Bergmann liked Functionalism. Indeed, he considered methodological behaviorism to be the consummation of the basic functionalist thesis. Nevertheless, he also found in it the threads of some extremely objectionable notions, many, if not all of which, were personified by Dewey and expressed or implied in his famous paper on the Reflex Arc (1896).

Philosophers will immediately understand Gustav's distaste for Dewey if I simply note that Gustav considered his views an outgrowth of Hegelian Idealism. Dewey couldn't accept the idealistic program explicitly, because he also had a certain respect for science, particularly in its pragmatic social aspects. So he ended up by rejecting philosophy. "That's a philosophy too." (I am quoting from classroom notes.)

On the psychological side, the Reflex Arc paper asserts, among other things, that there is nothing out there that can be clearly classified as stimulus or response. There are only series of changes. Psychically, the reflex arc is of one piece. The stimulus is born out of the response preceding it, and the response is born out of the stimulus preceding it. They are not two things, but properly understood, a unitary whole.

You will recall what I said earlier about that phenomenological view that identifies changes in stimuli with changes in behavior. This is the anti-analytic hallmark of Gestalt Psychology, and Dewey, however unwittingly, propounds it. Put another way, what is important is not the stimulus, but the meaning of the stimulus as indexed by the behavior. What may be inferred from behavior, then, is not only the perception of the stimulus but the very fact and nature of the stimulus. This total conflation of stimulus and response leaves the field of psychology exclusively to mental states. Their antecedents are a matter of indifference, and their behavioral consequences are a matter of course. For Gustav, this kind of thinking represents bad philosophy, bad science and certainly, bad psychology.

Lewin

As I noted earlier, Gustav came to the University of Iowa to assist Lewin in his application of the postulates and theorems of topological geometry to the explication of psychological phenomena. They quickly discovered that their views of theoretical psychology were antithetical in general, and Gustav quickly decided that in particular the use of topological mathematics for the construction of psychological theory was at best selectively metaphorical and at worst uninformed. Nevertheless, he properly limited his classroom exposition to critiques of tenets shared by other gestalt psychologists. With all this, he considered Lewin's position to be different from and, in some respects, better than that of the other towering representatives of Gestalt. For one thing, he applauded Lewin's focus on motivational concepts, which he attributed to the influence of the Wurzberg School and its emphasis on mental set. For another, he considered that Lewin was relatively undogmatic in his treatment of the concept of psychological field forces as a system of interdependent variables. As Lewin himself put it, not every region of the life space invariably affects every other region.

It should be noted that Kenneth Spence (1944) explicitly recognized the value of Lewin's experimental contributions to the formulation of R–R Laws, namely relations between behaviors and subjects' phenomenological reports, and in the complex area of human social behavior, the fruitfulness of hunches based by Lewin on phenomenological data.

Freud

Somewhat curiously, despite Bergmann's assignment of Freud to absolute preeminence in the history of psychology and his publication (1943) of a paper on psychoanalysis in the journal *Mind,* my classroom notes indicate that he devoted relatively little time to the substantive aspects of psychoanalytic theory. On the other hand, his year-long course was replete with parenthetical references to Freud, as in the case of his discussion of mental contents and acts. In this regard, the tripartite division of mind refers not to structure, as many suppose, but to mental acts, of which Id, Ego and Superego are the agents.

In his article in *Mind,* Gustav asserted that the same basic ideas and the same frame of reference underlie both psychoanalysis and the experimental psychology of learning. In my own courses in Theories of Personality, I have argued, more or less in the Miller–Dollard tradition, that the primary process might be understood, operationally, in terms of the principles of biogenic drives, especially as they relate to perception, and the secondary process, in terms of learning and acquired drives. But these kinds of translations reflect my own theoretical preferences—biases, if you will. I have found precious few psychoanalysts of any persuasion who are enthralled by these ideas.

I have already indicated that adherents of both structuralist and gestalt views may be on very shaky grounds when they claim to know what is going on in other people's heads. This liability to psychologists' error has been remarked as well in what Meehl (1982) has called "the nagging persistence of Wilhelm Fliess's Achensee Question." As everyone knows, Achensee was the residence of Wilhelm Fliess, a somewhat shady gentleman who carried on a long correspondence with Freud. The question he raised, as you have guessed, concerned the possibility that Freud's expositions of what was going on in his patients' heads were nothing more than descriptions of what was going on in Freud's own head.

Watson

Watson's solution to the problem of identifying other persons' conscious contents was to throw out the baby with the bath water. Gustav's (1956) opinion of this solution is stated in what is perhaps, among neobehaviorists, his most frequently quoted sentence:

> Watson's particular mistake was that in order to establish that there are no interacting minds, which is true, he thought it necessary to assert that *there are no minds,* which is not only false but silly. (p. 266)

Gustav's general evaluation of Watson, as exemplified in his influential paper, "The Contribution of John B. Watson" (1956), was by no means wholly commendatory. But he insisted that Watson's one great virtue outweighed his many sins. As usual, Gustav made the necessary distinctions: Watson was an experimental psychologist, a philosopher of psychology (that is, a methodologist, in Gustav's terms), a social philosopher, and a metaphysician. Gustav judged, as an outsider, that his experimental work was distinguished but not of transcendental importance. (It is a wry twist of history that, in current texts, Watson's most frequently cited research, fear conditioning in little Albert, is often presented somewhat inaccurately.) He considered Watson's social philosophy deplorable and his metaphysics, silly. Furthermore, he noted that these four sides of Watson often interfered with each other to the logical detriment of each. What was left was his methodological prescription which, in Gustav's opinion, gave him a place "second only to Freud, though at a rather great distance, . . . [as] the most important figure in the history of psychological thought during the first half of the century. Nor is his impact limited to the science of psychology" (1956, p. 265).

METHODOLOGICAL BEHAVIORISM

I have always rather believed that Gustav gave Watson more credit than he deserved, in that the clarification of the postulates of methodological behaviorism owes largely to Gustav's own work. Within psychology, its meaning has probably been conveyed even more cogently through the teaching, research, and writing of representatives of what came to be known as the Yale–Iowa tradition—notably, Clark Hull, Kenneth Spence, Neal Miller, Howard Kendler, Abe Amsel, Jud Brown, and Greg Kimble. (To the many others who should be mentioned, *Pace!*)

In a paper devoted mainly to Bergmann's teachings, it seems most appropriate to turn to one of his own statements (1956) of what methodological behaviorism is about:

> Combine . . . Watson's good thesis, that there are no interacting minds, with the great Functionalist truism about process. What follows is the thesis of methodological behaviorism. It must *in principle* be possible to predict future behavior, including verbal behavior, from a sufficiency of information about present (and past) behavioral, physiological, and environmental [including social-environmental] variables. This is the thesis. Let me also state one of its corollaries. Speaking commonsensically or, for that matter, clinically, we often attribute to a person a certain state of mind. We say that he or she perceives something, remembers something, plans something, is sad or gay, and so on. Nor is there any doubt, commonsensically, that we know what we mean when we assert such things, or, for that matter, that sometimes we are even right. It follows that it must *in principle* be possible to coordinate to any such statement another one, however complex, which mentions only behavioral, physiological, and environmental items, such that they are either both true or both false. Otherwise one would have to maintain that we can, literally and not metaphorically speaking, directly observe other people's states of mind. (p. 270)

Even though the progenitors and proponents of behaviorism conceived in the foregoing way are not entirely among the departed, the death or disappearance of behaviorism is announced with some regularity, or at least on a kind of mixed variable interval schedule (cf. Koch, 1964). I emphatically agree with Skinner (1969) that such obsequies show an unseemly haste:

> Behaviorism, as we know it, will eventually die—not because it is a failure but because it is a success. As a critical philosophy of science, it will necessarily change as a science of behavior changes, and the current issues which define behaviorism may be wholly resolved. [At the moment,] . . . as methodological behaviorists and operational psychologists put it today [,] behavior is . . . defined as a field which can be successfully analyzed apart from the world of mind [though] . . . the existence of [that] . . . world is admitted, with or without the implication that we can know about it in some other way. (p. 267)

Kenneth Spence (e.g., 1956) believed that this general conception of psychology in fact accords with that of most psychologists in this country. This view includes the precept that the terms employed by the scientist, no matter how abstract, must ultimately be referable to a basic set of terms that have direct experiential reference and that have a high degree of intersubjective agreement among observers. These terms and the abstract concepts defined from them are used to provide for explanatory and predictive statements in the form of general laws. Cronbach and Meehl (1955) have put the matter clearly:

> 1. Scientifically speaking, to "make clear what something *is*" means to set forth the laws in which it occurs. . . .

3. A necessary condition for a construct to be scientifically admissible is that it occur in a nomological net, at least *some* of whose laws involve observables. Admissible constructs may be remote from observation, i.e., a long derivation may intervene between the nomologicals which implicitly define the construct and the . . . nomologicals [referring to observables]. These latter propositions permit predictions about events. The construct is not "reduced" to the observations, but only combined with other constructs in the net to make predictions about observables. (p. 290)

The specification of the observable events and methods of measurement of key concepts in statements of laws is sometimes referred to, not altogether correctly, as *operational definition*. Even psychologists who would blanch at the very suggestion that they are following a behavioristic line speak of "operationalizing" their concepts. (Have you ever heard a more repulsive neologism?) These concepts are included precisely to permit the confirmation or disconfirmation by means of public observation of statements containing them. Perhaps, as some philosophers of science maintain, it would be even better to talk about the falsification of statements. Within this formulation of methodological behaviorism, even the classical problems of mental analysis may be treated behavioristically. Spence used to maintain, partly on these grounds, that although such conceptualizations are behavioristic in outlook, they are probably better described as "objective psychology."

ON "SUBJECTIVE BEHAVIORISM"

To some, the flexibility of this formulation and of correlative notions of what constitutes "theory" in psychology represents a retreat—some would characterize it as ignominious, others as merely prudent. George Miller and Robert Buckhout (1973) have this to say:

Many psychologists, even those who admire the hardheaded, quantitative posture of S–R theory, have come to the reluctant judgment that simple S–R connections are often more plausible than real. . . . Faced with this dilemma, one must either broaden the meaning of stimuli and responses so as to include perceptions and acts, which is to retreat from the hardheaded objectivity of true behaviorism, or propose an alternative element that will be easier to define and study. Many psychologists [they mean Hull, Spence, Neal Miller and those of like persuasion] have broadened their definitions of stimulus and response to include unobservable events and processes that play much the same roles in their theories as perceptions, images, ideas, and intentions played in the older psychologies. . . . They have adopted a contradictory position which we call subjective behaviorism . . . a term general enough to include anti-Hullians, who . . . were trying to fit something between S and R which represented the organism's active role in interpreting the stimulus and in effect modifying S through his evaluation of the feedback resulting from responding. (pp. 250–251)

The textual dissection of the corpus of this message would take a very long while, so I content myself here with picking at only a few of the extruding bones.

1. Every time you hear or read the phrase "simple S–R connections," you may be sure that what is meant is "*simplistic* (i.e., stupid) ideas of S–R connections," and that Watson—the publicist, not the psychologist—or some unnamed surrogate, is about to be flogged once again. Who besides Watson ever supposed S–R connections are simple? Not Thorndike, who is most likely to have used the term *S–R connections;* not Pavlov, who considered conditioned reflexes a function of rather complicated if mythical physiological arrangements; and assuredly not Skinner, who doesn't consider himself an S–R psychologist at all.

2. If the explanation of behavior exclusively in terms of simple (additive) connections between stimuli and responses were plausible, that is, if (contrary to fact) one could explain and predict behavior by use of such notions, they would be real—as real as real can be. As Boring (1933) has observed, "*Whatever exists as reality for psychology is a product of inductive inference*—usually from experimental data. To say that these realities are hypothetical constructs is not to alter the truth. . . . Their validity is attested by their power of physical subsumption. The realities are always tentative and have to make their way and prove their worth. There is no other scientific meaning for reality" (p. 7). I am aware that this conventionalist view of reality is not the only view and that some able analysts hold other views on technical philosophical grounds. But I don't believe Miller and Buckhout were making a technical philosophical point.

3. As for those psychologists who purportedly came to the reluctant judgment that simple S–R connections won't work and therefore broadened the meanings of stimuli and responses, in retreat from true behaviorism, I can vouch at first hand that Spence and his students, for example, have in publication and in the classroom consistently held to conceptions of S–R that are quite different from those imputed above to "true" behaviorists. We have never supposed that S–R means that immediately present and identifiable stimuli *impel* responses, in a long-discredited sense of causation as "force," nor that immediate external stimuli are the *only* determinants of responses. These matters are discussed in detail by Greg Kimble (1967) in a chapter entitled "The basic tenet of behaviorism." Whether we were "true believers," in the usual invidious meaning of that term, may be open to question. But we certainly never considered ourselves in retreat from "true" behaviorism.

4. Concerning the adjective "reluctant," I wonder what future generations of graduate students will think when they read that the so-called neo-behaviorists *reluctantly* came to the conclusion that they had better include in their theoretical

formulations unobservables, much on the order of perceptions, ideas, intentions, and the like. I suppose they will envision an historical era in which figures such as Tolman, Hull, Spence, Neal Miller and their students were driven, kicking and screaming, to the distasteful task of dealing with such notions as sign-gestalt expectations, habit strength, drive strength, and fractional anticipatory responses, to say nothing of emotion, frustration, conflict and a host of other hypothetical mediating processes (cf. Farber, 1964). If so, they are going to have a hugely distorted view of this phase of the history of psychology. It is the case, rather, that such notions were actively pursued, with the encouragement of philosophers of science such as Bergmann and Feigl. They were conceived as calculational devices appearing in laws ultimately tied to observable antecedents and consequents. However history eventually judges the usefulness of this enterprise, it will not accurately attribute the systematic use of these concepts to the existentialist demands of intuition or phenomenological testimony. For example, whatever one thinks of Hull's (1930) treatment of knowledge and purpose as habit mechanisms, it suggests, as Brodbeck (1968) has noted, that "the explanation of purposive behavior may not be a purposive explanation, and the explanation of a (mental) function may not be a functional explanation" (p. 140). And that is why labeling this sort of approach *subjective behaviorism* misconstrues its salient methodological feature.

ON CONSCIOUSNESS

It is very far from the case that, as one writer (Robinson, 1976) has complained, the concept of consciousness has been legislated out of behaviorism even though "it is that by which a real and knowable world becomes real and knowable in the first place" (p. 409).

In his initially more sober formulation, Watson (1913) himself did not at all deny the existence of consciousness, but did deny that it is the unique subject matter of psychology. "The separate observation of 'states of consciousness' is . . . no more a part of the task of the psychologist than that of the physicist. We might call this the return to a nonreflective and naive use of consciousness. In this sense consciousness may be said to be the instrument or tool with which all scientists work" (p. 176).

Kenneth Spence (1948), referring to the clarification of the relationship of consciousness to the data and constructs of science by the logical positivists and psychologists such as Boring, Pratt, and Stevens, strongly concurred that "the data of all sciences have the same origin—namely, the immediate experience of the scientist himself" (p. 68). He noted, as well, that most behavior scientists have continued to make use of the observation of such internal mental activities as thinking, desiring, emotional reactions, perceiving, etc.

in the form of the objectively recordable verbal reports of their subjects. Indeed, the scientist himself, in certain circumstances, may assume a dual role and serve as both subject and experimenter. In this event his own introspective report is recorded as a linguistic response and becomes a part of the objective data. To some critics of the behavioristic viewpoint, this acceptance of the verbal reports of their subjects as a part of the data has seemed to represent an abandonment of the strict behavioristic position and a return to the conception that psychology studies *experiential* events as well as overt behavior.

Such a contention, it seems to me, fails to note a very important difference in the two positions. The introspectionist, it should be recalled, assumed a strict one-to-one relationship between the verbal responses of his subjects and the inner mental processes. Accordingly, he accepted these introspective reports as *facts* or *data* about the inner mental events which they represented. The behavior scientist takes a very different position. He accepts verbal response as just one more form of behavior and he proposes to use this type of data in exactly the same manner as he does other types of behavior variables. Thus he attempts to discover laws relating verbal responses to environmental events of the past or present, and he seeks to find what relations they have to other types of response variables. He also makes use of them as a basis for making inferences as to certain hypothetical or theoretical constructs which he employs. In contrast, then, to the introspectionist's conception of these verbal reports as mirroring directly inner mental events, i.e., facts, the behaviorist uses them either as data in their own right to be related to other data, or as a base from which to infer theoretical constructs which presumably represent internal or covert activities of their subjects. (pp. 69–70)

In this general context, more than a few of you will recall that Kenneth made good use of a verbal paper-and-pencil test of anxiety as a basis for inferences about drive level (cf. 1958).

In sum, to say that consciousness can be dispensed with in a functional analysis of behavior assuredly does not get rid of it. Of course, if conscious events appear as a concept in a functional analysis of behavior, it is appropriate to ask how they can be explained or predicted. Like observable behaviors, conscious contents and processes are consequent to antecedents. Consequents are one thing. Antecedents are another. No one supposes that behavior doesn't exist because it can be accounted for by its antecedents or that, because it can be accounted for, it is the same thing as its antecedents. To explain doesn't mean "explain away." So much for the notion that to be a "true behaviorist" you must deny that consciousness is real and knowable.

UNDERSTANDING AND CONTROL

One of the pseudomethodological tenets traditionally held by many behavioral scientists of both S–R and Skinnerian varieties concerns the importance of environmental/situational variables in determining behavior. The extreme form of this position has had some scientific knocks lately, by demonstrations that innate, species-specific response tendencies limit the capacity of animals and human beings to acquire certain behaviors under certain environmental conditions, even under contingencies that would typically be considered favorable. It is clear that not all stimuli are equipotential in respect to all modes of response. I find it puzzling why such findings, which in a general sense are not exactly new, should so elate those who prefer to emphasize the primacy of intraorganismic factors, inasmuch as they emphasize the role of particular aspects of the environment in the production of particular, albeit unlearned, modes of response. It should be noted that, despite individual predilections, methodological behaviorism is in principle neutral on the issue of nature versus nurture.

More fundamental than the objection that animals and human beings will do what comes naturally, despite any contrived environmental architecture, is the objection that, when you come right down to it, animals and especially human beings will do as they damn well please. There is no use, according to Miller and Buckhout (1973), trying to control people by arranging favorable contingencies for their behaviors:

> In real life people may choose their own versions of Skinner Boxes, choosing to have their behavior controlled by an environment controlled by someone else. But just as they choose to be controlled they can and *do* choose *not* to be controlled— dropping out, tuning out, or rebelling for reasons that only the man himself can give accurate evidence on. It is this "semiautonomous" man that Skinner doesn't understand. . . . Indeed, many people reject or run away from the good life, a behavioral fact that Skinner chooses to ignore. (p. 270)

It is useless to argue that such rejection indicates that the contingencies are aversive rather than reinforcing and that the sensible thing to do is to find other contingencies. The protagonists are committed on ideological grounds to the belief that such arrangements can't be made or that, if they could, it would be immoral to do so or, at least, that it would violate the principle of man's freedom and dignity.

It is nevertheless the case that, if the determinants of behavior were known, and if enough of them were susceptible to manipulation, then it would be possible to control behavior. Clearly, in respect to important kinds of human (and animal) behavior, neither of these conditions obtains to any great degree at present. But that is beside the point of the ideological objection. The outrage is over the very idea that the determinants *might* become known, that they *might* be manipulable, and that anyone would even consider such eventualities as desirable. One commentator (Beldoch, 1972) has this to say:

> The psychologists have not speeded up the process of obtaining wisdom, only greatly increased the need for it. It becomes increasingly clear that our times are

> witness to the possibilities of terror. With their benign smiles, gentle manner, and blind minds, the psychologists would lead us straight for the sun. (p. 18)

Reading this, I was rather disappointed that this picture had not been properly rounded out by a suitable depiction of the torments of eternal hell fire.

I have indicated elsewhere (1964) that the essential ingredient in such views is a distrust of science. Not a few of those who bemoan our lack of knowledge concerning the causes and remedies for social and personal disorders—violent conflict, drug abuse, political corruption, ethnic and religious intolerance, occupational and educational disabilities, to name just a few of our current concerns—are the same people who condemn the use of those procedures best calculated to achieve that knowledge, namely, the methods of science.

Perhaps psychologists have been particularly inept in their attempts to understand and deal with these matters. I am quite certain that current institutional conflicts between psychological practitioners and researchers can only retard those efforts.

It seems fitting to conclude with a comment by Kenneth Spence in the first chapter of his Silliman Lectures (1956).

> The science-oriented psychologist merely asks that he be given the same opportunity to develop a scientific account of his phenomena that his colleagues in the physical and biological fields have had. If there are aspects of human behavior for which such an account cannot ever be developed, there are not, so far as I know, any means of finding this out without a try. (pp. 20–21)

In the original presentation of the first section of this paper at the centennial celebration of the Iowa Psychology Department, I appended the subtitle "Staying the course." Its reference to Bergmann's presentation of History and Systems is obvious. I also believe it to be a good prescription for those who adhere to the tenets of methodological behaviorism.

REFERENCES

Beldoch, M. (1972). Science as fiction (Review of Beyond freedom and dignity). *Psychotherapy and Social Science Review, 6,* 12–18.

Bergmann, G. (1943). Psychoanalysis and experimental psychology: A review from the standpoint of scientific empiricism. *Mind, 52,* 122–140.

Bergmann, G. (1956). The contribution of John B. Watson. *Psychological Review, 63,* 265–276.

Bergmann, G., & Spence, K. W. (1941). Operationism and theory in psychology. *Psychological Review, 48,* 1–14.

Boring, E. G. (1933). *The physical dimensions of consciousness.* New York: Appleton-Century.

Boring, E. G. (1936). Temporal perception and operationism. *American Journal of Psychology, 48,* 519–522.

Boring, E. G. (1950). *A history of experimental psychology* (2nd Ed.). New York: Appleton-Century-Crofts.

Bridgman, P. W. (1927). *The logic of modern physics.* New York: Macmillan.

Brodbeck, M. (1968). Purpose and function: Introductory comment. In M. Brodbeck (Ed.), *Readings in the philosophy of the social sciences* (pp. 139–143). New York: Macmillan.

Cronbach, L. J., & Meehl, P. E. (1955). Construct validity in psychological tests. *Psychological Bulletin, 52,* 281–302.

Dewey, J. (1896). The reflex arc in psychology. *Psychological Review, 3,* 357–370.

Epitaph (1987). Commemorative address by L. Addis, University of Iowa. (Mimeographed)

Farber, I.E. (1964). A framework for the study of personality as a behavioral science. In P. Worchel & D. Byrne (Eds.), *Personality and personality change* (pp. 3–37). New York: Wiley.

Feigl, H. (1969). The Wiener Kreiss in America. In D. Fleming & B. Bailyn (Eds.), *The intellectual migration* (pp. 630–673). Cambridge: Harvard University Press.

Hull, C. L. (1930). Knowledge and purpose as habit mechanisms. *Psychological Review, 37,* 511–525.

Kendler, H. (1987). *Historical foundations of modern psychology.* Chicago: Dorsey Press.

Kimble, G. A. (1967). *Foundations of conditioning and learning.* New York: Appleton–Century–Crofts.

Koch, S. (1964). Psychology and emerging conceptions of knowledge as unitary. In T. W. Wann (Ed.), *Behaviorism and phenomenology* (pp. 1–41). Chicago: University of Chicago Press.

Koffka, K. (1935). *Principles of Gestalt psychology.* New York: Harcourt Brace Jovanovich.

McGeoch, J. A. (1935). Learning as an operationally defined concept. *Psychological Bulletin, 32,* 688.

Meehl, P. E. (1982). *Subjectivity in psychoanalytic inference: The nagging persistence of Wilhelm Fliess's Achensee Question.* Paper presented at the Midwestern Psychological Association Convention, Minneapolis, MN.

Miller, G. A., & Buckout, R. (1973). *Psychology: The science of mental life* (2nd ed). New York: Harper & Row.

Pratt, C. C. (1939). *The logic of modern psychology.* New York: Macmillan.

Robinson, D. N. (1976). *An intellectual history of psychology.* New York: Macmillan.

Skinner, B. F. (1931). The concept of the reflex in the description of behavior. *Journal of General Psychology, 5,* 427–458.

Skinner, B. F. (1969). Behaviorism at fifty. In B. F. Skinner (Ed.), *Contingencies of reinforcement: A theoretical analysis* (pp. 221–268). New York: Appleton-Century-Crofts.

Spence, K. W. (1944). The nature of theory construction in contemporary psychology. *Psychological Review, 51,* 47–68.

Spence, K. W. (1948). The postulates and methods of "behaviorism." *Psychological Review, 55,* 67–78.

Spence, K. W. (1956). *Behavior theory and conditioning.* New Haven: Yale University Press.

Spence, K. W. (1958). A theory of emotionally based drive (D) and its relation to performance in simple learning situations. *American Psychologist, 13,* 131–141.

Spiker, C. (1976). *Gustav Bergmann on the logic of psychological concepts.* Paper presented at the American Psychological Association Convention, Washington, DC.

Stevens, S. S. (1935). The operational basis of psychology. *American Journal of Psychology, 47,* 323–330.

Tolman, E. C. (1936). Operational behaviorism and current trends in psychology. *Proceedings of the 25th Anniversary Celebration, University Southern California* (Pp. 89–103).

Watson, J. B. (1913). Psychology as the behaviorist views it. *Psychological Review, 20,* 158–177.

3 Psychology at Iowa Before McGeoch and Spence

Ernest R. Hilgard
Stanford University

In celebrating 100 years of psychology at the University of Iowa, I address my remarks chiefly to the first 50 years before there was an infusion of new leadership through the arrival of Kenneth Spence with other newly employed faculty. He came as an associate professor in 1938, to be followed by John McGeoch as Professor and Department Head in 1939. McGeoch unfortunately had his career cut short by his premature death in 1942. My good friend Kurt Lewin, who had first charmed me at the International Congress at Yale in 1929, was about to arrive in the then Child Welfare Research Station, but he was also prominent in psychology generally. I should perhaps have included him in the title of my chapter because in one sense those of us from the outside saw the most dramatic new arrivals at the time to be McGeoch, Spence, and Lewin. Upon McGeoch's death Spence began his many years of leadership. Lewin had been responsible for bringing Gustav Bergmann, a philosopher from Vienna, to help him formalize his topological psychology, but Bergmann found Spence's theorizing more congenial. Robert Sears came to head Child Welfare in 1942 to serve until 1949, when he left for Harvard before coming to Stanford in 1953. Because those I have just mentioned belong to the second 50 years of psychology at the University of Iowa, I have little more to say about them here. These newcomers found strong traditions established at Iowa before they arrived. I am fortunate to have lived long enough to have known some of the leaders from the earlier period.

PROFESSOR GEORGE THOMAS WHITE PATRICK
(1857–1949)

Professor George Thomas White Patrick, born in 1857, is the acknowledged founding father of psychology at Iowa. He graduated from Iowa in 1878 and went East for his advanced degrees, earning a Bachelor of Divinity degree from Yale and a PhD degree from Johns Hopkins, after 2 years in residence there from 1885 to 1887. He came immediately to Iowa where his first appointment is commonly referred to as Professor of Philosophy and Psychology, although his initial title was actually Professor of Mental and Moral Sciences and Didactics. The Hopkins degree was not awarded until 1888, after his first year at Iowa. In the meantime he had returned to take his final examination. At Johns Hopkins he was in the good company of those whom G. Stanley Hall had attracted there: Burnham, Cattell, Dewey, Donaldson, Hyslop, Jastrow, and Sanford. Of those, Hall took Burnham, Donaldson, and Sanford along with him to Clark University; Cattell went to the University of Pennsylvania; Dewey's first appointment was the University of Michigan, Jastrow's at Wisconsin. Although Hyslop was later ranked as among the top 30 psychologists by Cattell in his American Men of Science, he was better known to those interested in psychical research than to psychologists. He wrote six books on that topic between 1905 and 1913.

Professor Patrick belonged to the first generation of American-trained PhDs to establish laboratories without being initiated in Europe. In keeping with the strong tradition of some study in Europe, he did indeed find an opportunity to further his philosophical studies in Leipzig in 1894.

He lived out his career at Iowa, becoming Emeritus in 1928. Later he moved to Palo Alto, California, where he lived quietly. I had not known of his presence in our community until George Stoddard took me along for a pleasant conversation with him in the early 1940s. He died there in 1949, at the age of 92. I understand that his bust is placed in the Union Building.

The beginnings of philosophy and psychology at Iowa were very simple (Patrick, 1932). For the first 6 years (1887–1892), Professor Patrick occupied one room in the Old Capitol, then the Administration Building. Some equipment was purchased in 1888, and the formal beginning of a psychological laboratory has been dated as 1890 because that is the first year that funds were provided for laboratory equipment—the sum of $175 plus the promise of an additional $75 per year. Of course Patrick had been teaching psychology since 1887, so that specifying founding dates is always a bit arbitrary. A list of apparatus appears in the annual catalog of the University for 1891–1892, and a detailed account in the catalog for 1894–1895. Carl Emil Seashore wrote of an initial appropriation of $500 for laboratory equipment, but this probably refers to the first regularly budgeted money for the laboratory, increasing to $2,500 when he was writing (Seashore, 1942).

The next move of philosophy and psychology was to 14 North Clinton Street, previously occupied by the Homeopathic Medical School, and later by the School of Music. Five rooms were assigned to philosophy and psychology from 1892–1896. The rooms consisted of a lecture room, a library/reading room, and three laboratory rooms.

Patrick worked alone until 1895, when J. Allen Gilbert came as his assistant, fresh from a PhD at Yale under Ladd and Scripture. He lasted only 2 years, was unhappy in psychology, and went on to study medicine. Patrick initiated the *University of Iowa Studies in Psychology* in 1894, and Gilbert joined him as a co-editor during his last year at Iowa.

Gilbert was followed by Seashore, who had taken his Yale PhD the same year as Gilbert, but had stayed on as a postdoctoral assistant for the 2 years that Gilbert was at Iowa. He came in 1897 as an assistant professor of philosophy, an academic title that had been denied Gilbert.

With the coming of Seashore, Patrick gradually withdrew from psychology, although he had made a number of contributions to it. His title was changed to Professor of Philosophy in 1903, although he apparently did not relinquish the headship of the joint Department of Philosophy and Psychology until 1905. He continued as a Professor of Philosophy until he became Emeritus Professor in 1928.

DEAN CARL EMIL SEASHORE (1866–1949)

I turn next to Dean Seashore, whose long shadow falls on all aspects of the history of psychology at Iowa.

As already noted, he arrived as an assistant professor of philosophy in 1897. By 1902, he was Professor of Psychology, as he and Patrick more or less divided the fields of philosophy and psychology between them. Then in 1905, he took over the headship of both Philosophy and Psychology which remained joint departments until 1927, when the departments became separated. He then remained head of the newly created Psychology Department until 1937—that is, until the end of the first 50 years of psychology at Iowa. Concurrently, from 1908–1936, he was Dean of the Graduate College, at which date he became Emeritus, but was still to be heard from. He was succeeded by George Stoddard, who served from 1936–1942 as Dean of the Graduate College while also Director of the Child Welfare Research Station. However, when Dean Stoddard left for an appointment as President of the State University of New York, Dean Seashore was invited back again to become Dean of the Graduate College *Pro Tempore,* from 1942–1946. He died in 1949 at the age of 83.

I was with Dean Seashore on a number of occasions, particularly at the intimate annual meetings of the small group known as the Society of Experimental Psychologists, which he frequently attended. One other occasion was a symposium held in 1935 at the University of Southern California (USC) in Los

Angeles. The Symposium celebrated the 25th anniversary of the inauguration of graduate studies at USC and it was appropriate to have a distinguished graduate dean present at the symposium.

His son, Robert H. Seashore, with an Iowa PhD in 1925, was at the time a Visiting Professor of Psychology at USC. He was given the unusual privilege of reading the citation when his father was awarded one of his many honorary doctorates, and it was he who placed the hood over his father's shoulders.

An amusing visit was made to a movie studio during the symposium. Figure 3.1 shows the Seashores, father and son, along with the other participants in the symposium visiting the studio. Most of us will recognize child star Shirley Temple, in the middle. At that time she was being filmed for *Captain January*, with a childhood playmate of mine, Buddy Ebsen, in the title role. Dean Seashore is on the right of her as we view the figure, and Robert Seashore is next to

FIG. 3.1 Symposium on Convergent Trends in Psychology, University of Southern California, November 22–23, 1935, under the chairmanship of Milton Metfessel. Dean Seashore is in the middle of the back row, on the right side of Shirley Temple, with his son Robert Seashore looking over his shoulder. Milton Metfessel is further to the right, between Edward Tolman and Mary Cover Jones. Hilgard, in his early 30s, is on the other side of Shirley Temple. The others are West Coast psychologists and their spouses, except for the man with the striped tie who was the film director for Captain January.

him. I am located on the other side of Shirley Temple. There is another Iowa-related psychologist in the figure. Milton Metfessel, who chaired the Symposium, can be seen between Edward Tolman and Mary Cover Jones on the right in the back row. In 1929 Metfessel had left his associate professorship in psychology and speech at Iowa to head the psychology department at USC.

A small interchange with Dean Seashore early in our gathering has stuck in my memory. He asked to look at the back of my hands. He showed some disappointment because they were not suntanned enough. "I see," he said, "that you are not a golf player." He had been delighted to be able to play his rounds of golf in the California sunshine in November.

Seashore's importance to psychology and, indeed, to the University of Iowa as a whole, is too multi-faceted to be summarized briefly. I hope that his autobiography in the first volume of the *History of Psychology in Autobiography* (1930) and his *Pioneering in Psychology* (1942) are required reading for the graduate students who study at the University of Iowa.

THE HOUSING OF PSYCHOLOGY AT IOWA

I have mentioned the first housing of psychology in the Old Capitol and in five rooms at 14 North Clinton Street, all during the period when Professor Patrick considered himself to be a psychologist. But after Professor Seashore took over, more moves were in sight.

He began his laboratory work in the North Clinton Street quarters, and, as he put it, he was his own stenographer, wrote his own textbooks, invented the necessary apparatus, built his own bookcases, and served as general librarian. The old house was also occupied by the Department of Education, and the lecture room served as a departmental library for both psychology and education. His own office was in the workshop.

He found these somewhat primitive surrounding acceptable because a new laboratory was being built in Schaeffer Hall. He took especial pride in the room that he described as a "remarkable feature"—a light, sound, and jar-proof room built on a subfoundation and resting on a series of sandbaths in the second story. He had spent his first summer at Iowa supervising its construction. Schaeffer Hall had 12 rooms for psychology and two lecture rooms shared also with the Department of Education.

Seashore later saw that the abandoned university hospital could be remodeled to provide 300 rooms to accommodate Education, Psychology, Philosophy, and Child Welfare, with a joint library and other facilities. Psychology took about 75 rooms and Child Welfare 40 rooms. He renamed the building East Hall. There was also space available in University Hall, and an extended workshop shared with Physics in the Physics Building. Seashore's only regret was that he was not able to reinstall the remarkable room from Schaeffer Hall. An impressive dedication was held on December 30, 1930. At that time addresses were given by Professor Howard C. Warren of Princeton, Professor Walter Miles, an early Iowa PhD, then at Stanford University, but on his way to Yale, Professor Charles H. Judd, Dean of Education at the University of Chicago, Professor Edward A. Bott of the University of Toronto, and Professor Robert S. Woodworth of Columbia University—a distinguished group indeed. An account of the new laboratory was reported later by Professor Ruckmick (1937).

There were other facilities available to psychology in various parts of the university, but the new building was the central feature at the end of the 50-year period that I am discussing. Other spaces became available in later years.

THE IOWA CHILD WELFARE RESEARCH STATION

The Iowa Child Welfare Research Station was another of the many initiatives for which Dean Seashore was largely responsible. It became the Institute of Child Behavior and Development, the name having been changed by the Central Administration in 1963 to avoid misunderstandings surrounding the modern social welfare connotations of *child welfare*. I use the original name by which it was known during the years I am discussing. I had expected my colleague, Robert Sears, to discuss its history because he was its director from 1942 to 1949, but by reason of illness at home he withdrew from this program.

The idea originated as early as 1906 in the mind of Mrs. Cora Bussey Hillis, who viewed the research of the Agricultural College at Ames with respect. She visualized that a child research organization comparable to the Ames agricultural station, if connected with the University at Iowa City, could serve the same functions of research, teaching, and dissemination (Sears, 1975). She and women in the state continued to promote the idea through a formal organization known as "The State Organization to Promote the Establishment of the Iowa Child Welfare Research Station." A bill was introduced in the state legislature, but failed, and the cause was then taken up by Dean Seashore. He headed a committee called The University Committee on Research in Child Welfare, and prepared a report published in 1916 as a bulletin of the University of Iowa, in the Series on the Aims and Progress of Research, bearing the title, "A Child Welfare Research Station," with the subtitle: "Plans and Possibilities of a Research Station for the Conservation and Development of the Normal Child" (Seashore, 1916). With labor unions, service clubs, women's clubs, and others behind the campaign, this time it passed the legislature so that the plan was approved in 1917 with an appropriation of $50,000 to open the Station.

Bird T. Baldwin (1875–1928), with a Harvard PhD, and a postdoctoral summer in Leipzig followed by various academic positions, was immediately appointed the first Director, giving up his post in educational psychology at Johns Hopkins. World War I was declared before he could assume his duties, and he was needed in the war effort in Washington, so that the Station was not opened until 1919. He did yeoman service for 9 years, but died at the young age of 53 in 1928. He was before my time as a psychologist, and I regret that I never met him.

GEORGE D. STODDARD (1897–1981)

At the time of Baldwin's death, George Stoddard, with an Iowa PhD in 1925, had held an assistant professorship for 2 years. He was promoted to Associate Professor of Educational Psychology and made Acting Director of the Child Welfare Research Station for 1 year, 1928–1929, after which he became a Professor of Psychology and Director of the Station for 13 more years. In 1942 he left to become, in succession, the president of two universities—the University of the State of New York, and the University of Illinois—and completed his career at a third university as Chancellor and Vice President of the Long Island University. He died in 1981 at the age of 84.

Like his predecessor, Dean Seashore, he was available for other leadership appointments at Iowa. He succeeded Dean Seashore as Dean of the Graduate College when Seashore became Emeritus for the first time, and served from 1936–1942. After some difficulties in finding a suitable permanent replacement for Dean Seashore as Head of the Department of Psychology during those years, Stoddard filled this position and served as Graduate Dean for the year 1938–1939, before John McGeoch took over.

I knew George Stoddard quite well. Some of you, familiar with my history of psychology entitled *Psychology in America* (Hilgard, 1987), may be aware of an account I gave of a little service I did for him at a discussion at Stanford of the Yearbook of the National Society of Education that he edited with the title: "Intelligence: Its Nature and Nurture" (1940). Stanford, under Professor Lewis Terman's influence, and Iowa, under the influence of Professors Stoddard and Beth Wellman, took opposite sides on the relative contributions of heredity and environment. I was neutral, and was asked to chair a debate essentially between Terman and Stoddard, to be followed by a panel discussion. As Professor Stoddard was about to rise and reply to numerous criticisms by Terman, he whispered to me to interrupt him after he had answered a few points, to save time for the rest of the panel to join in. He had the audience with him, and when I interrupted him just as he was doing so well in his rebuttal, I received the boos, but he received the cheers. It had been a good move on his part, and I was glad to help.

Although this is later than the period on which I am focusing, I cannot refrain from mentioning my further experience with him, when he headed the United States Education Mission to Japan, in 1946, at the invitation of General MacArthur and the State Department. We were just about the first American civilians to appear in Japan after WW II, and we had a remarkable set of experiences in the month that we spent with Japanese educators, discussing with them the reforms

FIG. 3.2. The United States Education Mission to Japan, 1946, under the chairmanship of George D. Stoddard, with a stopover in Hawaii on the way to Tokyo. George Stoddard is in the middle of the front row. The row includes, beginning at the left, Frank N. Freeman, Hilgard, Emily Woodward, Stoddard, David H. Stevens (who represented the State Department), Wilson M. Compton, all members of the Mission, and Gregg M. Sinclair, President of the University of Hawaii, host to the Mission during its briefings during the stopover.

that the Japanese professors would like to see in Japanese education, with circumstances so favorable for change. The personal highlights for us were probably our luncheon with General MacArthur and Mrs. MacArthur at the Embassy and our opportunity to meet and shake hands with Emperor Hirohito. Figure 3.2 shows a picture in which George and I are together in the company of others. The picture was taken during briefings in Hawaii while en route to Tokyo, March 6, 1946. Unfortunately, this is not the whole group, but George Stoddard as the leader is in the middle of the front row. Some who are old enough may recognize Frank Freeman, at the left end of the front row. He had a distinguished career in education at the University of Chicago, and later as Dean of Education at the University of California, Berkeley. I am next to him, just half of my present age. The two at the far right of the front row are Wilson Compton, one of the three Compton brothers who were simultaneously presidents of universities, and President Gregg Sinclair of the University of Hawaii, our host in Hawaii, but not a member of the mission. I leave the subject of George Stoddard now to say something about the PhDs produced in the Department of Psychology and the Child Welfare Station.

THOSE WITH IOWA PHDS

A university achieves distinction for many different reasons, such as its libraries, laboratories, and other resources, but primarily for its faculty and the students who are served by the university. By their careers and accomplishments, the PhD graduates assure others of the competency of the faculty. Iowa psychology has a distinguished history of producing scholars who bear the Iowa PhD.

To see how old the tradition was, I looked up the first 10 PhD recipients in the *Psychological Register* of 1932 (Murchison, 1932). These degrees were granted between the years 1903 and 1910. There were not as many positions open for psychologists in those days, and to be listed in the *Psychological Register* the person had to be both alive and actively engaged in a psychological enterprise. I have not attempted to account for the three who are not in the Register, but I think it is remarkable that 7 of the 10 were listed in the book that came out 29 years after the first degree was granted among these 10. Here is the story of those of the first 10 who appeared in the *Psychological Register* of 1932:

- Mrs. Theodore W. Kemmerer (Mabel Clare Williams) had taught at the University of Iowa for 3 years prior to receiving the degree, and after her PhD, in 1903 remained on for a year, held a professorship at Coe College, and returned to Iowa where she became an associate professor by 1907, and continued to serve. She wrote a book entitled *Some Psychology* that appeared in 1930.
- Daniel Starch, with a PhD in 1906, had an interesting career both in academia and in applied psychology in the world of business. He remained at Iowa to teach for a year, then taught at Wellesley College for a year while doing some further study at Harvard, then taught for some years at the University of Wisconsin, and became a Professor of Educational Psychology at Harvard from 1920 to 1926. In 1932, at the time of the Register, he was Consulting Psychologist and Director of the Research Department of the American Association of Advertising Agencies. He continued in his independent work with his own agency, called by the name of Daniel Starch and Staff, Inc., in Mamaroneck, NY, until he became Chairman Emeritus in 1973 at the age of 90, shortly before his death.
- Franklin O. Smith, PhD 1912, became Professor and Department Head at the University of Montana.
- Walter Miles, PhD 1913, during the year 1913–1914 substituted for Professor Raymond Dodge at Wesleyan University. In the years 1914–1922, he had a most distinguished career in Boston at the Nutrition Laboratory of the

Carnegie Institution of Washington, where he could freely indulge the drive to invent apparatus that he must have acquired both under Professor Seashore and Professor Dodge. He then went to Stanford for the years 1922–1932, with some intervening years elsewhere, then to the Yale Institute of Human Relations until he reached retirement age, but he continued with service in Turkey for a time, and ultimately at the Submarine Base in New London, CT. He was President of the American Psychological Association in 1932, and a long-time member of the National Academy of Sciences and the American Philosophical Society, a distinguished career indeed.

- Thomas F. Vance, also PhD 1913, became a Professor at Iowa State College.

- Constantine F. Malmberg, PhD 1914, accepted a professorship at the Illinois State Normal University.

- Cordia C. Bunch, PhD 1920, after a career elsewhere, became a Professor of Applied Physics of Otology in 1930 at the Washington University Medical School in St. Louis.

These representatives of the very first PhDs from a university just getting under way in graduate studies are quite impressive. Iowa psychology has continued to have a distinguished history of producing scholars who bear the Iowa PhD. A fine account appears in the chapter entitled *Intellectual Progeny of Seashore and Science* by Donald K. Routh in the *Festschrift* for George Wischner that he edited (Routh, 1982).

THE FACULTY

As I mentioned earlier, distinguished students imply a distinguished faculty. What is surprising to contemporary students is how much was accomplished in the early days with a very small number of faculty members. As a very limited exercise in this respect, I have looked up the faculty as listed in the University Catalogs toward the end of the period of 50 years that I have made the topic of this chapter. I am passing over the many who came and went in the earlier years, without implying any disrespect for their contributions, in order not to lengthen this account unduly. So I begin with the Depression years following the stock market crash in 1929.

Dean Seashore remained as Department Head and Graduate Dean until he became Emeritus in 1936, but he was called back to duty, as we know. The years between 1929 and 1937 were relatively stable ones, so far as faculty continuity was concerned. The Department proper was manned by Seashore as Head, and three full professors: Frederic B. Knight, Professor of Education and Psychology, who had come following his Columbia PhD in 1920; Christian A. Ruckmick, with a 1913 PhD under Titchener at Cornell, had come from an associate professorship at the University of Illinois to a professorship at Iowa in 1924. Among his other accomplishments at Iowa, he edited the Iowa Studies in Psychology from 1928 to 1937. Lastly, Lee Edward Travis, Iowa educated with a PhD in 1924, had remained and attained his professorship in 1928. He was important in the coordination between the Psychology and Speech Departments, and headed the speech clinic. He had also done much to introduce electrophysiology.

There was only one associate professor at the time, Norman C. Meier, with an Iowa PhD in 1926, who had attained this rank in 1928. He became well known for his work in art appreciation. Lonzo Jones, who had just attained his degree, was a new assistant professor, the only one in the Department. There were two instructors who had not yet attained their PhDs, Herbert Jasper and R. E. Starbuck Miller.

Adding these up, there were four professors, one associate professor, one assistant professor, and two instructors—a total of eight, disregarding those in Child Welfare. Of these eight, only six were of assistant professor rank or above.

In Child Welfare there were numerous appointments for those not designated as psychologists. Among those called psychologists, George Stoddard had just reached the title of Research Professor, Beth Wellman had just become a research associate professor, and Harold Anderson was a research assistant professor. Ruth Updegraff had been at the Station since 1925 and had been appointed Research Associate after her PhD in 1928, and Orvis Irwin had just come as a research associate after completing his Ohio State PhD in 1929. If we add these up we find one at professor rank, one associate professor, one assistant professor, and two research associates designated as psychologists—a total of five psychologists on the staff, with only three of assistant professor rank or above.

Yet if we look at the Department in the years 1929–1935, when the staffs were little augmented, we see that from 5 to 14 PhDs were turned out each year with only a half dozen faculty members at or above the rank of Associate Professor, and in Child Welfare, an average of about four per year with the small staff of those at Assistant Professor rank or above.

As I have said, in the next few years after 1929, the staffs were little augmented. In the year 1935–1936, when Seashore was about to become Emeritus, he still headed the Department and the other full professors remained the same: Knight, Ruckmick, and Travis. Joseph Tiffin, with an Iowa PhD in 1930, had become an assistant professor of psychology and speech in 1931 and became the second Assistant Professor, leaving no assistant professors, because Jones had become an assistant dean of men. There were four instructors. Except for more at the instructor level, the size of the staff was little changed.

In Child Welfare, by the year 1935–1936, Orvis Irwin had been promoted to join Beth Wellman as a research associate professor. Ralph Ojemann was now listed as a research assistant professor of psychology, along with Harold Anderson and Harold Williams. Both Harold Skeels and Ruth Updegraff continued to be listed as research associates. So, again there had been only modest changes since 1929, for Ralph Ojemann had come that year, following his PhD at the University of Chicago. Wendell Johnson, with an Iowa PhD in 1931, had been made a research associate, and a speech clinician, and in 1933 became an assistant professor.

THE YEARS OF CRISIS AND TRANSITION

The next 2 or 3 years after 1936 became critical years for the Department of Psychology, best described as years of crisis and transition to new leadership. The occasion was of course that Dean Seashore was to become Emeritus in 1936, both as long-time Department Head and as Dean of the Graduate College. I do not know enough to explain the internal dynamics of those years, but I suppose that the end of a long period of dominance by a single strong individual often raises the question of successor. On the graduate dean side the transition was easy. George Stoddard was available, and he could continue as Director of the Child Welfare Research Station while taking over the graduate deanship in 1936. Things were not that easy in the Department of Psychology. I suppose that Professor Knight, although the senior in service at Iowa, because he was jointly in Psychology and Education, did not seem the most natural candidate for the headship. Professor Ruckmick, senior by 10 years to Professor Travis, may have thought that his turn had come, and Professor Travis himself was available.

I can only recount what happened. During the first year, 1936–1937, Seashore, instead of retiring, retained the department headship; and in the year 1937–1938, Travis acted as head during a turbulent year. There was bad blood between him and Ruckmick. Presently all the full professors and one associate had left, and Stoddard assumed the headship for the year 1938–1939. Professor Knight left in 1937 to become Director of Education and Applied Psychology at Purdue University, and Associate Professor Tiffin joined him there in 1938. Professor Travis left in 1938 for the University of Southern California to join Metfessel. Professor Ruckmick apparently did not fall as readily into an academic post, but he left in 1938 to become the general sales manager for the Stoelting Apparatus Company, possibly through Mr. Stoelting, who had been a close friend of E. B. Titchener under whom Ruckmick had studied at Cornell, and who were still alive at the time. Later Ruckmick became the Superintendent of Education in Ethiopia, and after that a lecturer at the University of Miami in Florida.

The decision was made to search outside the Department for new leadership, and the recruitment task fell largely on Dean Kay of the College of Liberal Arts and on Dean Stoddard. The initial successes were to add three new Associate Professors in 1938–1939 to join with Normal Meier as the only one remaining. These were Kenneth W. Spence, with a Yale PhD in 1933, to become an associate professor of psychology; James B. Stroud, with a University of Chicago PhD in 1930, to become an associate professor of educational psychology; and Dewey B. Stuit with a University of Illinois PhD in 1934, as an associate professor of psychology and Education. He later became the Dean of the College of Liberal Arts.

With the coming of John McGeoch, a Chicago PhD in 1926, who had had a distinguished career in several universities including Washington University, the University of Arkansas, the University of Missouri, and Wesleyan University in Connecticut, the Department was again on its feet. It was a sad event when McGeoch died in 1942, short of his 45th birthday, but he was ably succeeded by Kenneth Spence for the next 22 years, until 1964 when Spence left for the University of Texas.

I proposed to stop short of the McGeoch and Spence years because they belong to psychology at Iowa during the last half of its century during which its tradition of excellence has continued to flower. I hope that I have been fair to its roots in the first half.

ACKNOWLEDGMENTS

I wish to thank Professor Joan Cantor for supplying me numerous documents to assist me in the preparation of these remarks.

REFERENCES

Hilgard, E. R. (1936). A symposium on convergent trends in psychology held at the University of Southern California. *Psychological Bulletin, 33,* 146–147.

Hilgard, E. R. (1987). *Psychology in America: A historical survey.* San Diego: Harcourt Brace Jovanovich.

Murchison, C. (Ed.). (1932). *The psychological register* (Vol. 3). Worcester, MA: Clark University Press.

Patrick, G. T. W. (1932). Founding of the Psychological Laboratory at the State University of Iowa. An historical sketch. *The Iowa Journal of History and Politics, 30,* 404–416.

Routh, D. K. (Ed.). (1982). *Learning, speech, and the complex effects of punishment: Essays honoring George J. Wischner.* New York: Plenum.

Ruckmick, C. A. (1937). The psychological laboratory at the University of Iowa. *Journal of Experimental Psychology, 21,* 687–697.

Sears, R. R. (1975). *Your ancients revisited: A history of child development.* Chicago: University of Chicago Press.

Seashore, C. E. (1916). A Child Welfare Research Station. *Bulletin of the University of Iowa* (New Series No. 107). In the Series on Aims and Progress of Research, Prepared for the University Committee on Research in Child Welfare by the Chairman.

Seashore, C. E. (1930). Carl Emil Seashore. In C. Murchison (Ed.), *A history of psychology in autobiography* (Vol. 1, pp. 225–297). Worcester, MA: Clark University Press.

Seashore, C. E. (1942). *Pioneering in psychology.* (University of Iowa Studies, No. 398). Iowa City: University of Iowa Press.

Stoddard, G. D. (Chr.). (1940). *Intelligence: Its nature and nurture* (39th Yearbook of the National Society for the Study of Education, Parts 1 & 2). Bloomington, IL: Public School Publ. Co.

4 The Iowa Department of Psychology and the American Psychological Association: A Historical Analysis

Leonard D. Goodstein
American Psychological Association

GEORGE THOMAS WHITE PATRICK

In the Autumn of 1887 George Thomas White Patrick came to the University of Iowa as head of the Department of Philosophy and Psychology, then uniquely named the Department of Mental and Moral Science and Didactics. The two departments remained unified, although with a more traditional title, until 1927. Patrick immediately began the development of the University of Iowa Psychology Laboratories—the ninth such laboratory to be founded in the United States (Hilgard, 1987). The initial equipment was imported from Wundt's laboratory in Leipzig and served as the basis for introducing experiments into the elementary psychology course.

Patrick, an 1887 PhD from Johns Hopkins, was trained much more as a philosopher than a psychologist, but his association at Hopkins with G. Stanley Hall, James McKeen Cattell, Joseph Jastrow, and others introduced him to the new experimental psychology emerging in the German universities, a psychology that Patrick was to be instrumental in helping to import to the United States. Born on a farm in rural New Hampshire in 1857, Patrick moved with his family to Iowa at the age of 8. He received his BA degree from Iowa in 1878 and after teaching school in rural Iowa for several years, went on to Yale for an MA degree before entering Johns Hopkins as a doctoral student. When the opportunity arose to return to Iowa as its first professor of philosophy and psychology, Patrick gladly accepted and remained on the Iowa faculty until 1927 when he retired at the then mandatory age of 70. It is interesting to note that his sister, Mary, was the founding president of the American College for Girls in Constantinople (now Istanbul) and served in that post for 35 years.

Patrick, true to his initial training, remained more interested in philosophical than psychological matters, but was a vigorous supporter of the then emerging discipline of psychology at Iowa and elsewhere. Patrick can be seen as one of the historical figures that served as a bridge from philosophy to psychology in America (Seashore, 1949).

On July 8, 1892, some 5 years after the founding of the Iowa Laboratories, G. Stanley Hall, then president of Clark University, held a meeting of seven psychologists on the campus of Clark in Worcester, Massachusetts to found the American Psychological Association (APA). The organizing committee accepted 31 members, including George T. W. Patrick, into membership in this new and untested organization. The Iowa connection with the APA thus goes back to the founding of the Association, not quite 5 years after the founding of the Iowa Laboratories.

Although 13 of the 31 founders of the APA were eventually elected to the presidency of the APA, with both Hall and William James each elected twice (Hall in 1892 and 1924 and James in 1894 and 1904), Patrick apparently was not active in the APA. He was, however, active in the American Philosophical Association and was elected as the President of the other APA's Western Division for 1902. Although Patrick lived until the ripe age of 92—he died in 1949—Seashore (1949) characterized him as a, "semi-invalid, suffering from unexplained fatigue which kept him from physical exertion and made him limit his periods of mental work, take long vacations and retire early" (p. 452). Patrick's autobiography (1947)—a charming and witty document written at age 82 and published 10 years later as part of the Iowa Centennial—notes his interest and involvement in the American Philosophical Association, but he failed to mention any relationship with organized psychology. And, there is no record in the APA archives of Patrick's ever having attended an APA meeting or having been active in other ways. It is of interest to note that he mentioned the responsibilities of becoming president of the Western Division of the other APA—a post from which he resigned because of his illness—as one of the factors that led to his breakdown at age 45; he termed it *neurasthenia*. He was on leave from the University from the Spring of 1902 until the beginning of the Fall, 1911 semester when he recovered sufficiently to return to his teaching and writing.

Patrick's illness, however, did not interfere with his long and varied contributions to the literature of psychology. His publications include books on *The psychology of relaxation* (1916), *The psychology of social reconstruction* (1920), and *What is the mind?* (1928), as well as articles on such diverse topics as the psychology of women (1895), the psychology of profanity (1901), the psychology of football (1903), the psychology of war (1914), and the psychology of daylight savings time (1919). Patrick was also a very popular teacher, frequently described as "Iowa's unforgettable professor" by graduates of his era. At the Iowa Centennial Celebration in 1947, he was voted one of the five most popular professors of Iowa's first century.

CARL EMIL SEASHORE

Thus although George T. W. Patrick was the first link between Iowa and the APA, he was a weak link, and it was not until 1911 when Carl Emil Seashore became the APA's 20th president that the link was strengthened. Seashore had received his PhD in psychology from Yale University in 1895, having worked with George Trumbull Ladd, the APA's second president, and Edward Wheeler Scripture. He submitted his dissertation to Ladd, even though he had done the work under Scripture's supervision, a situation brought on by the politics of the Yale department at that time. Seashore stayed on at Yale as a post-doctoral fellow for 2 years and in 1897 joined the Iowa faculty as Assistant Professor of Philosophy and Director of the Psychology Laboratories.

A fellow classmate of Seashore's at Yale, C. B. Gilbert, had joined the Iowa faculty in 1895 following graduation, but found himself in continual conflict with Patrick, leading to his resignation in 1897. When Gilbert learned that Seashore was coming to Iowa to take his place, he wrote, "Seashore, you are going to hell" (Seashore, 1930, p. 260). But, as is often the case, one person's hell is another's paradise, and Seashore, one of the true pioneers of American psychology, remained at Iowa for the rest of his professional career, serving as Director of the Psychology Laboratories, Head of the Department of Psychology, cofounder of the Iowa Child Welfare Research Station, Dean of the Graduate School, as well as Acting President of the University on several occasions. He retired from the University in 1937 at the age of 71, but was recalled during World War II and again served as Graduate Dean *pro tem* from 1942 through 1946.

Seashore's research interests were varied, but were concentrated on the psychology of aesthetics, especially music. His autobiography (Seashore, 1930) proudly noted that he and his family were the first owners of a reed organ in Boone County, Iowa and that the singing of hymns was a daily ritual when he was growing up. His APA presidential address (Seashore, 1912), *The measure of a singer,* was an early attempt by Seashore to identify the elements necessary for success as a singer—such as discriminating pitch, timbre, intensity, and so on— and to describe procedures for measuring these elements. His later work on the psychology of music was much broader and included attempts to study the aesthetics of music.

Seashore was one of the early empiricists in psychology, continually attempting to extend the understanding of many human endeavors through the application of psychological research methods. These areas of study included child development, especially giftedness; speech and hearing, including speech pathology; education, including higher education; criminality; psychopathology; and the aesthetics of art and music. As a result of these interests, Seashore worked hard to establish linkages between his psychology departments and other units of the university, especially the College of Education, the Iowa Psychopathic Hospital, the College of Medicine, the departments of art, music, speech, physical education, and, of course, the Child Welfare Research Station. Although it is well known that he was one of those instrumental in the founding of the Station, it is less well known that he was also instrumental in the founding of the Department's Psychological Clinic and the Institute of Mental Health. The Clinic, founded in 1908 and modeled after that of Witmer's at the University of Pennsylvania, was developed as a training and research center, especially in the area of mental testing. After the founding of the Psychopathic Hospital in 1915, the Clinic served as an outpatient branch of the Hospital and was eventually completely assimilated into the Hospital. The Institute of Mental Health was also developed as a training and research unit within the Department, but one concerned with educational problems, especially disorders of speech and reading—the first such center in the country. Seashore saw all of these new operations as supporting graduate education in the University, under the leadership of the Psychology Department. And, under his leadership the Graduate College of the University of Iowa developed into a major institution with a well-deserved reputation for innovative, quality programs.

The APA annual meeting in 1911, the year of Seashore's presidency, was held in Washington, DC in conjunction with the meeting of the Southern Society for Philosophy and Psychology. The substantive program provides clear evidence that psychology was being applied to many varied fields as well as progressing as a basic science. The most important political issue to confront the governing Council was that of membership growth. The number of new members that could be elected each year had been reached, and some criteria for membership other than mere interest in psychology had to be established—a somewhat surprising conclusion for an organization with only 244 members.

At Seashore's urging, the Council set as requirements for APA membership both holding a position as a psychologist *and* having a record of published research. Applicants for membership henceforth would need to apply at least 1 month prior to the annual meeting and submit a statement of their professional position along with copies of their published research for review by the membership committee. The task of the committee over the next several decades became reviewing the published research of applicants and determining which of the applicants were worthy of being elected APA members. This change in the membership requirements was one step in the continual process of the APAs development as a professional association rather than a learned society (Goodstein, 1988).

Seashore remained an active and loyal member of the APA for the remainder of his life. As one index of that loyalty, Seashore proudly noted in one of his autobiographies that his eldest son, Robert, "holds the distinction of being the first son of a member of the American Psychological Association to be taken into that Association" (Seashore, 1930, p. 256). Robert, born in 1902, received his doctorate from Iowa, having written his dissertation under his father's direction. Carl Emil Seashore wrote (1964) of his pleasure in simultaneously serving as the director of Robert's dissertation, chair of his department, and as the dean of the graduate school awarding the degree. Robert Seashore died in 1951 at the age of 49, while serving as Chair of the Psychology Department at Northwestern University and a member of the APA Council of Representatives. Although the feat of having one's child become a member of the APA has been duplicated many times since, Seashore may be the only APA member to have a grandchild as well as a child become an APA member. Charles N. Seashore, now an independent consultant psychologist in Washington, DC and an APA member, is Robert's son and Carl Emil's grandson. It is worth noting that Carl's brother, August, although not a psychologist himself, was the father of two prominent psychologists, Harold Seashore, the long-time president of the Psychological Corporation, and Stanley Seashore, a long-time faculty member of the University of Michigan's psychology department. The contributions of the Seashore family to the discipline of psychology are clearly unparalleled.

In addition to his service over the years to APA, Seashore was also a member of the American Association for the Advancement of Science and served as the Vice President of the Section of Psychology. One of his many honors, one that specially delighted him, was his election to membership in the National Academy of Science—the first psychologist to receive that honor. His delight stemmed from the fact that he had earlier been rejected on several occasions from membership in the Society of Sigma Xi, the national honorary scientific society, on the grounds that psychology was not a science. He clearly won that war!

The 1930 meeting of the APA was held in Iowa City on December 29th, largely because of Seashore's insistence. The meeting had 382 registrants, 35% of the APA's total membership of 1,101 at that time. It boggles the mind to think of the impact on the Iowa City of today if 24,000 psychologists (35% of today's membership) suddenly descended on it!

Following the APA meeting, on December 30, there was a day-long program for which most registrants remained, dedicating the new psychology laboratories in East Hall (now Seashore Hall). At the day's final event, a celebratory dinner, Iowa's President Jessup and Seashore both spoke about the commitment of the University to the development of psychology in its many branches and to its application to all fields of human enterprise. The concluding action of the APA Council on December 29 was to formally vote appreciation to Dean Seashore and the faculty and students of the Department for their hospitality and support in the planning and conduct of the annual meeting and also to congratulate both the Department and the University for the fine new quarters that had been made available to the Iowa Department.

WALTER R. MILES

The 1932 meeting of the APA was held in Ithaca, New York under the presidency of Walter R. Miles, a 1913 Iowa PhD who had done his dissertation under

Seashore's direction. Miles received his BA in psychology in 1908 from Earlham College in Richmond, Indiana, where he served as the assistant in teaching the elementary psychology course. Without any further education at the time, he was offered a 1-year instructorship at William Penn College in Oskaloosa, Iowa. As Miles (1967) noted, one day there was a stranger in his classroom, Dean Carl Seashore from the University of Iowa Graduate School, out on a recruiting expedition for graduate students. He asked Miles to visit him in Iowa City and that visit resulted in Miles being accepted as a graduate student in psychology, where he worked under Seashore. It is interesting to note that, of the four doctoral degrees conferred at the 1913 Iowa commencement, two of them were in psychology and one each in chemistry/mathematics and political science/English, indicating the strength of Psychology compared with the other departments, even at that time.

When Miles completed his degree, he accepted a position as Associate Professor of Psychology at Wesleyan College in Middletown, Connecticut, where Raymond Dodge was professor and head. Miles' autobiography noted his pleasure in his election as an APA member in 1914. Miles went on to serve as director of the Carnegie Nutrition Laboratory, an affiliate of the Harvard Medical School, where he did some of the original scientific work on the effects of nutrition on behavior, and as professor at Stanford and Yale Universities. He had just moved to Yale in the Autumn of 1932 when he was preparing his APA presidential address. His address (Miles, 1933), *Age and human ability,* was an early report on the results of the Stanford Later Maturity Study on the changes in a variety of psychological function over the life span. This research is important as one of the first that demonstrated that there were no declines in many psychological functions over age and that some individuals show little if any decline at all. Following his retirement from Yale in 1953, Miles was a visiting professor at the University of Istanbul for 3 years and then Scientific Director at the Naval Submarine Base in New London, Connecticut, where he played a key role in the development of the Sea Labs program.

ALBERT BANDURA

From 1932 until Albert Bandura's election as APA's 83rd president in 1974, no Iowa alumnus or faculty member was elected as APA president. Not that there were not efforts. Kenneth W. Spence was on the ballot on several different occasions during the 1950s, but never succeeded in winning. The Department's influence on the APA was exercised through the presence of Iowans on most of the major boards and committees of the APA throughout this period, as well as in key editorial roles with APA journals. It is difficult to document or quantify this influence through an analysis of APA records, given the nature of the APA records and the time that would be required.

Bandura's presidential address (Bandura, 1974) was one of the important early landmarks in the development of a cognitive theory of behavior and behavior development, placing special importance on the role of imitation or modeling in such development. Bandura, a 1952 Iowa PhD, has been chiefly responsible for placing the concept of modeling or imitation on a solid empirical footing. In this connection, it is interesting to note that Seashore was an early and unheralded advocate of understanding the importance of imitation in human development, a position made quite directly in his autobiography (1930), suggesting the long historical roots to some contemporary ideas.

The most pressing political issues with which APA was contending during Bandura's term as president led to the development of a response to the proposed cuts in the budgets of both the National Academy of Science and the National Institute of Mental Health by the Nixon administration as well as a strategy for helping Congress use psychological research findings in the development of public policy. The former led to the birth of the American Association for the Advancement of Psychology—an external advocacy group primarily supported by the APA and its members—and the latter to the establishment of the Office of National Policy Studies within the APA central office. While both offices have subsequently been integrated into other APA central office structures, both were important interim steps in the further development of the APA as a professional association.

JANET TAYLOR SPENCE

The most recent APA president with Iowa roots is Janet Taylor Spence who served as APA's 93rd president in 1984. Her presidential address, "The Rewards and Costs of Individualism" (Spence, 1985), is a fascinating attempt to understand some of the changing patterns of our society in social psychological terms. Spence's term as the APA's president was highlighted by the efforts to integrate *Psychology Today* (PT) into the APA management structure. The acquisition of PT was clearly one of the most divisive and expensive decisions ever made by the Association. Spence found herself attempting to implement a decision that she had initially opposed and one that became "mission impossible." I take some pleasure in noting that I personally have been largely responsible for the sale of PT to a small publishing group early in the Spring of 1988, removing this vexatious problem from the APA once and for all.

CONCLUSION

It seems clear to me that the Iowa Department of Psychology has been an important factor in the development of the APA, as well as in the development of the discipline of psychology. One of the 31 founding members (3%) was an Iowa faculty member and three Iowa graduates and one Iowa faculty member (4%) have been presidents of the APA. Although the numbers are small, the influence has been large, to say the least.

The three Iowa PhDs who have been presidents of the APA place Iowa in ninth place in the order of frequency of presidential production. Columbia and Harvard are tied for first, each with 15; Johns Hopkins and Yale are tied for third place, each with 7; Chicago and Leipzig are next with 5 each. Should one more Iowa PhD be elected the APA president, Iowa would vault into seventh place, although why anyone so well-educated would wish to do so these days is a mystery to me.[1]

When I agreed to undertake this project tracing the Iowa–APA connection, I had no idea of what I would uncover. It turns out that I learned a good bit more about Iowa than about the connection, but that is not inappropriate, given the circumstances. I thoroughly enjoyed myself in this journey back into time and I am delighted to have this opportunity to share the results of this expedition with you.

ACKNOWLEDGMENTS

I gratefully acknowledge the help of Dibya Choudhuri of Smith College, Ludy T. Benjamin of Texas A & M University, and Jeanette T. Goodstein of the Society for Research in Child Development, for their help in various stages of the preparation of this chapter.

REFERENCES

Bandura, A. (1974). Behavior theory and the models of man. *American Psychologist, 29,* 859–869.

Goodstein, L. D. (1988). The report of the Executive Vice President: 1987. The growth of the American Psychological Association. *American Psychologist, 43,* 491–498.

Hilgard, E. R. (1987). *Psychology in America: A historical survey.* San Diego, CA: Harcourt Brace Jovanovich.

Miles, W. R. (1933). Age and human abilities. *Psychological Review, 40,* 99–103.

Miles, W. R. (1967). Autobiography. In E. G. Boring & G. Lindzey (Eds.), *A history of psychology in autobiography* (Vol. 5, pp. 231–252). New York: Appleton Century Crofts.

Patrick, G. T. W. (1895). The psychology of women. *Popular Science Monthly, 46,* 209–225.

Patrick, G. T. W. (1901). The psychology of profanity. *Psychological Review, 8,* 113–127.

Patrick, G. T. W. (1903). The psychology of football. *American Journal of Psychology, 14,* 368–381.

Patrick, G. T. W. (1914). The psychology of war. *Popular Science Monthly, 87,* 156–168.

---

[1]Subsequent to this writing Charles D. Spielberger was elected to serve as APA's 100th President in 1991, raising questions about how well we actually did educate him!

Patrick, G. T. W. (1916). *The psychology of relaxation*. Boston: Houghton Mifflin.

Patrick, G. T. W. (1919). The psychology of daylight time. *Scientific Monthly, 9*, 385–396.

Patrick, G. T. W. (1920). *The psychology of social reconstruction*. Boston: Houghton Mifflin.

Patrick, G. T. W. (1928). *What is the mind?* New York: Macmillan.

Patrick, G. T. W. (1947). *George Thomas White Patrick: An autobiography*. Iowa City, IA: University of Iowa Press.

Seashore, C. E. (1912). A measure of a singer. *Science, 35*, 201–212.

Seashore, C. E. (1930). Autobiography. In C. Murchison (Ed.), *A history of psychology in autobiography* (Vol. 1, pp. 225–297). New York: Russell & Russell.

Seashore, C. E. (1949). George Thomas White Patrick: 1837–1949. *American Journal of Psychology, 62*, 451–452.

Seashore, C. E. (1964). *Psychology and life in autobiography*. (Privately printed, available from Charles N. Seashore, 4445 29th St., NW, Washington, DC 20008.)

Spence, J. T. (1985). The rewards and costs of individualism. *American Psychologist, 40*, 1285–1295.

5 Defining Being Motivated: Alternative Operational Formats

Judson S. Brown
Oregon Health Sciences University, Portland, Oregon

Unexorcised remnants of the nostalgic spell cast by the Iowa Centennial Celebration have led me to devote the first part of this chapter to a personal account of the ways in which my views of emotion, frustration, and motivation were modulated by interactions with colleagues and students at Iowa. Some of the outcomes of these experiences, especially as they have affected my conceptions of operational definitions of the attribute of being motivated, are detailed in subsequent pages.

In the Fall of 1946, shortly after the end of World War II, I was hired as an assistant professor of psychology at Iowa. Much of the preceding 4 years had been spent in the Army Air Forces working with Arthur W. Melton on the design and construction of psychomotor tests for the selection of pilots, bombardiers, and navigators. This activity, of necessity, was applied in nature and made little use of the "purer" psychological knowledge I had acquired at Yale from Neal E. Miller, Donald G. Marquis, and Clark L. Hull. Quite understandably, as I began my work, I was apprehensive. I had delivered no classroom lectures while in the service, and my inadequate mastery of current trends in academic psychology, along with a lack of old, well-thumbed lecture notes, added fuel to my feelings of insecurity. The stress of the situation was enhanced by the fact that Kenneth Spence waited until just a week or two prior to the start of the semester to tell me what courses I would be asked to teach. As I recall, he finally said that I would be responsible for an undergraduate course in experimental psychology and a "traditional" graduate-level course entitled "Action and Emotion." Although the former offered few challenges, the latter posed substantial threats. "What in the world," I asked myself, "did those who concocted that title mean by the term *action?*" At Yale, obviously, I had studied *behavior* but never anything called *action.* Turning to the library for help, I discovered that the title was apparently a hangover from the days when psychologists sought to delineate, typically by introspection, the "mental" antecedents to overt action. A chapter entitled something like "The Determinants of Action," in the then-popular advanced-general textbook by Boring, Langfeld, and Weld, supported this interpretation. There the essence of the problem was portrayed as that of how the "will" functions to generate overt behavior and how reflex and voluntary actions might be distinguished. With but limited time for course preparation, and hampered by a Yale-induced bias against such terms as *volition,* I was forced to find unconventional ways of meeting my obligations.

Fortunately, G. R. Wendt's monograph called Methods of Recording Action came to my attention. Its title jibed with that of the course, and its content coincided with my war-time activities in the design and construction of electromechanical testing devices. So, for the first half-dozen or so sessions we discussed such matters as basic electricity and electronics; specific instruments for the measurement of reaction time, skin resistance, and eye blinks; and devices for the measurement and control of visual, auditory, and other types of stimuli. I suspected that the "founding fathers" of that course might not have approved of my stratagem but I had no other choice. And because many of our graduate students had scant knowledge of the "hardware" aspects of laboratory research my "action" was not entirely without merit.

While "treading water" in this way, I hastened to amass some lecture notes on spontaneous activity, reflex and voluntary factors in classical conditioning, tropistic behavior, purposive behavior, exploratory behavior, and more. Consequently, by the time I had completed my review of Wendt's material I was prepared, after a fashion, to turn to topics of more direct "psychological" significance.

The topic of *emotion* presented a different challenge. The term was familiar, to be sure, but it was not one with which I felt comfortable. At that time, most writers accepted, quite uncritically, the idea that emotions, though covert, were existential *reals* that served as important determinants of behavior. This, despite the fact that attempts to obtain reliable counts of the numbers and types of emotions, largely through introspective forays, had generated little but voluble disagreement. Moreover, extant theories of emotion were vague and unproductive. So great was the uncertainty that some writers, notably Duffy (1934), Meyer (1933), and Skinner (1938) had argued that the concept should be expunged entirely from the lexicon of psychology. To be successful, any scientific enterprise must be able, at the very least, to obtain accurate tallies of whatever phenomena are under investigation. But anger, joy, apprehension, and their alleged kin cannot be seen by the scientist in the same immediate sense that an eyeblink or a knee-jerk is seen. In my lectures on emotions, therefore, I spent far more time questioning their scientific utility than in emoting over their conceptual virtues.

Over a period of several years I wrestled with these issues without achieving satisfactory solutions. But with the astute help of I. E. Farber, I came to the tentative conclusion that emotions, whatever their "real" natures, could be treated within a theory of behavior as intervening variables. This notion was presented in a theoretical paper (Brown & Farber, 1951) where, to exemplify the approach, we outlined an "emotional" interpretation of frustrated behavior. Therein we suggested that frustration, considered as an emotional state (not clearly defined), could be regarded as the outcome of either (a) the simultaneous evocation of two competitive excitatory tendencies, or (b) the arousal of a single excitatory tendency and an incompatible inhibitory tendency. The effects of the production of frustration on observable behavior were assumed to be increased drive, plus the generation of frustration-specific internal stimuli. A number of fragmentary empirical findings, especially those showing increased vigor of responding during periods of nonreinforcement, were cited as supporting evidence.

During this era, Farber and I, with the able assistance of some of our graduate students, notably Frank N. Marzocco, Harry I. Kalish, John J. Meryman, and Alfred Jacobs, were conducting experiments designed to show that fear, vaguely described as a reaction to a CS that has been paired with an aversive US, was capable of potentiating some responses and, when reduced contingently after the occurrence of an instrumental response, could reinforce that response (Brown & Jacobs, 1949). The latter effect, of course, had been demonstrated by Miller's (1948) classic experiment on the reinforcing effect of fear reduction and was forecast by Mowrer's (1939) theoretical treatment of anxiety. Our observations, that a putative fear-arousing situation or event seemed to potentiate the *reflex-startle* reaction to a percussive sound, enabled us to develop a technique whereby strength of fear could be mapped on a moment-to-moment basis. Thus, we observed (Brown, Kalish, & Farber, 1951) that the magnitude of the acoustic startle in rats, though that response was never directly reinforced, varied concomitantly with operations believed to affect the acquisition, extinction, and spontaneous recovery of conditioned fear. On the theoretical side, the results were interpreted as manifestations of the energizing effect of an acquired source of drive and as consistent with Hull's assumption of a multiplicative relation between drive and habit strength. The procedure has since proved useful in a variety of settings and is now commonly described as the Potentiated Startle effect (Davis & Astrachan, 1978).

Throughout these years, however, I held to the view that emotions, drives, and the like, were, in some unclear sense, existential "reals" whose "true" nature might ultimately be revealed, albeit obliquely, by techniques such as the *potentiated startle* method. This same attitude perseverated during the writing of my book on motivation (Brown, 1961), although at that time I was beginning to feel some skepticism as to its soundness. This was due, in part, to comments that Frank Marzocco had made in one of our discussions of motivation. To my astonishment he once argued that an adequate theory of behavior might be constructed entirely devoid of the concept of drive. The conceptual seed planted by this comment, nourished by the insights of others, for example, Estes (1958), germinated and emerged in the form of a chapter in my book entitled "Motivational and Associative Interpretations of 'Motivated Behavior.' " Remnants of traditional views remained, however, because I still imagined that I would recognize "real" motivational phenomena were I to see them.

Throughout the course of these events the content of Action and Emotion underwent dramatic changes. Action with its purposive auras melted away, but a trace of emotion remained, albeit disguised as motivationally potent conditioned fear. Most significantly, *motivation* became the key descriptor for the course. Concern with the possible motivational consequences of learned behaviors led me to examine the *acquired drive* problem in the Nebraska Symposium on Motivation (Brown, 1953). There I raised the question of whether it makes sense to speak of an acquired drive *for* something. Doing so smacked undesirably of teleology and seemed to imply an unmanageably large roster of learned drives— as large, obviously, as the list of things that organisms are said to learn to need or desire. Moreover, extant theories of classical and instrumental conditioning failed to provide adequate models for the process of acquiring a drive *for* any particular something. Simple Pavlovian conditioning paradigms were unsatisfactory inasmuch as unconditioned stimuli capable of evoking a drive *for* a particular object, such as a new car, could not be identified. In attempting to explain money-seeking behavior, I suggested that what one learns as a child is to be *anxious* in the presence of cues that have been associated with the aversive consequences of *not* having money when it is needed. The anxiety conditioned to cues denoting a lack of money was seen as providing the drive in what had been loosely called a "drive *for* money." This version had the merit of being devoid of the purposive connotations of that phrase. The so-called drives for power, prestige, affection, and more, were also interpreted as manifestations of learned anxieties conditioned to deficit-indicating cues.

I have already mentioned one of the turning points in my thinking about motivation, namely, Marzocco's suggestion that a drive concept might not be required at all by an adequate theory of behavior. But there was a second idea of even more significance that I attribute to Farber. During the final months of the preparation of my book, he read the manuscript with a degree of critical insight and understanding that was superb. In those days I believed that since motivation was, in some sense, really "there," the task of the psychologist was to identify the empirical phenomena that "reflected" its "true essence" most accurately. Farber, however, argued that it would be much better to attempt to identify whatever phenomena would generate the *most useful definition* of motivation. That advice troubled me for some time, probably because I failed to grasp its significance. I am now convinced that it provides a significant key to the clarification of this and other conceptual puzzles. It occupies central stage in the discussion of specific definitions that follows.

Subsequently, Farber's caveat was underscored by Brodbeck's (1963) characterization of the nature of concepts. She stressed the idea that a concept names what is the same in different individuals, that is, a character they all exemplify. As she noted, whereas laws are discovered, concepts are not. The latter, being names, are *bestowed,* not found. This has led me to speak of *motivated* rather than *motivation* because the adjectival form better serves as a label to be bestowed on individuals who share some character in common. The task of reliably identifying "motivated" individuals, as we see later, is one in which operational definitions play a central role.

Finally, while exploring the implications of Farber's advice I encountered Bergmann's (1957) views on the significance, or lack thereof, of operational definitions. As he pointed out, the meaning of a term defined operationally might be perfectly clear and have unambiguous empirical reference, yet be utterly useless if it failed to enter into lawful relations with other concepts. Significant concepts are those that have been defined precisely and have also been shown to have predictive fertility. I come back to this point later on.

In brief, then, the foregoing ideas are perhaps the more significant ones derived from my long and pleasant immersion in the rich intellectual climate of Iowa. The way is now open to reflect on how my thinking about motivation has been affected and, I believe, improved by these ideas.

In the language of a behavioral science, terms such as *intelligent, anxious, rigid, motivated,* and their various kin, are commonly said to qualify as concepts. As I have observed, a concept is perhaps best characterized as a word, introduced to indicate that some identifiable attribute or property is shared by otherwise different individuals or entities. Once methods have been perfected for deciding reliably which individuals are to be labeled *intelligent, motivated,* or whatever, degree of sharing can then be readily determined. Such labels are given referential meaning by being connected to observable events, for example, specific kinds of testing situations, assorted treatments, response dimensions, and more.

The foregoing sentence epitomizes the essence of *operational definitions.* Were we to formulate such a definition it might assume the following "if . . . then . . ." conditional form:

X is motivated $\equiv$ if X is tested by means of the Iowa Motivation Test, then X gets a high score.

Here the adjective *motivated,* the attribute label, occupies the position of the predicate in the sentence "X is motivated." The three-bar sign stands for *means the same as.* By convention, therefore, the meaning of the three-word sentence at the left is identical to the meaning of the longer sentence at the right. The statement at the left is formally termed the *definiendum;* the one at the right, the *definiens*. Such a formulation tells us what we must do, that is, administer the test, and what outcome we must observe, that is a high score for X, in order to decide that X is to be labeled as *motivated*. As I note shortly, the kinds of operations that have been described in definientia of motivated vary widely and have significantly different implications. But comments on the operational format itself take precedence.

First, because the definiendum and the definiens mean the same thing, in any statement where the word "motivated" appears, that word can be replaced by the longer definiens without change of meaning. To say that the two statements are interchangeable in this way is to say also that the defined term is expendable. The assertion that "X is motivated" adds nothing new to what the definiens says. Hence the term *motivated* is redundant. Its introduction, *after* the definiens has been articulated, serves only one important function, that of *abbreviatory convenience*.

Second, from a different perspective, the definiens tells us precisely how we can know when the sentence with motivated as its predicate, is true or false for any particular individual. The definiens consists of two parts, an "if . . ." and a "then . . ." component. Each component can be independently determined to be true by observation, but *both* must be true for the conjoint definiens to be true. And it is only when the definiens is true that the definiendum "X is motivated" can be said to be true. Because the definiendum and the definiens have identical meanings, either both must be true or both must be false. If the "if . . ." component is true, but the "then . . ." portion is false, the definiens is false. If the "if . . ." phrase is false, the outcome is indeterminate.

Third, as an abstract term, *motivated* cannot be defined by ostension, that is, by the simple act of pointing. But if we decide to introduce such a term, its meaning can be accurately conveyed by a good linguistic definition. It is important, therefore, to be sure that the procedures and measurements described in the definiens be concrete and replicable. If these operations lie in the public domain, reasonable consensus can be reached among qualified observers as to which, if any, of the individuals under scrutiny merit being categorized as motivated.

Fourth, by means of a relatively simple expansion of the definiens, provision can be made for defining *degrees* of the attribute in question. Appropriately chosen levels of performance on the specified test would make it possible to arrange individuals on a scale of "motivatedness" and, as a result, to search for laws relating degree of that property to degree of some other. Success in deriving such laws would greatly enhance the *significance* of the definition.

Finally, whoever decides to formulate operational definitions of this kind must decide whether a vague, time-worn term like *motivated,* or some new unfamiliar term, should be entered into the predicate of the definiendum. In either case, one must also decide what kinds of operations would be likely to result in the best or most significant laws. The first of these points is discussed later on, but the second, to which I have already alluded, constitutes the focus of the following discussion.

A survey of extant treatments reveals that although formal definitions of the attribute motivated are almost nonexistent, reasonable guesses can be hazarded as to the kinds of operations that would have been included in the definientia had they been articulated. I have found it useful to group these into four major classes or types according to whether they emphasize Past Treatments (Type PT), Current Treatments (Type CT), Organic Measurements (Type OM), or Response Measurements (Type RM). The first of these highlights prior events such as food or water privation or intense noxious (usually) stimulation. The second invokes current treatments, especially intense external and/or internal stimuli. The third entails the measurement of electrical or other organic phenomena, whereas the fourth relies on the recording of overt responses to a test situation of some kind. As I have noted, a choice from among them involves variegated theoretical implications, research strategies, and conceptual interpretations.

Table 5.1, wherein the four types serve as column headings, summarizes the more important aspects and implications of these definitions. The entries in the first row are illustrative (fictitious) operational definitions of the attribute motivated, with corresponding features appearing in succeeding rows.

It is evident from the entries in the first and second columns that the two *treatment* paradigms (PT and CT) are much alike, differing only with respect to whether the treatment of record was administered (or occurred) prior to, or at the present time. And even this distinction is blurred by the possibility that past treatments may contribute importantly to a definition because of past-treatment residua persisting into the present.

The PT format is consistent with a long-standing assumption of students of animal behavior, namely that a food-deprived animal will be motivated (driven). Likewise, being sexually motivated has been viewed as deprivation-dependent (in part), being motivated to sleep has been scaled by reference to hours without sleep, and being fearful has been defined by reference solely to the number of antecedent CS-US pairings in an aversive conditioning paradigm. The two treatment styles differ from the two *measurement* varieties in that, for the former, no treatment outcomes are stipulated (Row 2). The definientia for the PT and CT cases consist of single statements devoid of *then* or contingent clauses. Despite that lack, such one-proposition definitions can be unambiguous. Through their use, individuals can be reliably tagged as being motivated and the possibility of useful laws can be explored. Hull (1943, 1952) did not view motivation as an individual-difference parameter and did not formulate an explicit operational definition of either drive or "being motivated." Had he done so, it would probably have been cast in the PT mold because of the greater compatibility of that style with his theoretical stance. The following comments on his approach to motivation are offered in support of this supposition.

TABLE 5.1
Type of Definiens

	Type PT *Prior treatment*	*Type CT* *Current Treatment*	*Type OM* *Organic Measures*	*Type RM* *Response Measures*
1 Example	X is motivated $\equiv X$ has been food deprived	X is motivated $\equiv X$ is exposed to a loud noise now	X is motivated $\equiv$ if X's organic state is measured, then X gets a high score	X is motivated $\equiv$ if X is given the m Test, then X gets a high score
2 Defined contingently?	No—outcomes not measured	No—outcomes not measured	Yes—outcomes measured	Yes—outcomes measured
3 Sensitive to individual differences?	No	No	Yes	Yes
4 Manipulation of level of motivation	Directly by investigator	Directly by investigator	Indirectly by sampling or by m.v. introduction	Indirectly by sampling or by m.v. introduction
5 Identification of motivational variables	By assumption for each variable	By assumption for classes of variables	By noting changes in organic states	By noting changes in test responses
6 Locus of arbitrariness	Choice of prior treatment	Choice of current treatment	Choice of organic state to be measured	Choice of test items and responses to be measured

In Hull's system, the concept of drive (D), construed as an intervening variable, was given referential meaning, by being "anchored to both antecedent and consequent events" (1943, p. 22). This is shown in the paradigm:

$$AC....f....D....f....Rs$$

Here drive (D) is assumed to be an increasing (sigmoid) function (f) of such antecedent conditions (AC) as time of food or water deprivation. Both antecents and consequents are, to be sure, represented in this schema, but D is not, in fact, *anchored* to both sets of observable conditions. Were we to translate the essence of this conception into a formal definition it would be of the PT style, drive being *defined* by antecedents only. Time of deprivation would appear in the definiens, but responses would not. Drive depends on what has happened to the individual, but not, in any way, on the frequency or vigor of his or her responses.

I have already noted that Hull did not use the adjectival forms *driven* or *motivated*. Had he done so he might have paid more heed to the place of individual differences either within or among strains or species. As indicated in Row 3, the PT format, appropriate to his treatment, is insensitive to individual differences. This claim is buttressed by the conclusion that all individuals who have been treated the same way must be identically motivated. Identical treatments define identical levels of being motivated and different treatments define levels that are different. This holds regardless of differences in genetic background, sensory acuity, gender, prior experience, or whatever. If such factors were to be added to the definiens of a treatment definition it would mean that the attribute is no longer being defined in terms of treatment alone.

A special feature of both the PT and CT formats is that they foster rather simple—some might say simple-minded—experimental manipulations of degree of being motivated (Row 4). If, by definition, being motivated increases with deprivation duration or other manipulable variable, then the effect on performance of (defined) level of motivation can be determined directly. I incline to the view that the rash of drive-manipulation studies that followed the publication of Hull's formulation were designed in this way because of his implied PT-style drive definition.

The kind of format one chooses also has implications for the task of identifying motivationally relevant variables (Row 5). If being motivated is asserted, as in a PT definition, to be an increasing function of time of food privation, then privation duration becomes, willy nilly, a motivational variable. It becomes so, not because of its role as an energizer of responses, or some other outcome, but by arbitrary (definitional) asseveration. This conclusion fits every definition that relies exclusively on some kind of prior or current treatment. Definitions that incorporate observations of outcomes, whether of organic states or responses, do not, in this way, irrevocably concretize the motivational status of some particular variable. This point is developed in more detail later. There it is argued that, in the most general sense, an empirical variable qualifies as concept-relevant provided its introduction is associated with reliable changes in the defined attribute.

One more aspect of the PT format seems worthy of comment. To say, for example, that "X is motivated" is to mean "X has been food deprived" is doubtless too vague to qualify as a good definition. Whoever might try to satisfy the conditions of that definiens would need to know exactly how extended the deprivation regimen would have to be for X to qualify as an exemplar of the attribute motivated. The length of the privation period could either be specified arbitrarily, or it could be determined following empirical tests of the effects of different starvation periods on one or another dependent variable. The first of these options has little to recommend it, inasmuch as neither very short nor very long deprivation intervals would appear likely to lead to *significant* definitions. The second option would involve the recording of either physiological or behavioral changes associated with food-free regimens of varying lengths. But if the information gained through such experiments were made a part of the definiens, the result would be a new definition, not of the simple *treatment* style, but of the *outcome* variety. Such a definition might take the following form: "X is motivated" (means) "if X is deprived of food for not less than 2 and not more than 100 hours then X drools when food is presented." I hardly need add that the same line of reasoning applies when the definiens describes a current noxious stimulus. For such a CT definition to be useful, some specification of the critical physical intensity of the stimulus appears to be mandatory.

Examples of the CT format are to be found in Hull's (1952) construct of stimulus intensity dynamism (V), introduced to encompass the alleged motivational aspects of conditioned stimuli; in Spence's (1958) air-puff-augmented drive; and in Miller and Dollard's (1941) assignment of drive properties to intense current stimuli. For these latter authors, most stimuli, whether external or internal, possess not only cue properties, but, if intense enough, drive properties as well. To define *being motivated* or *driven* in this way involves the implicit assumption that the designated stimulus, or class thereof, is a motivational variable. I have already noted some of the implications of the "if intense enough" qualifier contained in the preceding sentence.

Although the examples given of PT and CT styles are real, it seems fair to observe that some sort of outcome measurements may have been implied by those who favored these styles. Perhaps, therefore, the definitions, if fully expanded, would have included procedures for determining drive thresholds and for deciding the motivational relevance of assorted empirical variables. Miller and Dollard, indeed, ruled out some stimuli such as ultrasonic frequencies, invisible light waves, and radio waves, regardless of their intensities, because they do not elicit *measurable* reactions.

Regardless of how the most meaningful stimulus-intensity levels might be determined, they would doubtless vary with degree of sensory adaptation, prior experiences with the stimuli, organic conditions, and so forth. It is also likely that significant interactions between the specific stimulus under scrutiny and the stimulus dimensions of some reference tasks would be encountered. An intense sound might facilitate reaction time to a visual stimulus but not to a tactual one.

The entries in Row 6 of the table indicate that, whereas arbitrary decisions are involved in formulating every type of definition, the locus of arbitrariness differs. In the PT and CT style, patently, it lies in the choice of the specific conditions to be described in the one-part definientia. For the OM version, it lies in the election of the particular organic phenomena to be measured; and with the RM format it lies in the choice of the test task, the responses to be measured, the test-scoring procedures, and so forth. I expand on this point in discussing the last two types of definition.

Various aspects of definitions that specify either organic measurements (OM) or response measurements (RM) are listed in the third and fourth columns of the table, respectively. Duffy (1934), Lindsley (1957), and Malmo (1958), favored OM procedures such as the measurement of electrical potentials in the CNS, especially in the ascending reticular formation. Some sort of criterial outcome would naturally be required for the truth of the definiens to be established (Row 2), and a wide range of individual differences in measured potentials and hence in levels of the defined character would be anticipated (Row 3). Measurements such as these clearly lend themselves to the rank-ordering of individuals and to the delineation of properties suitable for combinations in lawful relations. Moreover, levels of organic states, whether chronic or phasic, would presumably be sensitive to a variety of modulating conditions such as diet, fatigue, chronic illness, and such more. Organic *responses,* such as skin-resistance *changes* to phasic stimuli, could be used in a definition that would combine aspects of both the OM and RM styles.

Typically, the operations described in RM-type definitions include some kind of alleged motivational test that is administered under standardized conditions and scored in a specified manner. An early example is provided by the work of Warden (1931) who developed the Columbia Obstruction Box as a device for *measuring* the drive levels of animals. He favored the term *incentive drive* and defined it quite explicitly in terms of the frequency with which rats (primarily) would cross an electrified grid to reach an incentive. Janet Taylor (1951) constructed the Manifest Anxiety Scale with the expectation that test performance would provide useful definitions of drive levels in college students. McClelland, Atkinson, Clark, and Lowell (1953) explored the idea that differences in the strength of the "achievement motive" might profitably be defined by storytelling responses to pictures on a modified Thematic Apperception Test. Although, in these examples, the topographies of the test situations and test instruments differed widely, measurements of overt responses were involved in all. Such behavioral outcomes could serve, in principle at least, in the "then . . ." propositions of definitions of being motivated. It will be evident that a close parallel can be identified in the field of intelligence testing. There one is said to have an IQ of such and such, provided he or she has been tested by means of a specified test, and in consequence, has been observed to reach a criterial level of performance.

As the entries in Row 4 indicate, levels of motivation can be manipulated within the constraints of either the OM or the RM formats. One way of doing this is by sampling. Once a large group of individuals has been tested, and motivational scores assigned, subsamples with different average score levels can be drawn from the parent population. This procedure was followed by Taylor (1951) who, treating motivation as an individual-difference parameter, cut out high- and low-anxiety (drive) samples from a larger group for subsequent testing in eyelid-conditioning and other situations. Involved here was the tacit assumption that the defined levels of motivation would remain essentially invariant over time. As critics of this procedure have pointed out, groups constituted on the basis of test scores in this way may differ not only with respect to the defined attribute, but also in other unknown ways inasmuch as membership in a group is not randomly determined.

In principle, at least, level of motivation can also be manipulated by introducing conditions of established motivational relevance into experimental situations as independent variables. Expanding on a suggestion made above, the motivational relevance of a variable can be established by noting whether its introduction, during a testing interlude, either *augments* or *diminishes* organic levels or test responses stipulated in definientia (Row 5). Consider an environmental variable such as room temperature. If that condition has been found reliably to affect scores on a motivational test then it becomes a bona fide motivational variable. As such it can be introduced into other situations and its effects determined.

To suggest that a variable qualifies as motivational, despite leading to *decreases* in the defined attribute, contrasts with the common idea that only conditions that augment motivation should so qualify. In effect, the position taken here is that an independent variable becomes motivational provided only that it *modulates* defined levels of motivation. But for this to prove useful, it is essential that the outcome-defined attribute has already been shown to enter into significant laws with other attributes. Variable-induced change in scores on a *useless* test would have no value.

Experiments designed to screen variables for motivational relevance would require proper controls (counterbalancing, random sampling, etc.) for any possible confounding effects of fatigue, response bias, practice, and more. Such experiments might profit from the use of factorial designs involving the simultaneous manipulation of two or more variables. Those designs might yield interactive effects of interest even in the absence of main effects. For instance, noise level might qualify as a motivational variable in combination with a headache-inducing drug, but not alone.

Variables selected as motivational because they *elevate* performance scores on a defining test would not necessarily be expected to augment performances in other non test situations. If the defining test for rats, say, involved bar-pressing, a conditioned *fear-arousing* CS might qualify as a motivational variable because it *suppresses* bar-pressing. But that same CS, without logical contradiction, could *amplify* rate of shuttle avoidance. Consistency of effects as between a motivation-defining task and any other would be expected only when the stimulus envelopes of the two tasks are similar and much the same skills are required. In addition, a variable that might be termed "motivational" because of its effects on a defining test might not be so classed were a different test to be used. The motivational status of any variable would thus be *test specific*. It would also be *subject specific* in some cases. A conditioned stimulus that evokes a performance-degrading autonomic reaction from one individual, thus justifying the label motivational, would probably not so function for others who have not been similarly conditioned.

Special problems attend attempts to determine the motivational relevance of variables such as genetic endowment, socio-cultural status, educational level, and the like. This is because these variables are seldom amenable to manipulation and control by an investigator. With either the OM or the RM formulations, correlational analyses could be employed to illuminate the relations of such factors to the defined attributes. Neither the PT nor the CT schemes, however, lend themselves to the use of either correlational or experimental procedures for the screening of variables. Yet an advocate of either scheme could assert, by definition, that individuals in a certain socio-economic group are, say, more highly motivated than the members of a different group. Such an assertion would be no more arbitrary than Hull's declaration that food-deprived animals are more highly motivated than satiated ones.

One factor affecting the choice of a definitional format is the general behavior theory one favors. If the theorist holds that all instances of overt performance reflect the joint contributions of motivation (drive) and habit, then test-situation behavior, as in the realization of the RM alternative, would not be acceptable as a way of defining drive unless habit strength values were accurately known. Perhaps this is why Hull chose to "define" drive in terms of antecedent conditions alone.

One way of circumventing this difficulty is to define, not drive, but motive, where motive embodies both drive and habit or their conceptual counterparts. McClelland and his associates (1953) followed this course, arguing that it was important to measure, not drive (motivation) alone, but a construct combining both an activation process and a guiding element. He made no attempt, strictly speaking, to measure a directionless drive like Hull's D. Warden (1931), likewise, chose to define a "directed push" toward an incentive, a notion that parallels Hull's excitatory potential rather than his D.

It may also be possible to resolve this issue without having to abandon the advantages of a measurement–style definition by electing the OM rather than the

RM alternative. It might be reasonable to suppose that the level of an organic state does not reflect the joint inputs of drive and habit inasmuch as no *overt* behavior is being emitted.

Regardless of theoretical preferences, performance on any so-called motivational test will inevitably be affected by the repertoire of skills the subjects bring to the task. If complex, highly coordinated manual movements are essential to good task performance, the resulting scores will be modulated by practice in making those, or similar movements. Inescapably, ratings of motivational levels would also vary with sensory acuity, motor coordination, perhaps verbal fluency, and other factors seldom considered to be of motivational significance. However, even if levels of performance-defined motivation are multiply determined, this does not imply that the procedure is useless. Intelligence-testing performance is also multiply determined and varies with socio-cultural variables (Garcia, 1981), alleged motivational factors (Hayes, 1962), and more. In the final analysis, if performance levels on tests, whether used to define intelligence or motivation, lead to useful laws and theoretical integrations, the use of such *confounded* scores can be defended. Definitions that rely on outcomes will probably yield more or better laws than definitions based on either antecedent or contemporary treatments, but this remains to be seen.

This discussion would surely be incomplete without some reference to the traditional distinction between primary and secondary processes in motivation. In a general sense, the question this issue raises is that of how to incorporate the distinction between innate and acquired factors into definitions of being motivated. One possibility would be to formulate two different definitions with distinctive definientia and definienda. The adjective *motivated* could be qualified with subscripts or by modifiers such as *innately* and *secondarily*. The definiens for *innately motivated* would make no reference to a need for prior learning whereas that for *secondarily motivated* would. Another possibility would be to inject the innate-learning distinction into descriptions of motivational variables while retaining a single motivational attribute. Certain variables would thus be labeled *primary* or *innate* provided their effectiveness as modulators of motivational levels could be shown to be independent of prior learning. Other variables, such as the CSs in classical conditioning paradigms, would be cast as *secondary* variables by virtue of their dependence on prior CS–US pairings. This second possibility is consistent with the suggestion that having many different drives may be conceptually overwhelming.

In closing, it seems appropriate to consider the question of whether psychology should retain, and seek to redefine, such inexact terms as motivation and emotion, or whether they should be allowed to rot away through disuse. During the early years of this century it became evident that everyday concepts of this kind were too imprecise to satisfy the new breed of "tough-minded" psychologists born of the Watsonian revolution. Yet others deemed these constructs to be of such great "social" and theoretical significance that their retention was mandatory. The emergence of the operationist formula seemed to provide a way of resolving the issue since any word, no matter how thickly encrusted with contradictory meanings, could be honorably retained provided it was *redefined* in an operationally immaculate manner. Torgerson (1958), for example, maintained that every student of behavior should begin his scientific endeavors by accepting, *as significant,* the common sense concepts of tension, motivation, attitude, learning ability, emotion, and intelligence, despite their vagueness. These "linguistic fossils," to use Bergmann's delightful descriptor, were then to be "purified" through the cleansing action of operational redefinition. Unfortunately, this philosophy of redefinition encourages investigators to choose operations derived from, and hence compatible with, their own idiosyncratic ideas of what the word *should* mean. Consequently, the adequacy of any new definiens for an old term is judged, not by its capacity to generate useful laws, but by its congruence with imprecise traditional conceptions. I was at Iowa when Janet Taylor chose to redefine drive in terms of scores on her Manifest Anxiety Scale, and I vividly recall that some of her colleagues dismissed her proposal on the grounds that "That's not what drive *really* is, at least not to me!" More recently, Mandler (1979) writing on emotion, has complained that "Not even our positivistic friends have been able to formulate an acceptable operational definition" (p. 279). Of course not! Like motivation, emotion is an amorphous, literary, hand-me-down, and whoever tries to redefine it in terms of operations that will be congruent with the preconceptions of Mandler or others will be doomed to failure. New definitions of old words can never encompass the kaleidoscopic array of diverse meanings with which such words are freighted. And the more explicit the redefinition, the less likely it will be that more than a very few can relinquish their long-standing, solidly ingrained ideas and accept the new.

Some of these difficulties stem from what might be called "the mystique of operational definition." For various reasons, behavior scientists were led to believe that precise definitions would increase their understanding of complex phenomena and accelerate the formulation of useful laws. But a statement about what a word shall mean, even though unambiguous, does nothing to advance the scientific enterprise. A definition does not tell us which observations are best nor how to make good sense of them. If sets of operations fail to yield significant laws, the introduction of linguistically equivalent words in a formal definition cannot fill the vacuum. Making observations and classifying the results under the control of theoretical speculations and objective criteria are the first steps in science. Introducing either new or old words to stand as the linguistic equivalents of the verbal descriptions of operations is not an absolutely necessary second step.

Logically, definition follows *after* operations have been developed and have been described in words. No matter what term is used as the predicate of a definiendum, its scientific contribution is merely that of abbreviation. It is an abbreviation for words that describe empirical operations already concretized.

The sequential order involved in redefining old words is the reverse of this. Oddly enough one begins, not with verbal descriptions of operations in need of abbreviation, but with abbreviations for *unknown* statements. One is then faced with the nearly impossible task of trying to identify whatever it is that the abbreviation is a "shortened version of." And the task is made even harder by the fact that we have no way of knowing when we have hit on the right solution.

It will be evident from the foregoing that the practice of attempting to redefine "linguistic fossils" has its drawbacks. Perhaps it is better to begin by gathering various kinds of data in the search for meaningful laws with little thought of trying to redefine an old word. This is not to be construed, however, as a plea for the rejection of theory and support for "dust-bowl" empiricism. But it is a plea for the rejection of the "village-gossip" level of theory that uncritically accepts layman notions as "significant" despite lack of scientifically acceptable evidence. Moreover, in rejecting the idea that the layman's "psychological" concepts should be redefined operationally, I am not denying the need for precise definitions of all abstract terms when accurate communication becomes necessary. In particular, I am not advocating the use of "open" definitions in which imprecise words like *motivation* and *anxiety* are deliberately left without formal definition in the belief that they will eventually accrue precise meanings through participation in nomological networks. As others (Bechtoldt, 1959; Brodbeck, 1963) have observed, even the simplest of laws cannot be formulated in the absence of reliable ways of identifying exemplars of the attributes under consideration. To obtain such laws it is not mandatory that the operations described in a definiens be equated in meaning to some particular attribute label, whether old or new. But once suitable operations have been described, reliable segregations of individuals into groups can be effected and the possibility of forming useful laws can be explored.

ACKNOWLEDGMENTS

I am especially grateful to both Charles C. Spiker and Joan H. Cantor for their keenly insightful and critically helpful comments on various parts of this paper. The preparation of the final sections has been accelerated by adapting portions of an unpublished manuscript to which D. Chris Anderson made important contributions.

REFERENCES

Bechtoldt, H. P. (1959). Construct validity: A critique. *American Psychologist, 14,* 619–629.
Bergmann, G. (1957). *Philosophy of science.* Madison: University of Wisconsin Press.
Brodbeck, M. (1963). Logic and scientific method in research on teaching. In N. L. Gage (Ed.), *Handbook of research in teaching* (pp. 44–93). New York: Rand-McNally.

Brown, J. S. (1953). Problems presented by the concept of acquired drives. In *Current theory and research in motivation: A symposium*. Lincoln, NE: University of Nebraska Press.

Brown, J. S. (1961). *The motivation of behavior*. New York: McGraw-Hill.

Brown, J. S., & Farber, I. E. (1951). Emotions conceptualized as intervening variables—with suggestions toward a theory of frustration. *Psychological Bulletin, 48,* 465–495.

Brown, J. S., & Jacobs, A. (1949). The role of fear in the motivation and acquisition of responses. *Journal of Experimental Psychology, 39,* 747–759.

Brown, J. S., Kalish, H. I., & Farber, I. E. (1951). Conditioned fear as revealed by magnitude of startle response to an auditory stimulus. *Journal of Experimental Psychology, 41,* 317–328.

Davis, M., & Astrachan, D. I. (1978). Conditioned fear and startle magnitude: Effects on different footshock or backshock intensities used in training. *Journal of Experimental Psychology: Animal Behavior Processes, 4,* 95–103.

Duffy, E. (1934). Emotion: An example of the need for reorientation in psychology. *Psychological Review, 41,* 184–194.

Estes, W. K. (1958). Stimulus-response theory of drive. In M. R. Jones (Ed.), *Nebraska symposium on motivation* (pp. 35–69). Lincoln, NE: University of Nebraska Press.

Garcia, J. (1981). The logic and limits of mental aptitude testing. *American Psychologist, 36,* 1172–1180.

Hayes, K. J. (1962). Genes, drives, and intellect. *Psychological Reports, 10,* 299–342.

Hull, C. L. (1943). *Principles of behavior*. New York: Appleton–Century–Crofts.

Hull, C. L. (1952). *A behavior system*. New Haven: Yale University Press.

Lindsley, D. B. (1957). Psychophysiology and motivation. In M. R. Jones (Ed.), *Nebraska symposium on motivation* (pp. 44–105). Lincoln, NE: University of Nebraska Press.

Malmo, R. (1958). Measurement of drive: An unsolved problem in psychology. In M. R. Jones (Ed.), *Nebraska symposium on motivation* (pp. 229–265). Lincoln, NE: University of Nebraska Press.

Mandler, G. (1979). Emotion. In E. Hearst (Ed.), *The first century of experimental psychology* (pp. 275–321). Hillsdale, NJ: Lawrence Erlbaum Associates.

McClelland, D. C., Atkinson, J. W., Clark, R. A., & Lowell, E. L. (1953). *The achievement motive*. New York: Appleton–Century–Crofts.

Meyer, M. F. (1933). That whale among the fishes—the theory of emotions. *Psychological Review, 40,* 292–300.

Miller, N. E. (1948). Studies of fear as an acquirable drive: I. Fear as motivation and fear-reduction as reinforcement in the learning of new responses. *Journal of Experimental Psychology, 38,* 89–101.

Miller, N. E., & Dollard, J. (1941). *Social learning and imitation*. New Haven, CT: Yale University Press.

Mowrer, O. H. (1939). A stimulus-response analysis of anxiety and its role as a reinforcing agent. *Psychological Review, 46,* 553–565.

Skinner, B. F. (1938). *The behavior of organisms*. New York: Appleton–Century–Crofts.

Spence, K. W. (1958). A theory of emotionally based drive (D) and its relation to performance in simple learning situations. *American Psychologist, 13,* 131–141.

Taylor, J. A. (1951). The relationship of anxiety to the conditioned eyelid response. *Journal of Experimental Psychology, 41,* 81–92.

Torgerson, W. S. (1958). *Theory and methods of scaling*. New York: Wiley.

Warden, C. J. (1931). *Animal motivation: Experimental studies on the albino rat*. New York: Columbia University Press.

6 Iowa and Aggression

Leonard D. Eron
University of Illinois at Chicago

This is not a chapter about aggression at Iowa. Rather, it is an account of a series of laboratory studies on aggression conducted by my students and me while I was a faculty member at the University of Iowa. For the past 35 years my research and scholarship have been concerned primarily with gaining an understanding of how individuals learn to be aggressive. The studies which have gained most prominence have been field studies, primarily two large-scale longitudinal investigations. One of these comprised 875 eight-year-old subjects from a semi-rural area in New York State who have been followed for 22 years to date (Eron, Walder, & Lefkowitz, 1971; Huesmann, Eron, Lefkowitz, & Walder, 1984; Lefkowitz, Eron, Walder, & Huesmann, 1977). The other is a 3-year longitudinal study of 700 subjects ages 6 and 8, living in a Chicago suburb. They were followed for 3 years (Eron, Huesmann, Brice, Fischer, & Mermelstein, 1983). The latter study has been replicated in four other countries: Australia, Finland, Israel, and Poland (Huesmann & Eron, 1986). This research has yielded important insights into the learning conditions for aggression. However, equally important, although perhaps not as well known, is a series of laboratory studies done while I was on the faculty at the University of Iowa. This 100th anniversary volume affords me an opportunity to summarize these studies in one chapter, to indicate their importance in shaping an understanding of how aggressive behavior can develop as a problem-solving strategy in children, and to acknowledge the contributions of my former students, a very bright, competent, and dedicated group of young persons with whom I had the privilege of working while at Iowa. The researches were carried out primarily as doctoral dissertations and masters' theses. Unfortunately, with a few exceptions, they have largely remained unpublished, although I have often referred to the findings in my own writing.

First-wave data for the 22-year study just mentioned were collected in the Spring of 1960, 2 years before I joined the faculty at Iowa. My colleagues and I were interested at that time in relating a youngster's aggressive behavior as observed in school to its antecedents as seen in the childrearing behaviors of the parents. In developing a theoretical rationale and a design for this study we were influenced by the pioneering childrearing research of Robert Sears, also a former faculty member at Iowa (Sears, Maccoby, & Levin, 1957; Sears, Whiting, Nowlis, & Sears, 1953). Closely associated with me in developing and implementing this design over the years has been Leopold Walder who received his PhD at Iowa in 1954. Before 1960 we had spent a substantial amount of time devising a paper-and-pencil measure of aggression for children and a face-to-face interview with parents. Our definition of *aggression* was "an act which injures or irritates another person", that is, hostile, acting-out, interpersonal aggression, with no indication of intent. This definition did not connote more socially acceptable aspects of the term such as ambition, achievement, and striving to get ahead. In 1960 we tested 875 children in 38 classrooms and interviewed 80% of their mothers and fathers (Eron, Walder, & Lefkowitz, 1971). Our measure of aggression was a peer-rating procedure in which every child in the class rated every other child on 10 items of aggressive behavior. The reliability and validity of this scale have been demonstrated in a number of studies. The parents' interview was a closed-end, precoded questionnaire individually administered in a face-to-face situation. The interview was designed to obtain information on four types of antecedents to aggression: instigators to aggression, contingent response to aggression, identification, and socio-cultural variables. And indeed we found that data obtained from parents on each of these variables related to aggression of the children in school.

One of the surprising findings in 1960 was the moderately high positive relation we obtained between punishment and aggression (Eron, Walder, Toigo, & Lefkowitz, 1963). This is not what would have been expected at that time from theoretical explanations based on laboratory studies with animals and nursery school children. When such subjects are punished for aggressive behavior in given situations, they tend not to act aggressively subsequently when they are in similar situations. By further detailed analyses of our data we found that such a relation between punishment for aggression and aggression indeed existed, but only for a subsample of the population—boys who are highly identified with their fathers (Eron et al., 1971). For boys who have a very close identification with their fathers there is a negative relation between punishment and aggression—the more they are punished, the less aggressive they are; for boys with moderate or low identification, however, the relation is in the opposite direction. The more these boys are punished, the more aggressive they are. Only when a boy is closely identified with his father does punishment have its intended inhibitory effect on the behavior. Perhaps the same punishment is experienced more intensively by a boy who is closely identified with his father so that the inhibiting effect of the punishment overcomes any instigating effect it might have. The unfortunate fact is that only a minority of the boys in the study had this close an identification with their fathers.

One explanation of the survey findings is that punitive parents serve as models for aggressive behavior when the son is not highly identified with the father. This seemed especially likely when we determined that the positive relation between punishment and aggression in the larger group of subjects was due largely to the physical punishment items. It was really only physical punishment by the parent that related to the child's aggression (Eron et al., 1971). When the parent punishes a child physically, the punishment becomes very salient to the child; it is an obvious motor act that he sees, hears, and feels. It is therefore not surprising that it is copied and that it stands out as a way of solving problems.

Another explanation of the positive relation between punishment and aggression would be that punishment is just another frustration, another instigator to aggression. However, punishment did not relate in the same way as did our other measured instigators (e.g., rejection, lack of nurturance, and parental disharmony). We found, for example, that results were different with punishment and instigation depending on whether mothers or fathers provided the information on these variables. With mother as the informant, punishment was the best predictor to contemporaneous aggression. With father as the informant, instigation was the best predictor. Furthermore, when identification was kept constant (as we had done in investigating the punishment–aggression association) there was no consistent relation at all between instigation and aggression. It was only punishment that operated in this interactive way with identification (Eron et al., 1971). Thus, punishment very likely does not act as an instigation, but rather punishment operates by providing a model of behavior for the child to copy.

Indeed from all these studies it seemed as if we were dealing with two disparate kinds of subjects who, when grouped together in an experiment, might cancel each other out to give no results—one group that is low aggressive and highly identified with parents and another that is high aggressive and less identified. Put them together, and you get unexplainable results. If you do not know in advance what the relevant variables are, these variables will not be stable from sample to sample and results will be anomalous.

It was at this point that I arrived at Iowa and had the opportunity to begin studying the development of aggression in the laboratory and to pursue these questions under standard laboratory conditions. For the psychologist interested in establishing a causal model for a particular behavior, the laboratory of course is the ideal setting. Independent variables can be manipulated and their effect on the dependent variables of interest can be measured. The survey study shows only which conditions are correlated with different levels of aggression; it does not manipulate these levels. Accordingly an apparatus was developed which would permit us to manipulate and measure aggression and its antecedents, concomitants, and consequences in the laboratory.

LABORATORY AGGRESSION

To study aggression in the laboratory it was necessary to design an apparatus that would give us an objective score that would relate positively and highly to the aggression measure we had developed in the field studies (Williams, Meyerson, Eron, & Semler, 1967). In this way each of the measures, independently obtained, could serve as a validity check on the other, and we could be more certain that we were referring to the same construct when we combined and contrasted results from the field and the laboratory. Thus, we designed an aggression machine after the manner of Buss (1966) who had also spent some time at Iowa in earlier years, but one that could be used with young children. This new apparatus was dubbed the Iowa Aggression Machine (IAM). Instead of electric shock we used noxious sound (Williams et al., 1967).[1] The child was led to believe that pushing buttons on a panel would deliver sounds of increasing noxious intensity to the earphones of a classmate. The choice of button (intensity of sound) made by the subject, as well as the latency, duration, and frequency of the subject's responses were all recorded automatically by pen recorders that were connected to the buttons and made ink tracings of the data. Automatic timers controlled the whole procedure.

The nature of this situation is such that it closely resembles the semantic definition of the peer-rating measure of aggression—"an act which injures or irritates another person" Eron et al. (1971). Furthermore, this machine situation seems to be consonant with the definitions of aggression used by many previous investigators. Dollard, Doob, Miller, Mowrer, and Sears (1939), in their quite specific definition, stressed both intent and the necessity of performing the act toward another person before the act could be termed *aggressive*. Buss (1961) de-emphasized intent in his definition but specified that the response must be made in an interpersonal situation. In the least specific definition, Bandura and Walters (1959) maintained that the act had only to be potentially pain producing, that is, an act that could injure if it were aimed at a vulnerable object. Thus, because the nature of this button-pushing task does imply intent and is carried out in an interpersonal situation, it certainly comes within the scope of all these definitions.

The subjects were run three at a time. They were brought into the experimental room and told they were to play a cooperative game in which each subject in his or her own booth had to turn off one of a series of four amber lights by pressing the appropriate button under the lights. This was purposely made a very

---

[1]Thanks are due to Professor Milton Rosenbaum for his initial suggestions with regard to this procedure.

simple task so that all subjects would be sure to perform it correctly. The subjects were told that in order to win the game all three teammates had to complete three trials in a row correctly. After after trial subjects were informed by a light signal (called the mistake light) which teammate made an error, and they could inform that teammate of an error by pressing 1 of the 10 buttons next to the mistake light. The buttons were ordered according to the intensity of sound that they delivered, with sounds increasing in unpleasantness from left to right.[2] In the original experiment with the aggression machine, subjects were selected on the basis of their peer-rating aggression score—60 boys and 60 girls, half of whom had been rated as high aggressive and half as low aggressive. They were brought to the experimental room three at a time and fitted with earphones. Sexes were tested separately and there was systematic grouping of high and low aggressive children—either all three high aggressive, all three low aggressive, two highs and one low, or two lows and one high.

The children were told that each button caused a different sound to be heard by their teammate and the farther right the button, the louder the sound. Buttons 1, 5, and 10 were demonstrated to each subject by presenting sounds of approximately 100 Hzs delivered at 96 db., 105 db., and 110 db. sound pressure level, respectively, for a duration of 1 second.

Eighteen trials were administered, on the first 15 of which subjects were led to believe that they were solving the problem correctly but their teammates were not (on their own panel the mistake light never lit up, but the lights for their teammates did). The last three trials were rigged as success trials for all teammates. Thus, in each of the first 15 trials, subjects were required to depress one of 10 buttons graded in intensity of the sound they could deliver to the earphones of their teammates. Actually, the apparatus was switched off after the demonstration and no one received any sound; after the experiment each subject was told the apparatus had broken down so no one had received any sound at all.[3]

The aggression score, automatically recorded by a moving pen, was the numeral of the button pushed (intensity of aggression), length of time the button was depressed (duration), the time elapsing between onset of the mistake light and the button-pushing response (latency), and the number of times the button was pushed (frequency). It was found that high peer-rated aggressive subjects of both sexes pressed the button at significantly greater intensities, for longer dura-

---

[2]In a later experiment (Peterson, 1971), third-grade subjects were actually asked to rate the sounds for unpleasantness, and indeed the results were very consistent with the a priori judged irritability of the sounds.

[3]The machine used with third graders was adapted for college-age subjects by Hedges (1967). In this adaptation, sawtooth noises of approximately 75, 95, and 115 db. were used. These noises were judged by audiology experts to be extremely noxious at high amplitudes, but not harmful. All the instructions were given to the subject through earphones via tape recordings and in experiments with college students, the noxious sounds were actually delivered to the subjects' earphones as noxious stimulation in addition to the demonstration, when warranted by the particular experimental design.

tions, with shorter latencies, and more frequently than low aggressive subjects. These results thus provided the validation with an overt measure of aggression that we sought for the peer-rating procedure. To my knowledge it was the first demonstration that button pushing on an "aggression machine" related to the characteristic aggression level of the subject as measured by paper-and-pencil procedures.

There were some other interesting findings. Boys always obtained significantly higher intensity scores than girls, but there was no difference for latency, duration, or frequency. It seems that girls are stimulated to aggression as quickly and as frequently as boys and maintain the aggressive response for as long as boys; they just do not hit as hard as boys. In nonlaboratory studies this difference could be attributed to less developed musculature. This result, however, would indicate that the lower intensity of girls' aggressive responding must be a function of learning rather than constitution, since the required muscular effort for button-pushing is minimal. Further it was demonstrated that scores on this apparatus are unaffected by the sex of the experimenter or the extent of his or her verbally aggressive interactions with an assistant during the instruction procedure (Marcus, 1965).

In one of the first studies with the aggression machine, Leonard Meyerson (1966) sampled two groups of boys, one high and one low aggressive as determined by scores on the peer-rating instrument. These subjects were then split into three groups, one of which watched a film in which two college-aged men were playing at the aggression machine. One of the men seemed to be making mistakes, and the other man was pushing very high intensity buttons (far to the right) in order to notify him—this was called *similar aggression*. In the second film the same two young men were playing a board game; one made a mistake and the other got up and throttled him—this was called *nonsimilar aggression*. In the third film the two men were at the aggression machine; one player was making no mistakes and thus his teammate was not pushing any buttons—this was called the *control condition*. There was an effect for only one group, the low-aggressive children who saw the similar aggressive film. They pushed very high buttons (far to the right of the "aggression machine") when they played the game with the machine. The low-aggressive children in the nonsimilar aggression condition showed no effect, nor did the high-aggressive children in either the similar or nonsimilar conditions. It seems that a specific response had to be learned, and it was learned by the low-aggressive subject who saw the model performing the aggressive act without getting punished for it (i.e., no one administered or harmed the model physically for pushing high buttons). This finding suggests that the effect of the film was rather narrow; that is, only the specific aggressive behaviors shown were influenced by the content of the film. These results contradict previous findings of the generality of aggression arousal following observation of an aggressive act.

AGGRESSION ANXIETY

Aggression anxiety was invoked as a construct to explain the foregoing findings (i.e., the influence of the aggression movie on the aggression machine score of low aggression boys but not high aggression boys). The Meyerson data suggest that the difference is accounted for by the reduced anxiety (i.e., increased permissiveness of the situation after the showing of the machine aggression movie). Observation of a model performing a specific aggressive behavior without subsequent punishment to the model lowered inhibition and the low aggressive subjects responded as high aggressive subjects. In other words, aggression anxiety is presumed to be present when there has been a history of punishment for aggression. As Mowrer (1939) stated, when someone is punished for aggression, it can be assumed that feelings of anxiety will thereafter be associated with the cues for aggression. However, whether or not punishment can cause aggression anxiety seems to mainly depend on whether or not it is severe enough. In the case of a parent using physical punishment in reaction to a child's aggression, as just pointed out, it is only when the child is highly identified with the parent that punishment is negatively correlated with aggressiveness. It is likely that such a close relationship between parent and child would have the effect, from the child's point of view, of increasing the intensity of the punishment to a very high level and thus increasing the level of anxiety about the consequences of being aggressive in the future. Such a theoretical model suggests that regardless of identification, an intense enough punishment should inhibit aggressive behavior. However, none of the punishments parents used and reported for that study were intense enough to inhibit the aggressive behavior of a child who was not already identified with his parents.

A good way to study aggression anxiety is by looking at retaliation or threat of retaliation. Nancy Edwards (1967) did a study in which she sampled high and low aggressive male and female subjects (i.e., college students, who in their initial encounter with the aggression machine, pushed high or low buttons). Half were placed in a retaliation situation; they were told that after they corrected their partners, their partners would have the opportunity to correct them. The other half were placed in a nonretaliation situation. They were told that when they finished correcting their partners, the experiment would be over. Again she found that it was only the low-aggressive men who were affected by this experimental manipulation. When there was no chance of retaliatory punishment, the low-aggressive male subjects pushed buttons just as high as the high-aggressive males. For the high-aggressive males it made no difference whether they were in the retaliation or nonretaliation conditions; they continued to push buttons at the same level as on the selection task. The same goes for both high and low females. They were unaffected by the retaliation condition—it was as if they were not sensitive to cues of punishment. Because girls learn very early in life to be nonaggressive, the opportunity for punishment for aggression rarely arises. Thus, they do not build up sensitivity to such cues as retaliation and they probably learn nonaggressive behaviors other than sheer avoidance of retaliation. Edwards' study indicates that those behaviors that avoid retaliation in a likely retaliatory condition are attributable to what we have here referred to as *aggression anxiety*. In our later writings we have changed the name of that variable to the more parsimonious term, *aggression avoidance*. Barbara Honhart (1970) demonstrated that threat of retaliation affected physiological arousal in her subjects (all males), for example, increased heart rate when subjects were in the threat of retaliation condition. Also she found no evidence of catharsis (i.e., tension reduction as indicated by physiological measures or lowered instigation to aggression as measured on the aggression machine) subsequent to delivery of aggressive responses on the machine by the subject.

Rolf Peterson (1971) controlled aggressive levels of both his 8-year-old subjects and their targets in an attempt to define more explicitly the conditions under which the possibility of retaliation affects aggressive behavior. Following the results of Meyerson (1966) and Edwards (1967), he expected aggression to be reduced when the target of aggression had a high potential for retaliation, especially if the subjects were low aggressive. He selected boys who were high or low aggressive on the peer-rating measure (e.g., in the upper or lower 25% of the class), and he put half in a retaliation situation and half in a nonretaliation situation. Each subject had both a high-aggressive target and a low-aggressive target—selected by the subject himself on the peer-rating inventory as well as by the others in the classroom. He found that the highest buttons were pushed by the high-aggressive subjects when they were in the retaliation condition with a high-aggressive target. The next highest group—almost as high as the first group—were the low-aggressive subjects with a low-aggressive target in a nonretaliation situation. Thus, when the low-aggressive subject is doubly assured he will not get any punishment because his target is another low-aggressive boy who is not likely to hit back hard, even if he had a chance to do so, and when he is quite sure there will not be any retaliation anyway, he is almost as aggressive as the most aggressive of the high-aggressive boys. It seems that the only thing that keeps the low-aggressive boy from being more aggressive is fear of punishment. The high-aggressive boy, however, is most aggressive when he is in a situation where he expects retaliation from another high-aggressive boy. It is almost as if he invites punishment or is operating on the theory that offense is the best defense—"I'll get my licks in before he gets back at me." Apparently, the prospect of being aggressed against serves as a discriminative stimulus that elicits aggression in these boys. One expects that under these conditions aggressing in the past has led to reinforcement. The high-aggressive subject seems to seek out the possibility of punishment. This might help explain the persistence of aggressive behavior over time despite the severest sanctions for such behavior (Eron, Huesmann, Dubow, Romanoff, & Yarmel, 1987; Huesmann, Eron, Lefkowitz, & Walder, 1984).

A study by Randall Daut (1969) demonstrated that performing aggressively on the Iowa Aggression Machine led to an increase in aggression anxiety in his subjects (female college students). Aggression anxiety was assessed from TAT (Thematic Apperception Test) stories told by the subjects immediately after they were forced by way of instructions to deliver noxious sounds of various intensities to the earphones of a peer. Half of Daut's subjects were instructed to push high buttons (which they were told delivered noxious sounds), and half the subjects were instructed to push low buttons (which they were told delivered mild sounds). The measures of aggression anxiety were two ratio scores from Pittluck (1950) that took into account expressions both of unmodified physical aggression and of the defense against the expression of aggression. For both measures of aggression anxiety, the subjects who had been instructed to push high buttons had significantly higher scores than the subjects who had been instructed to push low buttons. These results support the hypothesis that commission of an aggressive act increases aggression anxiety at least in these female subjects. Daut commented that, of the subjects forced to push high buttons, several remarked that the sound must have really been annoying and two refused to push the high button, one pushing it briefly and then returning to low buttons. These observations corroborate the presence of aggression anxiety in subjects forced to act in an aggressive manner (i.e., to push high intensity buttons).

Another aspect of gender that is important in determining the intensity of aggressive expression is the sex of the target of aggression. Although aggression is frequently reinforced within the young male peer culture (Hess & Handel, 1956), aggression against girls is regularly punished by parents and other socializing agents. Buss (1966) found that college males are significantly less aggressive (in terms of intensity of shock administered) toward female targets than toward males. He also found that females are more aggressive toward males than males are toward females. Thus, the taboo against aggressing toward females exerts a more potent influence on the intensity of the aggression response than does the inclination of males generally to be more aggressive than females.

This taboo is learned early in life and persists at least until college age, but an experiment by Lawrence Hedges (1969) with the Iowa Aggression Machine demonstrates that it is unlearned or disinhibited easily. Of his subjects, all of whom were males, half had a female target and half had a male target in the traditional aggression machine situation in which the subject corrects the "errors" of a confederate by administration of noxious stimuli (in this case, loud sound). During the instruction phase, which was presented on videotape, half of the subjects saw a male model delivering high intensity noxious tones to a male target and half to a female target. A third manipulation had to do with the possibility of retaliation. Control groups who were tested with no video target and no retaliation manipulation responded to either male or female targets. Hedges found that, generally, subjects obtained significantly higher scores when responding to a male target than to a female target in both the control and the experimental groups. However, those subjects who observed a female target being administered high intensity sounds administered significantly higher intensity sounds to female targets than those who observed a male target. Furthermore, those subjects who had an actual male target but observed a female target being corrected pushed buttons of significantly higher intensity than subjects who observed a male target. In fact, the group with the actual male and observed female target had the highest scores of all. It seems, then, that if it is permissible in a specific situation to be aggressive toward a female target, it is indeed permissible to be aggressive toward a male. Observation of a male model responding aggressively toward a female seems to be a sufficient condition for disinhibiting a long-standing prohibition against being aggressive toward females.

With his random selection of subjects, Hedges did not replicate Edwards' (1967) findings of disinhibition of the aggression response when there is assurance of no retaliation. However, in a post hoc analysis, he selected subjects who were high and low aggressive according to Edwards' criteria, based on initial responses on the aggression machine, and corroborated her findings exactly: Low-aggressive subjects who are assured that there is not possibility of retaliation respond as aggressively as high aggressive subjects.

James Williams (1966) demonstrated that it was possible to induce a hostile attitude in his fifth-grade student subjects that would then influence the magnitude of their responses in the aggression machine situation. Hostile and nonhostile attitudes were learned by subjects through pairing of one nonsense syllable with hostile words and another nonsense syllable with nonhostile words. Subsequent to this learning task, the subjects were introduced to the aggression machine. Either the hostile nonsense syllable or nonhostile nonsense syllable was used as a ready signal for informing their partners of errors. Those subjects who had learned the hostile pairing made significantly more aggressive responses after the hostile ready signal than did control subjects who had the same pairings but for whom the discriminative stimulus was the color in which words were typed. They also made significantly more aggressive responses than a second control group of subjects who received pairings of active, nonhostile words with one nonsense syllable and passive words with the other. The two control groups did not differ in aggressive responding. Thus, it was necessary to learn a specific hostile attitude that mediated the aggressive response. Exposure to a similar number of hostile stimuli or learning a high-activity concept did not affect aggressive responding. The nonsense syllables themselves were later rated by the subjects, and the same relations found for the motor aggression response were found in the polarization of evaluative ratings of the two nonsense syllables. These results were interpreted by Williams (1966) "as indicating that the nonsense syllable associated with hostile words during training later evoked the hostile attitudinal response which mediated more intense motor aggressive and evaluative rating responses" (p. 57). To repeat, it was necessary to learn a specific hostile attitude that then mediated the aggressive response.

This series of studies redirected our thinking from a rather mechanistic explanation of the learning of aggression in terms of drive reduction and the association between instigation, punishment, and aggressive responses toward a greater emphasis on the cognitive mediators between the situational and response variables. It was apparent that what was going on inside the heads of our subjects was important in determining the magnitude of their responses on the aggression machine. As I. E. Farber (1963) has succinctly stated, "things people say to themselves determine the rest of the things they do" (p. 196). And it is how individuals interpret the situation they are in, and the likely consequences of any responses both to themselves and the ones with whom they are interacting, that determines the quality and strength of that response. Further, these interpretations are a function of past learning, attitudes, and norms of behavior built up over time. As I have written before (Eron, 1982, 1987), aggression is a multideternined behavior. There are genetic, constitutional, physiological, temperamental, characteralogical, and situational variables, all of which are implicated in whether or not an individual will make an aggressive response at any given time and how intense that response will be. The studies described here, conducted in the Iowa psychological laboratories, have added to our understanding of how situational, characterological, and attitudinal variables contribute to aggressive behavior.

REFERENCES

Bandura, A., & Walters, R. H. (1959). *Adolescent aggression*. New York: Ronald Press.

Buss, A. H. (1961). *The psychology of aggression*. New York: Wiley.

Buss, A. H. (1966). Instrumentality of aggression, feedback and frustration as determinants of physical aggression. *Journal of Personality and Social Psychology, 3*, 153–162.

Daut, R. L. (1969). *TAT aggression anxiety as a function of prior aggression and the stimulus properties and sequence of the cards*. Unpublished honors thesis. University of Iowa, IA.

Dollard, J., Doob, L. W., Miller, N. E., Mowrer, O. H., & Sears, R. R. (1939). *Frustration and aggression*. New Haven, CT: Yale University Press.

Edwards, N. (1967). *Aggressive expression under threat of retaliation*. Unpublished doctoral dissertation, University of Iowa, Iowa City, IA.

Eron, L. D. (1982). Parent-child interaction, television violence and aggression of children. *American Psychologist, 37*, 197–211.

Eron, L. D. (1987). The development of aggressive behavior from the perspective of a developing behaviorism. *American Psychologist, 42*, 435–442.

Eron, L. D., Huesmann, L. R., Brice, P., Fischer, P., & Mermelstein, R. (1983). Age trends in the development of aggression, sex typing, and related television habits. *Developmental Psychology, 19*, 71–77.

Eron, L. D., Huesmann, L. R., Dubow, E., Romanoff, R., & Yarmel, P. W. (1987). Aggression and its correlates over 22 years. In D. Crowell, I. M. Evans, & C. R. O'Donnell (Eds.), *Childhood aggression and violence* (pp. 249–262). New York: Plenum.

Eron, L. D., Walder, L. O., & Lefkowitz, M. M. (1971). *Learning of aggression,* Boston: Little-Brown.

Eron, L. D., Walder, L. O., Tiogo, R., & Lefkowitz, M. M. (1963). Social class, parental punishment for aggression and child aggression. *Child Development, 34,* 849–867.

Farber, I. E. (1963). The things people say to themselves. *American Psychologist, 18,* 185–197.

Hedges, L. E. (1967). *Aggression as a function of gender and noxious stimulation.* Unpublished master's thesis, University of Iowa, IA.

Hedges, L. E. (1969). *Aggressive responses as a function of target cues and the possibility of retaliation.* Unpublished doctoral dissertation, University of Iowa, IA.

Hess, R., & Handel, J. (1956). Patterns of aggression in parents and their children. *Journal of Genetic Psychology, 89,* 199–212.

Honhart, B. B. (1970). *An investigation of catharsis: overt aggression and heart rate as functions of retaliation and arousal and opportunity for aggression.* Unpublished doctoral dissertation, University of Iowa, IA.

Huesmann, L. R., & Eron, L. D. (1986). *Television and the aggressive child: A cross-national comparison.* Hillsdale, NJ: Lawrence Erlbaum Associates.

Huesmann, L. R., Eron, L. D., Lefkowitz, M. M., & Walder, L. O. (1984). The stability of aggression over time and generations. *Developmental Psychology, 20*(6), 1120–1134.

Lefkowitz, M. M., Eron, L. D., Walder, L. O., & Huesmann, L. R. (1977). *Growing up to be violent: A longitudinal study of the development of aggression.* New York: Pergamon Press.

Marcus, J. L. (1965). *Examiner effects on two measures of aggression in children.* Unpublished master's thesis, University of Iowa, IA.

Meyerson, L. J. (1966). *The effects of filmed aggression on the aggressive responses of high and low aggressive subjects.* Unpublished doctoral dissertation, University of Iowa, IA.

Mowrer, O. H. (1939). A stimulus–response analysis of anxiety and its role as a reinforcing agent. *Psychological Review, 46,* 553–565.

Peterson, R. (1971). Aggression as a function of retaliation and aggression level of target and aggressor. *Developmental Psychology, 5,* 161–166.

Pittluck, P. (1950). *The relation between aggressive fantasy and overt behavior.* Unpublished doctoral dissertation, Yale University, New Haven, CT.

Sears, R. R., Maccoby, E. E., & Levin, H. (1957). *Patterns of child rearing.* Boston: Row Peterson.

Sears, R. R., Whiting, J. W., Nowlis, V., & Sears, P. S. (1953). Some child rearing antecedents of aggression and dependency in young children. *Genetic Psychology Monographs, 47,* 135–234.

Williams, J. F. (1966). *Semantic mediation of motor aggression.* Unpublished doctoral dissertation, University of Iowa, IA.

Williams, J. F., Meyerson, L. J., Eron, L. D., & Semler, I. J. (1967). Peer rated aggression and aggressive responses elicited in an experimental situation. *Child Development, 38,* 181–190.

7 The Development of Developmental Psychology

Tracy S. Kendler
University of California, Santa Barbara

I was asked to present a retrospective and prospective view of developmental psychology, including a discussion of Iowa's influence on the field as a whole and on myself personally. After being presumptuous enough to agree, I wondered how in the world to do so briefly and coherently until I hit upon the idea of treating the field itself as a developing entity in which the end product is a mature science.

To define scientific maturity, I drew upon Thomas Kuhn (1970), who is notorious for the importance he assigned to scientific revolutions. He is less celebrated for asserting that a science has to become mature before such revolutions are possible. Maturity, he maintained, is arrived at in two stages. The first stage is preparadigmatic. Sooner or later, a paradigm emerges that heralds the transition to the mature, "normal" science stage.

"Normal science" is a pattern of research based on past scientific achievements that a particular scientific community acknowledges as the foundations for its further practice. Acceptance of Mendel's theory by the biological community is a good example. The consensus provides the paradigm, which consists of a strong network of conceptual, theoretical, instrumental, methodological, and quasi-metaphysical commitments. The network lays the basis for communication. The commitments provide the rules and standards for scientific practice. Acquisition of a paradigm and the normal science that follows is a sign of maturity in a scientific discipline.

In the beginning, the paradigm is largely an agreement about the expectation of future success, based on selected and still incomplete examples. Normal science consists of realizing the success by further articulating the paradigm itself and also by extending the domain to which it applies. In the mature, normal-

"

science stage, when the expectation approaches realization, an accepted pattern of research emerges, based on a common agreement among the members of the discipline about the importance of certain basic facts or laws and their explanatory theories. There is a consensus about the domains to which the paradigm applies. All members agree about what is important to know and there is general understanding about the appropriate instrumentation and experimental methodology for expanding that knowledge. Broad acceptance of a paradigm makes possible the abstruse knowledge, based on specialized research, that typifies the well-developed sciences.

Kuhn (1970) acknowledged that there can be scientific research without a paradigm. However, he noted, history discloses that where there is no paradigm, any or all of the possible facts can seem equally important. And early fact gathering is more like a random activity than the directed pursuit that characterizes the mature science. The search for the chemical basis of the gene is a fine example of directed pursuit in a mature science. Preparadigmatic research either produces a morass of easily collected facts or a number of conflicting schools, accompanied by incompletely resolved debates. Nevertheless, Kuhn held, preparadigmatic science has been essential to the development of many significant sciences.

Today, the field of developmental psychology has all the appurtenances of a developing science: serious researchers with respectable academic status, technologically advanced laboratories, its own division in the APA, its own independent society, and too many professional journals. But it is still in the preparadigmatic stage.

There is as yet no consensus about a valid theory of development that the field, as a whole, is busy either articulating or expanding to new domains. There is no general agreement about the basic, important facts every student should know. The literature is difficult, or impossible, to keep up with because every researcher is free to build anew; to create a new theory, starting from first principles, and justifying the use of each concept introduced. While this freedom can be exhilarating, it also generates confusion and eventual self-doubts.

Although the field has not yet reached maturity, there has been some development that can be sorted into four overlapping phases, beginning with the applied phase in which the University of Iowa participated importantly.

Why the immaturity? According to Sears (1975), a fellow Iowan, the history of child development is different from that of the more mature life sciences. The other life sciences, developed within the academic structure, depended on the scientists' intellectual curiosity, on their desire to know more about their own discipline. In contrast, early academic interest in developmental psychology was fostered by external pressures driven by practical concerns for the betterment of children. There is no clearer example of this beginning than the establishment of the Iowa Child Welfare Research Station.

The idea of a station devoted to science in the service of children traces back to 1906, when it was first promoted by a formal organization of the women of Iowa, led by Mrs. Cora Bussey Hillis. The Ames agricultural station, devoted to the use of science for the improvement of corn and hogs, was already a thriving research organization. Mrs. Hillis had lost some of her children. She thought she might have been spared this loss if there was a comparable organization devoted to children. Why not establish such an organization at the University of Iowa?

These trail-blazing women presently joined forces with some University of Iowa faculty and some enlightened legislators. Together they proposed a bill to the state legislature providing for a child welfare station in order to investigate the best scientific methods of conserving and developing the normal child, to disseminate the information acquired by such investigation, and to train students for future work in child psychology. The idea of applying science to humans was still novel enough to produce initial resistance in the conservative legislature. Still the campaign persisted until public pressure increased enough to get the bill passed by 1917.

The plans for the station, prepared by Carl Seashore, who was then both Professor of Psychology and Dean of the Graduate College at the University of Iowa, included five divisions of study. Four divisions concerned the physical well-being of children and the fifth fell under the rubric of "Education and Morals." The rationale for this division was as follows:

> the child comes into the world relatively without a character and what he shall be is determined by the influences of the home. Let those who are disposed to question this, study the formation of habits in the mind of any little child and he will see that child was not born with them, although he was born with a temperament. The habits are the direct result of the influences which are fixed in the home and a child's habits constitute its character. Yet our scientific theory of education begins in the schoolroom, overlooking the most important period before school. It is to remedy these conditions that we propose to have . . . a specialist who will develop the same sort of scientific aid in education that is now developed on such an elaborate scale in our schools and colleges of education. His specialty, if you please, will be limited to the investigation of those principles which can be of immediate use for education in the home . . . for guiding parents in the training of various types of children—subnormal, normal, and gifted. (Seashore, 1916, p. 13)

Bird T. Baldwin, an educational psychologist, was appointed first director of the station. After World War I ended, he set up the Preschool Laboratories of the Iowa Child Welfare Research Station for the purpose of obtaining scientifically valid and practically useful data on children between 2 and 6 years of age. The data were to provide tentative physical, social, and mental norms against which to evaluate and promote the education and development of the preschool child (Baldwin & Stecher, 1925). Some of you can remember that, beginning in the

1940s, this kind of normative information, extended and popularized by Arnold Gesell and Frances Ilg, became gospel for the parents of a whole generation of young children.

But, although normative data are useful for assessing the progress of children, they do not, by themselves, provide a scientific basis for remedial action. To meet this need, the Iowa Child Welfare Research Station later progressed to the second phase in the development of the discipline by pioneering in applied, semi-experimental research in naturalistic settings. Beginning in the 1930s, Stoddard, Skeels, Wellman, Updegraff, and their collaborators used experimental-control type of comparisons to investigate the effect of environmental stimulation on children's intelligence. Intelligence was measured by means of standardized IQ tests and the comparisons were based on long-term, real-life experiences.

In one set of studies, children who remained in an orphanage were compared with children adopted at an early age. In another set, children who attended nursery school were compared with children who did not. The general conclusion was that a markedly unstimulating (e.g., orphanage) environment, experienced for long periods, produced substantial losses in IQ. Preschool education produced some gains in IQ, depending on the amount and consistency of preschool attendance (e.g., Skeels, Updegraff, Wellman, & Williams, 1938).

These conclusions were attacked by the Terman cadre at Stanford, who were vigorously engaged in defending the constancy of the Stanford–Binet IQ scores. Subsequent research on early intervention programs, like Head Start, has shown the Iowans were correct because such interventions did raise the IQs of the children who participated. But the Californians may also consider themselves vindicated because the effect of this kind of early intervention on IQ scores gradually dwindled within 2 or 3 years. Now the question has taken a new, more developmental turn. We no longer ask whether the IQ of deprived youngsters can be affected by education—it can. We are now asking how do these interventions affect the subsequent course of development, or what can be done to maintain the salutary effects of early intervention (e.g., Garber & Hodge, 1989; Jensen, 1989).

The third phase in the development of the discipline can be labeled *experimental child psychology*. In this phase the emphasis shifted from using scientific methods for social purposes, like the betterment of children, to using children as subjects to test general psychological theories for the purpose of extending scientific knowledge. The third phase flourished at Iowa in the 1950s and 1960s under the able leadership of Charles Spiker, who established the first, very influential graduate program in experimental child psychology at the University of Iowa. But the ground was prepared for this development in the 1940s, when I was there, by earlier theorists like Kurt Lewin, who was a member of the Child Welfare Research Station, and Kenneth Spence, who was a member of the Psychology Department.

Both Lewin and Spence, along with their numerous disciples, believed that without theories it is impossible in psychology, as in any other science, to proceed beyond the mere collection and description of miscellaneous facts that have little predictive value. Truly successful application is contingent on the construction of valid theories. Valid theories require clearly defined constructs linked to observable facts. Moreover, to provide logical, experimentally testable derivations, the theories should be coordinated with mathematical concepts.

Each man had such a theory and they were both interested in extending the generality of their respective theories to children. This interest stimulated the emergence of basic, as opposed to applied, experimental child psychology, which was intended to provide a testing ground for general psychological theories applicable throughout the life span.

Such a program would be characteristic of a mature science of general psychology, were it not that, despite their mutual emphasis on the importance of theory, Lewin and Spence represented different, competing schools. Each school had a program comprehensive enough, and a following enthusiastic enough, to produce a paradigm for experimental psychology. But, sadly, in the long run neither succeeded in doing so.

Lewin was a Gestaltist and Gestalt theory was primarily directed toward perception. Perception was broadly conceived as encompassing cognition. Cognition, was, in turn, conceived to be the basis of behavior. Cognition, at any age, was seen as depending on how the perceiver interpreted the environment. In this sense, the Gestalt school antedates the current, cognitive school of psychology.

Lewin's particular formulation of Gestalt theory conceptualized the person–environment interaction as a topological "life space," where interacting forces operated to determine behavior (Lewin, 1954). The life-space model has not survived, but while Lewin was at Iowa, it provided the rationale for a productive, experimental child psychology program.

To mention the results of a few representative experiments, Lewin, Lippitt, and White (1939) found a strong tendency toward aggression in children exposed to experimentally manipulated autocratic atmospheres. But this aggression was usually diverted from the autocratic leader to the other children or toward material objects. Another experiment (Barker, Dembo, & Lewin, 1941) showed that frustration decreased the constructiveness of children's play. A third example is selected from a series of level-of-aspiration experiments. Level of aspiration was measured by presenting subjects with a choice of tasks that varied in difficulty. The more difficult the chosen task, the higher the level of aspiration exhibited. A sample experiment (Jucknat, 1937) showed that, with both children and adults, the direction and the amount of change in the level of aspiration depended on the degree of previous success and failure. Success raised the aspiration of both children and adults, whereas failure lowered it.

Although much of the research produced under the aegis of Lewin's theory included children, the data they yielded were not intrinsically developmental. Rather, the experiments were intended to test, articulate, and extend a general theory of behavior that applied to any age. Escalona (1954), one of his distinguished disciples, remarked that Lewin expected his concepts would help break down the barriers between various branches of psychology by creating a single, unified, general-process theory that would apply regardless of developmental status. As she put it, "In a sense Lewin's child psychology aimed at the destruction of child psychology as an independent discipline" (p. 971).

Kenneth Spence was a prominent member of the opposing, neobehaviorist school. Neobehaviorists produced explanatory theories about automatic, associative learning. Unlike radical behaviorists, members of this school constructed and tested elaborate, associative theories about the learning process and, in that sense, they were the forerunners of the current connectionist school. The principles guiding neobehaviorist theorizing were drawn from conditioning. Although human behavior was studied, laboratory animals were favored because they allowed for better controls and freer experimental manipulations.

Early in his career, Spence produced an influential theory about discrimination learning in animals (Spence 1936, 1937). After experimentally confirming some implications of this theory on infrahuman animal learning, Spence became interested in testing it on children. Under his direction, Kuenne (1946), a graduate student from the Child Welfare Department, performed some experiments to test the hypothesis that very young children tend to learn in accordance with the same learning principles as infrahuman animals, whereas older children tend to learn in a qualitatively different, more abstract way. This hypothesis was based on the assumption that learning in so-called preverbal organisms is controlled relatively directly by all perceptible elements in the impinging external stimulus. Among verbal subjects, control passes to a covert, mediating response that represents the relevant, and disregards the irrelevant, components of the stimulus complex. The hypothesis was confirmed by the data, but this interpretation was later challenged. Although the disputes that arose were never resolved, the mediating, representational-response notion anticipated the current emphasis on the importance of how information is represented.

Kuenne's research became the first of many experiments that investigated such mediation in children. A goodly proportion of these investigations were conducted by Iowans including David Ehrenfreund, Hayne Reese, Wendell Jeffrey, Sheldon White, Charles Spiker, Joan Cantor, Howard Kendler, and myself. The guiding hypothesis in most of this early research was that covert, mediating, representational responses are learned according to the same principles as the overt response. Experiments on mediation in children were, by and large, conducted in the experimental, child psychology mode, because they were explicitly intended to expand the scope of some general-process learning theory.

In another sense, this research paved the way for the fourth phase of developmental psychology by demonstrating that learning depends, in an important way, on the developmental status of the subject. Developmental status in this usage refers to both phylogeny and ontogeny. In the developmental phase one seeks developmental facts, or better yet, discovers developmental laws, and formulates developmental theories to explain them.

What do I mean by development? To cite Ernest Nagel, another distinguished philosopher of science, development—as used in the life sciences—refers to long-term, permanent, sequential changes in the structure or function of the organism. These changes result in novel outcomes for the individual, outcomes that increase one's capacity for self-regulation. Deterministic explanations of developmental changes are expected to be found in some alteration in the developing organism, or in the environment, or most likely, both (Nagel, 1957). Environment in this context is broadly conceived to range from the cellular to the social surround. Developmental changes in the structure and function of the brain, as manifested in both ontogeny and phylogeny, provide suitable examples.

My point is that, if there is to be a separate, mature discipline called developmental psychology, it will be because there are separate, basic, developmental laws to be discovered and explained. Let it be understood, however, that developmental laws do not replace general-process laws; they supplement them, just as the laws of genetics supplement the general laws of biology. This is the message of my retrospective review.

Now to the influence of Iowa on myself personally. I came to Iowa as a graduate student in 1940 eager to learn more about psychological theory. I chose Iowa for three reasons. I wanted to do graduate work with Lewin because my undergraduate training was Gestalt-oriented. Iowa was relatively inexpensive, an important consideration because the country was then in the midst of the Great Depression. Last but not least, the decision was made jointly with a fellow undergraduate named Howard Kendler.

Although Lewin's reputation in the Gestalt camp brought me to Iowa, and he was a co-sponsor with Chuck Strother of my master's thesis, as it turned out, the director of my PhD dissertation was Kenneth Spence. How that happened is another story. It is ironic that Spence tried to persuade me to do the experiment that Kuenne eventually did, probably because I was his first female, doctoral student. But I had an early feminist overreaction to being consigned to work with children rather than rats where, it seemed to me, the really basic work was occurring. I elected to do my PhD research on discrimination learning in rats. This research (T. Kendler, 1950) extended the application of Spence's theory to a new set of conditions and at the same time confirmed its capacity to explain a phenomenon claimed by Gestaltists to support their theoretical views.

In retrospect, it is clear that Iowa left an indelible impression on me because I later resumed research on discrimination learning, which I am still pursuing. There was, however, a long hiatus between getting the PhD and getting back to the laboratory again. The first part of the hiatus was filled by duties associated with World War II, including a stint in the Pentagon. The later part was occupied by duties associated with marriage and the young family Howard and I collaborated on. Presently, however, we also began to collaborate on what grew into a research program to investigate how children acquire the mediating, representational responses that had such marked effects on their learning.

Experiments with children required considerable piloting with suitable experimental procedures. It was very convenient to have available, not only our own two children, but a whole neighborhood of youngsters anxious to play the "games" we concocted. The games that evolved from this neighborhood piloting were discriminative transfer procedures designed to determine whether the effective stimulus for choice behavior consisted of the relatively direct, stable signals from the visual displays registered on the learner's sensorium; or whether the effective stimulus consisted of the relatively indirect signals generated by mediating, representational responses, which could change as the demands of the task changed.

The procedures consist of two phases. The first phase presents a discrimination problem to the subject that could be solved in either the direct or the mediated mode. The second phase is a transfer task from which one could infer which mode the subject used. There was prior evidence that rats respond to such discriminative transfer tasks in the direct mode (Kelleher, 1956) while human adults respond in the mediated mode (Buss, 1956; H. Kendler & D'Amato, 1955). Our plan was to find out how children acquired mediating responses.

The first experiment with children (T. Kendler & Kendler, 1959) suggested that kindergartners were in a transitional stage in which the fast learners responded in the mediational mode and the slow learners responded in the direct mode. This promising start led to a series of experiments that showed nursery school children tended, as a group, to respond relatively directly and nonselectively to the environmental input, whereas their elder counterparts tended increasingly to respond to how they represent the relevant components of this input.

We expected, at first, that the transition from the direct to the mediated mode would take place some time between 5 and 7 years of age. But as the data accumulated we discovered that the probability of responding in the mediational mode increased in a gradual, orderly manner over a surprisingly long age span. The span extended from about 3 years of age—the youngest group we worked with—up to young adulthood.

The developmental change was both replicable and orderly enough to fit a simple log function of age quite neatly (T. Kendler, 1979b). This function, extrapolated downward, crossed the X-axis at about 2 years of age, the same age that Piaget set as the beginning of the preoperational stage of development and also the age at which the Stanford–Binet test begins. The increase in the probability of responding in the mediational mode begun in early childhood continued to increase, in a growth-like, decelerating manner, up to young adulthood.

When we began this research we had assumed that the hypothetical, mediating responses were learned according to the same principles as overt responses. Our initial intention was to expand the application of a general-process learning theory to a new domain by finding out how children learn to mediate. Consequently this part of our work was done in the experimental child psychology mode. However, as these and other experimental data accumulated it began to look more and more as though we uncovered a developmental change—a long-term, permanent, sequential change in the structure or function of the organism that produces a novel outcome that increases the individual's capacity for self-regulation. By now, I also suspect that these changes are attributable to some alteration in the developing organism, modulated by some long-term environmental determinants. There is some reason to think that the human ontogenetic changes have their counterparts in the evolution of the central nervous system.

This is not the place to describe the evidence that led to these conclusions or to elaborate on the theory that I am evolving to explain and organize the accumulating data. It is fitting, however, that I acknowledge the influence of Iowa by sketching its outlines. The theory assumes the system that underlies discrimination learning can be decomposed into an information-processing and an executive component. The information-processing component encodes the displayed information into usable form. The executive component determines which choice the subject makes.

Each component can be further decomposed into two levels; each level operates in a different mode. To briefly describe lower level functioning first, information processing at the lower level is relatively direct and nonselective. To say processing is direct means that there is minimal interpretation of the information. To say it is nonselective means that all perceptible input, relevant or irrelevant, is processed simultaneously. Problem solving at the lower level consists of learning to make the correct choice according to gradual, automatic, general-process learning principles (T. Kendler, 1971; Rust & Kendler, 1987). I think Spence might have found this formulation acceptable because it is based on the continuity theory of discrimination learning he originally formulated.

The higher information-processing level acts on the output of the lower level to abstract and process further only the relevant features in the display. Which features are relevant can change with the context in which the display is presented. The higher executive level uses the information to formulate and test reasonable hypotheses about the solution to the problem (T. Kendler, 1979b). Higher level processes operate in accordance with the more rational, general-process principles that might have been acceptable to Lewin.

The theory is developmental in that it assumes that among humans the lower levels within each component develop relatively early and quickly. The higher levels begin to develop a little later but proceed much more slowly (T. Kendler, 1979a). The theory is not about successive stages that replace each other. Instead the lower levels remain functional throughout the life span where it continues to subserve perception and automatic learning. Nor is the emergence of the higher levels brought on by conflicts or inconsistency, as in Piaget's theory. I suspect that they emerge gradually as the child's nervous system matures and his or her experience expands.

I also suspect that as development proceeds these functional levels increasingly complement each other. The higher level processes are more efficient but they require more cognitive effort and their scope is more limited. The lower levels are less efficient but they subserve automatic learning and they can control more behaviors simultaneously than the higher level. When the two levels work harmoniously the higher level can generate correct solutions to problems which, if repeated often enough, become automatic and effortless thus clearing the way for higher level solutions to new problems.

Although some of the details necessary to articulate and test such a theory have been filled in, much more remains to be done. But it does provide an example of what I mean by a developmental theory and it certainly shows the influence of my Iowa training.

I close by considering the prospects for developmental psychology. I expect that the field will continue to thrive, at least for a while. But whether it becomes a mature, independent, scientific discipline depends on whether it makes progress toward developing its own paradigm. A mature developmental paradigm would enrich general psychology, just as genetics enriched biology.

I have contended that there has been progress toward maturity that can be divided into four overlapping phases. The good news is that each of these phases flourishes today. There are psychologists fruitfully engaged in applied research directed at the betterment of children. There are experimental psychologists engaged in the extension of general process theories to children. The developmental phase was very active while Piaget was alive. Currently, it seems more fashionable to attack his ideas than to elaborate them, but he continues to have his defenders.

The bad news is that together we do not form a mature science. We have not yet found a paradigm. There is no unifying developmental theory accepted and implemented by the community of developmental psychologists. Nor is there any agreement about the important facts or methods that should be included in any developmental curriculum. There is certainly no common direction governing basic developmental research.

I am disappointed but not discouraged. If the field is to grow into a "normal" science, it will depend on the realization of the developmental phase. There is still a possibility that a unifying theory will emerge which, I suspect, will be psychobiological in nature. What I can safely claim is that, if a unifying theory of psychological development is born, it will be because Iowans have made seminal contributions in the past and will continue to do so the future.

REFERENCES

Baldwin, B. T., & Stecher, L. I. (1925). *The psychology of the preschool child*. New York: Appleton.

Barker, R. T., Dembo, T., & Lewin, K. (1941). Studies in topological and vector psychology: II. Frustration and regression. University of Iowa Studies in Child Welfare, 18, No. 1.

Buss, A. H. (1956). Reversal and nonreversal shifts in concept formation with partial reinforcement eliminated. *Journal of Experimental Psychology, 52,* 162–166.

Escalona, S. (1954). An addendum—The influence of topological and vector psychology upon current research in child development. In L. Carmichael (Ed.), Manual of Child Psychology (2nd ed.; pp. 971–983). New York: Wiley.

Garber, H. L., & Hodge, (1989). Risk for deceleration in the rate of mental development. *Developmental Review, 9,* 259–300.

Jensen, A. R. (1989). Raising IQ without increasing g? *Developmental Review, 9,* 234–258.

Jucknat, M. (1937). Performance, level of aspiration and self-consciousness. *Psychol. Forsch., 22,* 89–179.

Kelleher, R. T. (1956). Discrimination learning as a function of reversal and nonreversal shifts. *Journal of Experimental Psychology, 51,* 379–384.

Kendler, H. H., & D'Amato, M. F. (1955). A comparison of reversal shifts and nonreversal shifts in human concept formation behavior. *Journal of Experimental Psychology, 49,* 165–174.

Kendler, T. S. (1950). An experimental investigation of transposition as a function of the difference between training and test stimuli. *Journal of Experimental Psychology, 40,* 552–562.

Kendler, T. S. (1971). Continuity theory and cue dominance. In H. H. Kendler & J. T. Spence (Eds.), *Essays in neobehaviorism: A memorial volume to Kenneth W. Spence* (pp. 237–264). New York: Appleton.

Kendler, T. S. (1979a). The development of discrimination learning: A level of functioning explanation. In H. W. Reese & L. P. Lipsitt (Eds.), *Advances in child development and behavior*, (Vol. 13, pp. 83–116). New York: Academic Press.

Kendler, T. S. (1979b). Cross-sectional research, longitudinal theory, and a discriminative transfer ontogeny. *Human Development, 22,* 235–254.

Kendler, T. S., & Kendler, H. H. (1959). Reversal and nonreversal shifts in kindergarten children. *Journal of Experimental Psychology, 58,* 56–60.

Kuenne, M. R. (1946). Experimental investigation of the relationship of language to the transposition behavior of young children. *Journal of Experimental Psychology, 35,* 471–490.

Kuhn, T. S. (1970). *The structure of scientific revolutions*. University of Chicago Press.

Lewin, K. (1954). Behavior and development as a function of the total situation. In L. Carmichael (Ed.), *Manual of Child Psychology* (2nd ed.; pp. 918–970). New York: Wiley.

Lewin, K., Lippitt, R., & White, R. (1939). Patterns of aggressive behavior in experimentally created "social climates." *Journal of Social Psychology, 10,* 271–299.

Nagel, E. (1957). Determinism and development. In D. B. Harris (Ed.), *The concept of development*. Minneapolis: University of Minnesota Press.

Rust, K. J., & Kendler, T. S. (1987). Lower level encoding: Holistic or nonselective? *Developmental Review, 7,* 326–362.

Sears, R. R. (1975). Your ancients revisited: A history of Child Development. In E. M. Hetherington (Ed.), *Review of child development research* (Vol. 5, pp. 1–73). University of Chicago Press.

Seashore, C. E. (1916). *A Child Welfare Research Station*. Bulletin of the State University of Iowa, No. 107, 1916.

Skeels, H. M., Updegraff, R., Wellman, B. L., & Williams, H. M. (1938). *University of Iowa Studies in Child Welfare, 15,* No. 4.

Spence, K. W. (1936). The nature of discrimination learning in animals. *Psychological Review, 43*, 427–449.
Spence, K. W. (1937). The differential response in animals to stimuli varying within a single dimension. *Psychological Review, 44*, 430–444.

8 Reflections on a Century of Research in Psychopathology

Norman Garmezy
University of Minnesota

The celebration of a century of contribution by a famed department of psychology is a noteworthy event. It is one that invites reminiscences, and for the latter half of this birthday party these often focus on the imposing figure of Kenneth Spence. Stories about the man abound and each of us has a personal one to tell. So I begin by adding to the lore.

I came to Iowa in the early summer of 1943—a refugee from infantry training that I had just completed at Fort McClellan in Alabama. The likelihood of this transition was heavily laden with chance. I had gone to the Personnel Section on the camp base to see whether there were any openings in the Air Force and was told that none were available. As I headed out the door to go back to my company (which as it turned out would have likely led to my becoming part of the invasion of Salerno) the clacking of a teletype machine sounded and the Lieutenant called out to me, "Hold it, soldier!" I watched as he read the message and then asked: "There's an ASTP program in personnel psychology starting at the University of Iowa. Would you like to go there?"

And that is the way I came to Iowa. It was another instance of what my colleague at Minnesota, Marvin Dunnette, once labeled "that giant roulette wheel in the sky." I was one of some 60-plus Army personnel sent to the Army Specialized Training Program at Iowa. Our task: To study for 6 months in a broadly based psychology program with the intention of completing the course sequence that, in part, emphasized personnel work. It was as you might have guessed more Spencian than military. However, I did end up subsequently in an Army replacement center assigning men to various tasks, and ultimately was assigned to the 28th U.S. Infantry Division which was appropriately named "The Bloody Bucket," and in time became M/Sgt. of the G–3, Plans and Training Section in the Headquarters Company of the Division.

Once assembled at Iowa we proved to be a heterogeneous group, which Dr. Spence quickly realized. So he gave the entire group a screening exam. I recall it was primarily a general math and statistics test that Spence used to subdivide the corps into four platoons.

The first platoon was made up of the high scorers and the assignments were distributed down to the fourth platoon on the basis of test performance. We were taught partially on this semisegregated basis in small groups, while there was a common attendance in the large lecture sections.

When the platoon lists were posted I found that I had been assigned to Platoon 1. With the usual degree of anxiety that I could identify later as trait, not state, I immediately went to Dr. Spence's office and asked to see him. Within minutes I was admitted. There sat Professor Spence behind his desk and I debated momentarily whether or not to salute him. (I wish I had!) It was the first time I was close to *the man*. He asked me what I wanted and our exchange was a brief one. In playlet form it went like this:

Pvt. G.:   "Dr. Spence, I have been assigned to Platoon 1, and I don't think I should be in it."
Dr. S.:   "Why?"
Pvt. G.:   "I don't know enough, sir."
[Little did I know then that I was questioning the validity of his screening test.]
Dr. S.:   [a therapist to his very core] "You are in the first platoon!"

Reflecting on this brief exchange I had to conclude that never in the history of warfare had so few ($N = 1$) owed so little to so few ($N = 1 + + +$).

Well, I survived and had a great time in the Department and in Iowa City. One extracurricular activity was the writing of an Army musical review with Larry Paulus (who later became head of the Ernie Pyle Theatre in Tokyo after the Japanese surrender), that sold out for two consecutive performances.

Some 2½ years later in Germany, I sat on my helmet one day and addressed a letter to Dr. Spence asking whether I might be able to come back to Iowa to study for the PhD in clinical psychology. This decision had been stimulated by Professor Charles Strother, whose lectures to our ASTP corps had convinced me that this would be my postwar chosen profession.

Somewhat later a letter came from Professor Dewey Stuit offering me an appointment as a counselor in the Student Counseling Office when the war ended. I returned to the States with the 28th Division which was to be refitted for the war in the Pacific, but the atomic bomb devastation of Hiroshima and Nagasaki brought the war to a rapid and unexpected end. Within a month my Division was disbanded and Edith and I, newly married, came to Iowa City. It was a dual decision for which we have both been always grateful.

Iowa was everything we had anticipated and hoped for. On the academic front I. E. Farber became my advisor and proved to be a fine one at that. When I went off to the Worcester State Hospital for a 1-year internship that stretched into a 3-year stay, Spence subsequently issued a ruling to deter anyone else from ever following in such inexplicable footsteps. However, over those 3 years I developed my dissertation titled "Stimulus Generalization in Schizophrenic Patients Under Conditions of Reward and Punishment." Farber became the most extraordinary thesis adviser in terms of his output of letters that had to serve as long-distance dissertation supervision.

Worcester was exactly the place for an Iowan to be. Eliot Rodnick was Chief Psychologist having replaced David Shakow who had accepted a joint professorial appointment at the University of Chicago and the University of Illinois. Rodnick had been trained in experimental psychology at Yale and had served as Clark Hull's senior research assistant. On graduating, he went to Worcester on Hull's advice because academic appointments in the late 1930s and early 1940s still bore the taint of religious preferences. The Academy was not his until later in the 1940s when he went to Duke University as Director of Clinical Psychology and subsequently became Chair of the Department.

Hull, Shakow, and Rodnick shared a vision that Worcester was an ideal setting for creating a program for studying the experimental psychopathology of schizophrenia, and Shakow (1977) had already shaped Worcester's experimental and clinical psychological contributions in that significant direction. All three men had perceived a bright future for such a linkage, and history has proved the correctness of this pioneering view.

For me, Iowa's training enabled the bridging of experimental psychology and psychopathology. Worcester was a fertile clinical soil in which to do so, and I remain forever grateful to my two distinguished mentors—I. E. Farber and Eliot Rodnick. Theirs was a joint helpfulness, wisdom, and support that covered 2 years and a span of some 1,400 miles.

Now for the present: When Dr. Cantor invited me to speak at this Centennial celebration we agreed on a topic that would emphasize research in psychopathology and some of psychology's more exciting contributions to this venture.

Because 1887–1888 was the first academic calendar for the Department of Psychology this had to serve as a starting point. So I went to the history books to see whether the founding of the Department of Psychology at Iowa was a singular great event or embedded amidst other worldly occurrences. What I found was that 1887–1888 were busy times. Some examples:

- In February, King Lobengula of Matabele accepted a British protectorate for his country.
- In March, Britain assumed a protectorate over Sarawak.
- In April, Britain established a protectorate over North Borneo and Brunei.

At last I realized that I had located the sources of risk and protective factors, not in psychopathology, but rather in political science.

The year 1888 was one in which Benjamin Harrison, Republican, defeated Grover Cleveland, Democrat, and (a) no one watched the lips of either candidate, and (b) neither parole patterns nor the American Civil Liberties Union were ever mentioned:

- It was the year in which the word "chromosome" was first used.
- Van Gogh painted Sun Flowers, and The Yellow Chair.
- Rimsky-Korsakov, who had nothing to do with Korsakoff's Syndrome, proved it by writing *Scheherazade*.
- Richard Strauss in turn wrote *Don Juan,* and Strindberg wrote *Miss Julie,* now modified as *Ms. Julie.*
- The first beauty contest ever was held in Belgium and the contestants muddled up the questions something fierce.
- Electrocution replaced hanging in New York State, but I was unable to find any comment on furlough programs in the Harrison–Cleveland exchanges.
- Of greater importance, 1887–1888 saw the appearance of the first two volumes of our oldest scientific publication, the *American Journal of Psychology,* under the ownership and editorship of G. Stanley Hall.

I searched the stacks of the University of Minnesota's library and located both of these volumes and examined their contents. My interest was in psychopathology as it could serve as a beginning for my 100-year inquiry into research in psychopathology. In the 1888 volume there were two articles of interest for this presentation. One was a detailed autobiographical case history furnished by a paranoic. This article was preceded by a section headed *Notes* which resembled, but were lengthier than, our current *Psychological Abstracts.* Virtually all focused on psychopathology, of which the several listed here are examples:

- A report of the *"timing of mental processes"* in insane patients and controls conducted in *Bechterev's* laboratory; the patients exhibited deficits.
- A German psychiatrist reported on "nervousness" as a reflection of the present generation, terming the behavior a *"diseased excitability of the nervous system made functional by injuries."* An illustrative case history was used to demonstrate support for the hypothesis.
- A report from the Bicetre Hospital indicated that epileptic seizures peaked between 8 p.m. and 8 a.m.
- A Professor Kern challenged the view of hereditary criminality and opposed the contemporary theories that would account for crime in general.

The 1888 gem that I found in the musty confines of the library stacks was a case study that appeared in the 1888 volume of the *American Annals of the Deaf*. It was an extraordinary case of resilience in a child whose great physical disadvantage was her blindness and deafness. The child described was Helen Keller. The account dealt with the training program that had been initiated to provide language for this extraordinarily gifted child.

This was further confirmation of a view of the case study that I have held and about which I have written (Garmezy, 1982), namely that this method although essentially a clinical one that differs in exactness from the more identifiable methods of science, is the first step in understanding human behavior. Indeed it is the fundamental base on which we have attempted to erect a science of such behaviors. In the article I have cited, I attempted to illustrate the applicability of single-case analysis to the heartland of our discipline—learning, cognition, physiological, and developmental psychology, and so on, citing Ebbinghaus, Galton, Stratton, Piaget, Cattell, and Freud among others. But it is in the field of psychopathology that the study of the single case has reached it zenith. The history of classification in psychopathology is the accumulation of single cases in the search for similarities focused on symptom expression. Without this prior base an experimental psychopathology of major mental disorders would have flagged.

However, it was not observations of disordered patterns of behavior alone that set the course for the scientific study of psychopathology, for concurrently the brain became a focus of interest for neuropathologists who studied the brains of deceased mental patients. The laboratory was the Asylum and it is not possible to look back on these 100 years without an examination of this site as the place where the struggle to create a science of psychopathology took place. Unfortunately, the Asylum was also the site of multiple violations of the human spirit.

In 1894, Weir Mitchell (1894), a distinguished neurologist, provided a blistering commentary on the state of the Asylum:

> Once we spoke of asylums with respect; it is not so now. We, neurologists, think you have fallen behind us, and this opinion is gaining ground outside of our own ranks, and is, in part at least, your own fault. . . . Where . . . are your careful scientific reports? You live alone, uncriticized, unquestioned, out of the healthy conflicts and honest rivalries that keep us (neurologists) up to the mark of the fullest possible competence. (p. 167)

We have two tracks to follow and these tell an interesting psychiatric story. One was the Weir Mitchell condemnation directed to psychiatry. But the Asylum was not always so wanting. Quite the contrary. In the closing quarter of the 19th century the dominant mode of treatment was *moral management* or *moral therapy*. Its roots were located in the French Revolution, when Philippe Pinel was appointed physician to the Bicetre, a "notorious hell-hole" in which male mentally ill patients were confined. Pinel literally struck off the chains that fettered the patients thus inspiring a famous painting by Robert Fleury. In its place he instituted a hospital regimen based not on mechanical restraints but on sympathetic understanding and early efforts at treatment. The history of this change and its subsequent effects in England and elsewhere have been detailed by Albert Deutsch (1949), a well-known journalist whose book, *The Mentally Ill in America,* had a great impact when it first appeared in the mid 1930s.

In America, transitions occurred that were socio-cultural in origin. In the closing quarter of the 19th century the aforementioned moral therapy was the prevailing form of intervention. Its roots were socio-cultural in origin. To the Asylum came the middle class and upper class essentially for needed rest and relaxation (Bell, 1980). Mental disorder, in the light of the demographics of the hospitals' census, was viewed as due to overwork and an excessive conscience. The needed treatment was perceived to require good food, a restful atmosphere, and the need to escape for a brief period from the pressures of the outside world. The Superintendent acted in *loco parentis* and behaved accordingly.

The roots of this form of treatment as perceived by Brendan and Winifred Maher (1985) was a consequence of the Industrial Revolution that took place in the latter half of the 19th century. In Great Britain the ruling aristocracy felt the encroachment of the successful entrepreneurial class. This rise was perceived as the consequence of "thrift, hard work, moral character, perseverance, and temperance" (p. 313).

Thus, rest from these strains was considered the appropriate treatment for the well-to-do and the rising class of movers of industrial growth. On the other hand, the workers' failures were believed to reside in shortcomings in the self. A mental illness merited dismissal. These "pauper lunatics," as they were termed, necessitated public institutions that received minimal expenditures for such unproductive masses. Charles Dickens would have portrayed the Asylum and its consequences in much the way he treated the factories that expended the lives of workers during the Industrial Revolution.

In Massachusetts where "moral treatment" too had been in vogue, the impoverished masses of Irish immigrants who came to Massachusetts seeking a promised land provided the impetus for the dissolution of moral treatment and a gradual transition to a genetic model for the etiology of mental disorders. Poverty and its consequences were not society's fault but were lodged in the shortcomings of the poor. The genetics of the day was a genetics of prejudice supported by the absence of an adequate scientific base.

Today there is a genuine revolution in science taking place with advances in molecular biology, molecular genetics, and the various neurosciences such as neurochemistry, neurobiology, and so forth. That is the present picture but it was not apparent in the late 19th century.

In the United States, social classes were also differentiated but in Maher's words, these categorizations were "less encrusted" (p. 313). We were less urbanized, less industrialized early in the 20th century, but above all the ethos of the nation bore a political-historical view that all Americans were presumed equal and this exercised an influence, even though the execution of the philosophy often left a great deal to be desired.

Further, publicity and media revelations of neglect and abuse resulted in efforts to improve the mental hospitals.

Two world wars and the evidence of a corps of "walking wounded" veterans added to the need for VA hospitals that provided a somewhat better milieu and treatment effort than had existed previously.

As the hospital improved, the scientific search to enhance an understanding of both etiology and treatment of mental illness also got underway. Numerous laboratories for psychiatric research were set up. In the VA the appointment of psychologists undoubtedly helped to create a research environment. Without an intent to be inclusive, famous settings such as the McLean Hospital, Worcester State Hospital, New York State Psychiatric Institute, "Psychopathic Hospitals" in Ann Arbor, Boston, and Iowa City, the Henry Phipps Psychiatric Clinic at the Johns Hopkins Medical School, and the Child Study Center at Yale all became foci for a new research enterprise. The last named is particularly important because of the neglect that marked psychiatric research on children's mental disorders.

A second track to be followed is not one of settings but rather of persons. In the list of illustrious contributors, Adolf Meyer deserves the highest grades for integrating psychology and psychopathology (Lief, 1948). Meyer, a Swiss pathologist, came to the United States and accepted a post at a state hospital located in Kankakee, Illinois. Meyer believed that the etiology of mental disorders would be resolved by an understanding of brain structures and their related functions. He concentrated initially on numerous postmortem examinations of the brains of deceased mental patients, but could find no consistent pattern of variation from the normal brain that might unlock the mystery of etiology. With this disappointment he turned his focus to an effort to study carefully living patients, leaving the laboratory and the multiple appraisals of tissue and organ systems. He turned his efforts to uncovering the pre-hospital histories of patients and pioneered the study of early childhood factors as influencing agents in adult mental disorders.

Meyer, like Freud, was an early life-span developmentalist in psychiatry, but his model differed. His effort to understand psychological modes of human functioning combined with his profound investment in biological processes led him to a new vision of *psychobiology*. To understand such functioning all available facts were to be used as a basis for treatment action.

Influenced by Jane Addams of Hull House fame in Chicago, and subsequently by John Watson at The Johns Hopkins University, Meyer turned to environment as an additional source of inquiry, in the course of which he created a diagnostic system that was organized around a concept of reaction types that emphasized both the plasticity and individuality of mental patients.

He was the foremost trainer of a new breed of young psychiatrists, and his disciples formed the structure and leadership of a new academic psychiatry. He created the Life Chart—a life span biographical account of health events stressors and correlated behaviors over time. One such chart appears in Figure 1. All psychiatric residents had to create Life Charts of their patients' histories in which

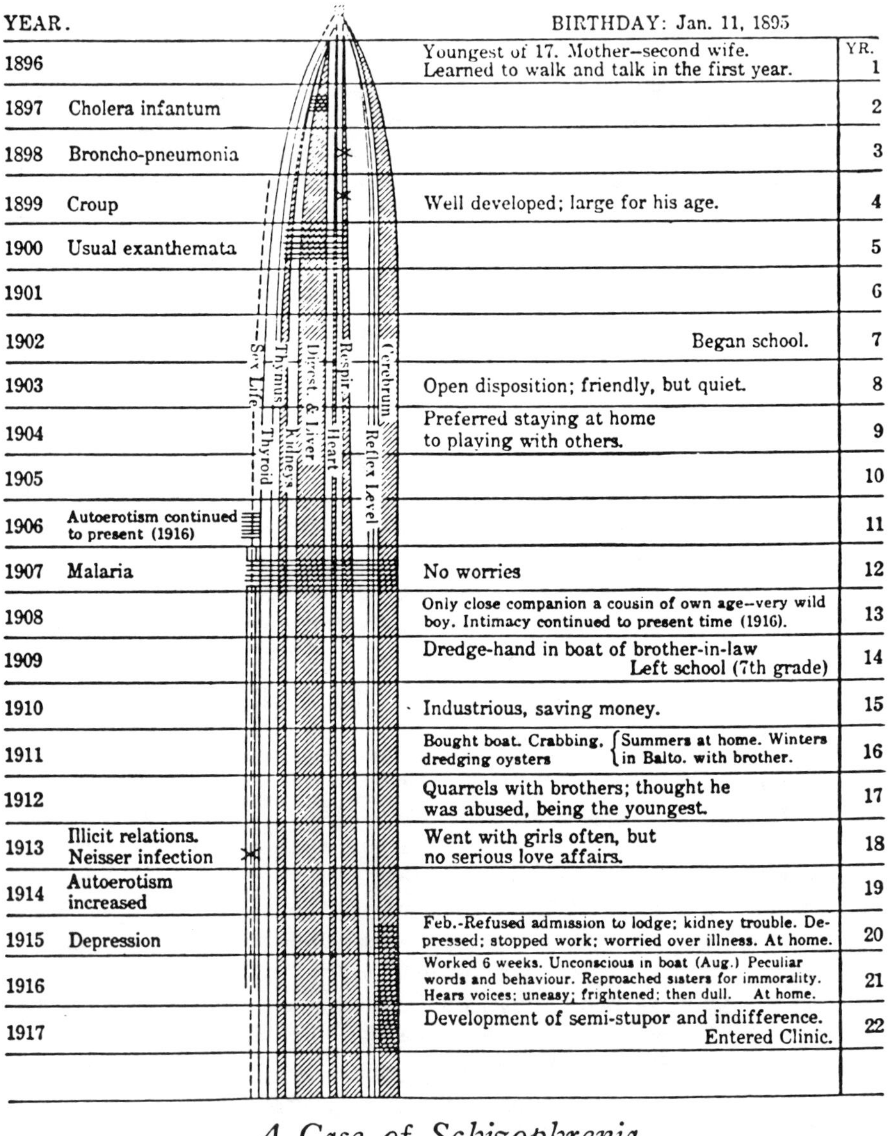

YEAR.		Sex Life / Thyroid / Thymus / Digest. & Liver / Kidneys / Respir. / Heart / Cerebrum / Reflex Level	BIRTHDAY: Jan. 11, 1895	YR.
1896			Youngest of 17. Mother—second wife. Learned to walk and talk in the first year.	1
1897	Cholera infantum			2
1898	Broncho-pneumonia			3
1899	Croup		Well developed; large for his age.	4
1900	Usual exanthemata			5
1901				6
1902			Began school.	7
1903			Open disposition; friendly, but quiet.	8
1904			Preferred staying at home to playing with others.	9
1905				10
1906	Autoerotism continued to present (1916)			11
1907	Malaria		No worries	12
1908			Only close companion a cousin of own age—very wild boy. Intimacy continued to present time (1916).	13
1909			Dredge-hand in boat of brother-in-law. Left school (7th grade)	14
1910			Industrious, saving money.	15
1911			Bought boat. Crabbing, dredging oysters { Summers at home. Winters in Balto. with brother.	16
1912			Quarrels with brothers; thought he was abused, being the youngest.	17
1913	Illicit relations. Neisser infection		Went with girls often, but no serious love affairs.	18
1914	Autoerotism increased			19
1915	Depression		Feb.-Refused admission to lodge; kidney trouble. Depressed; stopped work; worried over illness. At home.	20
1916			Worked 6 weeks. Unconscious in boat (Aug.) Peculiar words and behaviour. Reproached sisters for immorality. Hears voices; uneasy; frightened; then dull. At home.	21
1917			Development of semi-stupor and indifference. Entered Clinic.	22

A Case of Schizophrenia

FIG. 8.1.   A Meyerian life chart of a case of schizophrenia from Lief (1948, p. 420).

physical and social events, and various traumas were placed in juxtaposition with adaptive and maladaptive behavioral patterns; this provided a visual image of the role of stimulus events and possibly reactive behaviors of the patients.

The model was limited, the descriptive language system abstruse, the reaction typology essentially unvalidated, and the diagnostic system clearly ran counter to Kraepelinian formulations. But whatever its shortcoming, Adolf Meyer abetted a research orientation to psychopathology that facilitated the growth of psychiatric research.

There was another movement underway, the roots of which we can now perceive as the instrumental beginning of experimental psychopathology. In the 1880s, Emil Kraepelin—a giant in psychiatry's history—went to study in Wundt's laboratory and to participate in the experimental studies that were underway.

In 1890, when appointed to the Chair in Psychiatry at Heidelberg, he opened the first laboratory devoted to experimental research and broadened its content to include studies of motor activity, memory and learning, word association, and (in anticipation of the growing problems in this area) alcohol and drug addiction.

Kraepelin organized the psychiatric nomenclature and the achievement provides an interesting story that I wrote about (Garmezy, 1982) in an earlier publication:

> An interesting story can be told about the historical origins of Kraepelinian classification, which we can still identify as the precursor of American psychiatry's newest classification scheme (Diagnostic and Statistical Manual of Mental Disorders, 1980). I once marveled aloud to Manfred Bleuler about the incredible achievement of Emil Kraepelin, who in precomputer days gathered together the complexities of the disturbed human psyches that he saw and treated in his university psychiatric hospital setting. Bleuler replied that, as a young boy he had witnessed part of the annual pilgrimage of Kraepelin to a villa in northern Italy, to which he retired each summer when his duties at the university clinic had ended. Kraepelin would stop overnight at the Bleuler home in Zurich and spend the evening in discussions with Eugen Bleuler, Manfred's famous father. With him, Kraepelin carried many case folders, which he read over and over during his vacation respite in Italy, searching for common attributes that would allow him to aggregate the complexity of individual cases into homogeneous subgroups based on patients' symptoms. Vacation ended, Kraepelin would again stop at the Bleuler home on his way back to the university. The next summer, he would reappear with a new bundle of patients' case records. So, the Kraepelinian system evolved. It continues to evolve as more is learned about the similarities and differences among diverse groups of mental patients. But, the origin of this important scientific activity resides in the single case. (p. 8)

Psychology in relation to psychopathology also had its giants. In the 1920s and 1930s three great psychopathologists—the best of breed in the first third of this century—were also moving into laboratories that would speed progress in psychopathology. In my somewhat biased view I would identify these three as:

1. David Wechsler for his research in neuropsychology at Bellevue Hospital in New York City together with his major contributions to the assessment of intelligence and memory function;

2. David Shakow (who I consider to be the father of American clinical psychology), at Worcester State Hospital, demonstrated the multiple contributions that experimental psychology could provide by focusing on attentional functioning and set in relation to reaction time. Shakow used these findings to explain the oft observed deficit behaviors in schizophrenic performance, and developed explanatory constructs that could account for significant differences between schizophrenic patients and normal individuals; and

3. Joseph Zubin of the Psychiatric Institute of Columbia University who brought biometrics into juxtaposition with psychopathology, particularly schizophrenia, and provided systematic laboratory tasks marked by careful measurement and the variations evident in the performance of schizophrenic patients and control subjects.

I suppose as an adopted Minnesotan I would add two other names to this pantheon, that of Starke Hathaway and his most famous pupil, Paul Meehl, who created a powerful structured personality instrument—the MMPI—that enhanced precision in diagnosis, the roots of which (unacknowledged I fear) can now be found in contemporary structured interviews, now used by psychiatrists, to provide a more systematic appraisal to the diagnosis of various psychiatric disorders.

Here at Iowa, tribute should be paid to Arthur Benton, another founder of contemporary neuropsychology—a field of critical importance to the study of brain-behavior relationships that is now being advanced by the emergent technologies of brain imaging. Kudos too to John Knott for his advances in psychophysiology, to Charles Strother, a pioneer in the study of childhood psychopathology, and to Janet Spence, I. E. Farber, and Kenneth Spence for their theoretical and empirical contributions toward increasing our understanding of anxiety.

Although there were no specialists in the Psychology Department who probed the mysteries of schizophrenia, several illustrious graduates of the Department took their Iowa orientation and applied their wisdom to the experimental study of schizophrenia. I note particularly two of my contemporaries in our graduate student days—Bertram Cohen at Rutgers, and Gerald Rosenbaum formerly at Wayne State University and the Lafayette Clinic, now Director of the Clinical Psychology Training Program at San Diego State University.

I have undoubtedly omitted numerous Iowa names that warrant mention in this brief chapter, but one member of the Psychiatry Department occupies an important place in child psychiatry's relatively brief history. Richard Jenkins' work on the distinction between internalizing and externalizing symptomatology in child psychiatric cases sets forth a dichotomy, the significance of which has stood the test of time. This separation of symptoms has proved to be not only a powerful differentiator of presenting attributes, but it has provided a set of antecedents and consequents surrounding the dichotomy that has helped to differentiate the truly endangered child (the externalizers) from those (the internalizers) with less self-destructive potential. In terms of familial factors, manifest competence, school failure, outcome continuities in disorder, and the like, this dichotomy has remained a most productive one, and a tribute to Professor Jenkins' pioneering research efforts.

Now for some closing observations. This chapter has not sought to trace the 20th century's history of research in experimental psychopathology. Such a complete history has yet to be written. However, Brendan and Winifred Maher have written several chapters that are highly relevant to this venture. In two of the chapters they have traced the status of mental disorders over the centuries at various times, changes in treatment, the historical, cultural, and social trends that have influenced psychiatry, modes of diagnosis, and so forth (Maher & Maher, 1985). In Hearst's (1979) edited volume entitled *The First Century of Experimental Psychology,* the Mahers (1979) have also traced the research contributions of Kraepelin, Jung, and others and have cited the early research efforts at McLean Hospital, Worcester State Hospital and the New York State Psychiatric Institute. They have given considerable attention to the emergence of neuropsychology, to the paradigms provided by Pavlov's *experimental neurosis* and Watson's *conditioned phobia,* to the Hullian group at Yale who sought to put psychoanalytic theory to experimental test, to the later experimental studies of frustration and aggression, to the construct of mental set and schizophrenic's deficits on reaction time tasks, and to the emergence of risk research. Their excellent chapter provides an overview of the multiform contributions of psychology to the furtherance of research in psychopathology.

In *The Shaping of Modern Psychology,* Hearnshaw (1987) examined "medical influences" but provided minimal commentary on experimental psychological contributions to furthering psychiatric understanding. And I fear that Koch and Leary (1985), in their *A Century of Psychology as Science,* have attended not at all to the contributions of clinical psychology to the advancement of a scientific experimental psychopathology.

Several volumes have provided a history of the growth and development of clinical psychology. Hilgard (1987), in his *History of Psychology in America,* has written a superb chapter on clinical psychology, several pages of which are devoted to research on experimental psychopathology, focused largely on investigations related to the etiology of schizophrenia.

Two additional volumes have emphasized research progress in clinical psychology—Hersen, Kazdin, and Bellack (1983) and Kendall and Butcher (1982). In the Hersen et al. volume, Depue and Monroe (1983) begin their chapter on *Psychopathology Research* with this sentence: "Psychologists and psychiatrists

have been doing research on psychopathology for approximately four decades"
(p. 239).

I suspect that the time span is a lengthier one, if one focuses on the experimental study of schizophrenia. Shakow's first paper, published in 1932, dealt with aspects of motor coordination in schizophrenic patients. His article on mental set in schizophrenia using a discrimination reaction time task appeared in the *Psychological Bulletin* in 1936. The Worcester State Hospital program of research in schizophrenia was launched in 1929, and by 1969 had generated 439 references.

In these studies, the names of distinction include Hoskins, Jellinek, Shakow, Huston, Freeman, Rubin, Angyal, Rosenzweig, Gottlieb, Hanfmann, Rodnick, Hoagland, Hunt, Cameron, Kant, Malamud, Rotter, Roe, Pincus, Elmadjian, and others.

In paying tribute to these pioneers I once wrote:

> It is unlikely that there will ever be another research program in schizophrenia to match this one for the clinical-experimental sophistication and sensitivity of its investigators, the careful delineation of the characteristics of its subject samples, the attentiveness to environmental (ward and laboratory) attributes, the concern for diagnostic precision, the control of therapeutic effects, the unique inter-disciplinary flavor, the matchless rigor of its data gathering, and the staying power of its empirical findings. (Garmezy, 1971, p. 317)

Perhaps, in time, that paragraph will have to be revoked, but it does reveal the superb early scientific antecedents to our many current experimental investigations of schizophrenia.

On the developmental side there is also a more than a 70+-year research history that was initially focused on longitudinal studies of conduct disordered delinquent youth. This area too has had a long history involving psychology as a discipline that provided powerful forebears to the highly active current scene (Stone & Onque, 1959).

So a history has to be written of the contributions of psychological science to psychiatric disorders. In part, this history will also have to attend to the recent emergence of a developmental psychopathology rooted in the sciences of development psychology, child clinical psychology, child psychiatry, developmental biology, and developmental genetics (Cicchetti, 1989; Lewis & Miller, 1990). Child psychopathology is coming of age, and the scientific contributions that stem from psychology will once again attest to the power of our discipline as a contributor, not solely to the study of normative development, but also to the varieties of maladaptive behaviors and mental disorders that have plagued society over centuries.

REFERENCES

Bell, L. V. (1980). *Treating the mentally ill: From colonial times to the present.* New York: Praeger.

Cicchetti, D. (Ed.). (1989). *The emergence of a discipline*. Hillsdale, NJ: Lawrence Erlbaum Associates.

Depue, R. A., & Monroe, S. M. (1983). *Psychopathology research*. In M. Hersen, A. E. Kazdin, & A. S. Bellak (Eds.), *The clinical psychology handbook* (pp. 239–264). New York: Pergamon Press.

Deutsch, A. (1949). The mentally ill in America. New York: Columbia University Press.

Diagnostic & Statistical Manual of Mental Disorders, 3rd Edition (1980). Washington, D.C. The American Psychiatric Association.

Garmezy, N. (1971). Commentary. *Journal of Nervous and Mental Disease, 153*, 317–322.

Garmezy, N. (1982). The case for the single case in research. In A. E. Kazdin & A. H. Tuma (Eds.), *New directions for methodology of social and behavioral sciences: Single-case research designs* (pp. 5–17). San Francisco: Jossey–Bass.

Hearnshaw, L. S. (1987). *The shaping of modern psychology*. London: Routledge & Kegan Paul.

Hearst, E. (Ed.). (1979). The first century of experimental psychology. Hillsdale, NJ: Lawrence Erlbaum Associates.

Hersen, M., Kazdin, A. E., & Bellak, A. S. (Eds.). (1983). *The clinical psychology handbook*. New York: Pergamon Press.

Hilgard, E. R. (1987). *Psychology in America: A historical survey*. San Diego: Harcourt Brace Jovanovich.

Kendall, P. C., & Butcher, J. N. (Eds.). (1982). *Handbook of research methods in clinical psychology*. New York: Wiley Interscience.

Koch, S., & Leary, D. E. (Eds.). (1985). *A century of psychology as science*. New York: McGraw–Hill.

Lewis, M., & Miller, S. M. (Eds.). (1990). *Handbook of developmental psychopathology*. New York: Plenum Press.

Lief, A. (1948). *The common sense psychiatry of Dr. Adolf Meyer*. New York: McGraw–Hill.

Maher, B. A., & Maher, W. B. (1979). Psychopathology. In E. Hearst (Ed.), *The first century of experimental psychology* (pp. 561–621). Hillsdale, NJ: Lawrence Erlbaum Associates.

Maher, B. A., & Maher, W. B. (1985). Psychopathology II: From the eighteenth century to modern times. In G. A. Kimble & K. Schlesinger (Eds.), *Topics in the history of psychology* (Vol. 2, pp. 295–329). Hillsdale, NJ: Lawrence Erlbaum Associates.

Mitchell, S. W. (1894). Address to the American Medico–Psychological Association (May 16, 1894). *Journal of Nervous and Mental Diseases, 21*, 413–438. (Cited in Whitehorn, J. C. (1944). A century of psychiatric research in America. In *One hundred years of American psychology* (pp. 167–193). American Psychiatric Association. New York: Columbia University Press.

Shakow, D. (1977). *Schizophrenia: Selected papers*. New York: International Universities Press.

Stone, A. A., & Onque, G. C. (1959). *Longitudinal studies of child personality*. Cambridge, MA: Harvard University Press.

9 The Changing Icons in Personality Psychology[1]

Albert Bandura
Stanford University

When one is invited to address a Centennial gathering of graduate compatriots, the strong inclination is to say something cosmic. You will be happy to hear that I have fought that inclination and conquered it. What I have to say is concerned with more terrestrial issues. It is only fitting, on an occasion such as this, to touch briefly on one's initial experiences at being imprinted on Iowan psychology. When it came time to select a graduate school, I went to my trusty undergraduate advisor and asked, "Where are the stone tablets of psychology?" He replied without any hesitation, "Iowa, of course." To dispel any misgivings about a distant migration to the Midwest, he enumerated the renowned credentials of the Iowa faculty. As I departed from the University of British Columbia to Iowa City, my advisor's parting counsel was that Iowa is a distinguished but tough place. It was clear from his characterization that the Iowa Psychology Department was not Mr. Rogers' Neighborhood. It was, indeed, an intellectually lively and demanding place where major theoretical issues were pursued with a passion. It was refreshingly free of colorless eclecticism.

Much to my surprise, it was also a highly supportive and hospitable department. As a native Canadian, I did not qualify for fellowship stipends. Art Benton always managed to find ways to keep me adequately supplied with the coin of the realm. In recalling this fluid system of financial aid, I was reminded of a major tourist attraction in the San Jose area, the Winchester Mystery House, which was built by the heir of the rifleman. Mrs. Winchester was of the belief that she would continue to live as long as she added new constructions to her ever-

---

[1]Some sections of this chapter contain revised material from my article, "Human Agency in Social Cognitive Theory" (Bandura, 1989).

expanding mansion. As Art Benton created ongoing makeshift carpentry jobs for me, his home on South Court began to take on a Winchester look. I navigated through the Iowa graduate program with those temperamental Marchand calculators in one hand and a serviceable hammer in the other. When Jud Brown departed for summer consultancies to the Lackland Airforce program, I was keeper of his house and hound. His home got needless coats of paint as part of an unarticulated financial aid program.

At the end of my first year of graduate study it was evident that my undergraduate advisor needed some corrective feedback regarding the ethos at Iowa. I explained to him that my initial experiences in graduate study at Iowa reminded me of Mark Twain when he said of Wagner's music, "It's not as bad as it sounds."

The graduate training at Iowa served us well, whatever course our scholarly pursuits took. I recall attending a meeting convened by one of the National Institutes in Washington on applying learning theory to child development. It was heavily populated with Iowa graduates—Sid Bijou, Shep White, Jack Gewirtz, and myself. Although we worshipped at different theoretical altars, we all bore the distinguishing Iowa stamp—a strong commitment to theoretical analysis and respect for incisive experimentation. Many of the psychological contents of a given era are perishable. But commitment to a conceptual framework and rigorous tools of inquiry remain highly serviceable in the continuing search for informative muses.

PERSONAL CAUSALITY: PERSONAL DETERMINANTS VERSUS INDIVIDUAL DIFFERENCES

I was asked to comment briefly on what's doing within the vast boundaries of the sovereign domain of Personality. Because a person is, of course, centrally involved in virtually every psychological phenomenon, this could be a tall order that encompasses every branch of psychology. Indeed, the recent years have witnessed growing personality colonization of neighboring psychological territories and other disciplinary domains. To cite but a few examples, personal factors are very much involved in regulating attentional processes, schematic processing of experiences, memory representation and reconstruction, cognitively based motivation, emotional activation, and the efficacy with which cognitive and behavioral skills are executed in the transactions of everyday life (Bandura, 1986, 1988a; Bower, 1983; Cantor & Kihlstrom, 1987; Hamilton, Bower, & Frijda, 1988; Sternberg & Kolligian, 1990; Sorrentino & Higgins, 1986). A notable example of a fruitful interdisciplinary expedition of personality theory is the burgeoning research documenting the influential role played by psychosocial factors in human health and disease (Ader, 1981; Bandura, in press; Holroyd & Creer, 1986; Matarazzo, Weiss, Herd, Miller, & Weiss, 1984). The significant advances in knowledge of psychobiologic relations are helping to broaden the perspective on health functioning from a biomedical approach to a more comprehensive biopsychosocial one.

The influential contribution of personal causality to human functioning is often insufficiently recognized because the issue tends to be cast in terms of *individual differences* rather than *personal determinants*. The difference in these conceptions is illustrated by instances in which a personal factor is necessary for a given course of action, but it is developed to the same level in different individuals. For example, all librarians know how to read well and do not differ in this respect, but possessing the ability to read is essential for performing the librarianship role. In such cases, the differences between individuals is negligible but the personal competence is vital for successful performance. Personal determinants operate as dynamic factors in causal structures rather than as static entities that people possess in differing amounts. The alternative perspectives on personal causation reflect more than variations in semantic labeling. The individual differences approach is rooted in trait theory, whereas the personal causality approach is founded on a transactional model of causation. The implications of these alternative conceptions for measurement and causal analysis of personal determinants shall be addressed later in greater detail.

MODELS OF PERSONALITY

The conceptual models that have guided the study of personality have undergone considerable change over the years. At the time I was pursuing graduate study, the psychodynamic drive model was the dominant line of theorizing. In this view, which embraced a hydraulic motivational model, behavior was regulated by the interplay of inner impulses and restraining forces. Most of these inner motivators operated below the level of consciousness disguised by defensive mental operations. Much time was spent devising ways of detecting and altering the inner dynamic forces. Although these drive theories postulated a thorough psychic determinism, the unconscious mental life bore only a loose relation to human thought and action. The inner dynamics could not only produce any variety of effects, but they could even show up in opposite forms of behavior. Such versatile psychic determinants were not easily testable or refutable. The psychodynamic drive theories did not fare well under close empirical scrutiny. They had neither much predictive power nor much success in altering human behavior.

There has been some recent revival of interest in psychoanalytic theory stimulated by its assumed conceptual affinity with the computer model of mental processes. Psychoanalytic theory downgraded the role of conscious processes in the regulation of human thought, affect, and action. In the computer model, the neurophysiological machine goes about its computational cognitive activities without any consciousness at all. Some writers have attempted to forge an alliance between psychoanalytic theory and the newer emergent computer models in which computational power is distributed through parallel processing among microprocessors interacting with each other. In the assumed theoretical parallelism, the microprocessors become microminds endowed with the functional properties of the psychoanalytic inner agents (Turkle, 1988). People do, of course, eventually routinize cognitive operations to the point where they execute them with little accompanying awareness or shortcircuit them altogether. Thus, they often react with fixed ways of thinking unreflectively, and with habitual ways of behaving unthinkingly. However, there is a marked difference between nonconscious processing of information and a strife-ridden unconscious mental life that orchestrates behavior. Whereas the computer models have eliminated a self, psychoanalytic theory is heavily invested in an omnipresent unconscious self.

When I was in graduate school, there was also a bit of a side activity in the form of trait theorizing that was largely ignored and remained dormant until its revival in the seventies by the controversy over the cross-situational consistency of behavior. Trait theorists replaced drives with personality dispositions as the regulators of action. Trait theories do not address themselves much to issues of where dispositions come from, which factors modulate their strength, or the mechanisms through which they generate behavior and motivate and guide it. Rather, they have been concerned mainly with assessing personality traits and testing their predictive utility. Trait approaches did not excite personality theorists who prefer more substance in their theoretical gruel. If behavior is largely the product of a disposition, then actions should be fairly consistent across situations and stable over time. The major controversies revolve around this basic assumption, as well as disagreements about the number and kinds of prime traits that personality theory should embody.

Trait theories received secondary attention until Mischel (1968) shattered the trait icons with a large body of evidence showing that measures of personality traits usually correlate weakly with social behavior in different settings. Past behavior predicts future behavior in similar situations with moderate success, but conduct varies across situations differing in properties that affect the functional value of a particular form of behavior. For example, parents who are nonpermissive for aggression in the home but demand and reward such behavior outside the home have children who do not aggress toward family members but are quick to pick fights with teachers and peers (Bandura & Walters, 1959). The biasing factors that lead people to see behavioral uniformity when variability in behavior is the common pattern, itself, became the object of study. People are prone to mistake behaving similarly in the same setting over time as indicative of behaving similarly in different settings (Mischel & Peake, 1982). Social psychologists analyzed the readiness to attribute specific behavior to an underlying disposition as a basic defect in attributional judgment (Jones, 1976; Ross, 1977). Individuals view their own actions as varying under different situational circumstances and constraints but, based on limited observation, they are quick to see the behavior of others as springing from an underlying disposition.

Efforts to strip traits and dispositions of their causal sovereignty did not go uncontested. Proponents of the trait theories argued that seemingly different behaviors may be manifestations of the same underlying disposition. This argument had little persuasive force because no reliable criteria were provided for identifying the behaviors that are expressions of a particular root disposition and those that are not. A more common response to the limited yield of trait predictors was to fault the methods used to study relationships between trait indices and behavior. The prescribed methodological rectifications took several forms, as did the critiques of them.

Trait theorists attempted to extract cross-situational uniformity in behavior from behavioral variability by classifying people into consistent or variable types, by profile matching of personal attributes to the types of behaviors situations require for success, or by averaging ratings of different forms of the behavior performed at different times and in different places to get a truer index of a trait (Bem & Allen, 1974; Bem & Funder, 1978; Epstein, 1983). None of these methodological remedies provided a cure for predictive deficiency because variability in behavior is not a failing of method but a valuable property of human adaptiveness (Bandura, 1986).

Disappointment with the predictive and operative power of drive and trait theories led to a brief rise of interest in views espousing situationalism. In this perspective, human behavior is shaped and controlled by environmental forces (Lundin, 1961; Skinner, 1969). One-sided environmental determinism added further fuel to debates about which model of causation provides the best glimpse of the theoretical promised land. Many majestic trees were sacrificed and much ink was spilt in arguments over whether human behavior springs from inner dispositions or is situationally regulated. Because adaptive functioning requires both generality and discriminability of actions, framing the issue in such dichotomous terms made for thick journals and psychic scar tissue, but only thin progress. Whether people behave uniformly or variably depends on the interplay of self-generated and external sources of influence accompanying the behavior in different situations. Thus, if acting intelligently serves adaptive functions in diverse settings, people will act in consistently intelligent ways in situations that otherwise differ markedly. By contrast, if indignant demands bring punishment from police officers but better service from store clerks, people will behave authoritatively with clerks but cautiously with police. Therefore, social cognitive theory is concerned with explaining the mechanisms governing both behavioral generality and variability (Bandura, 1986).

Unidirectional causality emphasizing either dispositionalism or situationalism has since given way to reciprocal models of causation. Nowadays almost everyone is an interactionist. Therefore, the major issues in contention center on the type of interactionism espoused. At least three different interactional models have been posed, two of which subscribe to one-way causation in the link to behavior. In the *unidirectional model,* persons and situations are treated as independent influences that combine in unspecified ways to produce beha-

vior $\begin{matrix} P \\ \\ E \end{matrix} \!\!\nearrow\!\!\searrow\; B$. The basic problem with this causal model is that personal

and environmental influences do not function as independent determinants. They determine each other. People create, alter, and destroy environments. The changes they produce in environmental conditions, in turn, affect them personally. The unidirectional causality with respect to behavior is another serious deficiency of this model of interactionism.

The *partially bidirectional* conception of interaction, which is widely adopted in personality theory, acknowledges that persons and situations affect each other. However, it treats influences relating to behavior as flowing in only one direction. The person–situation interchange undirectionally produces behavior, but the behavior itself does not affect the ongoing transaction between the person and

the situation $\begin{matrix} P \\ \updownarrow \\ E \end{matrix} \!\!\searrow\; B$. A major limitation of this interaction model is that

behavior is not procreated by an intimate interchange between a behaviorless person and the environment. Such a feat would be analogous to immaculate conception. Except for their social stimulus value, people cannot affect their environment other than through their actions. Their behavior plays a dominant role in how people influence situations which, in turn, affect their thoughts, emotional reactions, and behavior. In short, behavior is an interacting determinant rather than a detached by-product of a person–situation interchange.

Social cognitive theory conceptualizes the interactional causal structure as involving *triadic reciprocal determinism* (Bandura, 1986). In this model of reciprocal causation, behavior; inner personal factors in the form of cognitive, affective and biological events; and environmental influences all operate as interacting determinants that influence each other bidirectionally

$B \;\rightleftarrows\!\!\nearrow^{\displaystyle P}\!\!\searrow\; E$. The mutual influences and their reciprocal effects do not

all spring forth simultaneously. It takes time for a causal factor to exert its influence. Because of the time lags in the operation of the triadic factors, it is possible to gain some understanding of how different segments of reciprocal causation operate without having to mount a Herculean effort to assess every possible interactant at the same time.

Different subspecialties of psychology center their inquiry on selected segments of reciprocality. Cognitive psychologists select the interactive relation between thought and action as their major sector of interest. They examine how conceptions, beliefs, self-percepts, and intentions shape and direct behavior. What people think, believe, and feel affects how they behave. The natural and extrinsic effects of their actions, in turn, partly determine their thought patterns and affective reactions.

Social psychologists examine the segment of reciprocality between the person and the environment in the triadic system. This line of inquiry adds to our understanding of how environmental influences in the form of modeling, tuition, and social persuasion alter cognitions and affective proclivities. The reciprocal element in this segment of causation has been of central concern to the subspecialty of person perception. People evoke different reactions from their social environment by their physical characteristics, such as their age, size, race, sex, and physical attractiveness. They similarly activate different reactions depending on their socially conferred roles and status.

Of all the different segments in the triadic causal structure, the reciprocal relationship between behavior and environmental events has received the greatest attention. Indeed, ethological, transactional, and behavioristic theories focus almost exclusively on this portion of reciprocity in the explanation of behavior. In the transactions of everyday life, behavior alters environmental conditions, and it is, in turn, altered by the very conditions it creates.

Clarifying how the various subsystems function interactively can advance understanding of important aspects of the superordinate causal system. What has been lacking is research on how the multiple reciprocal links of influences operate together and how the patterning and relative strength of the constituent factors in the causal structure change over time. We have recently conducted microanalyses of triadic reciprocal causation using a dynamic computerized environment in which individuals have to preside over an organization (Wood & Bandura, 1989). In this series of experiments, each of the major interactants in the triadic causal structure—cognitive, behavioral, and environmental—functions as an important constituent in the transactional system (Bandura & Jourden, in press; Bandura & Wood, 1989; Wood & Bandura, 1989a; Wood, Bandura, & Bailey, 1990). The cognitive determinant is indexed by self-beliefs of efficacy, cognized goals, and quality of analytic thinking. The options that are actually executed in the management of the organization constitute the behavioral determinant. The properties of the organizational environment, the level of challenge it prescribes and its responsiveness to behavioral interventions represent the environmental determinant. The constituent factors in the ongoing transactional system are measured repeatedly. The findings of this program of research have helped to clarify how composite causal structures operate and how the relative contribution of the constituent factors changes over time.

Efforts to elucidate how personal determinants contribute to psychosocial functioning have relied extensively on omnibus tests of personal attributes designed to serve diverse purposes. Such omnibus personality tests contain a fixed set of items, many of which may have little bearing on a particular phenomenon of interest. Moreover, in an effort to serve all purposes, the items are often cast in a general form requiring respondents to try to surmise what the unspecified particulars might be. For example, consider an item from one of the most widely used personality measures, the locus of control scale: "The average citizen can have an influence in government decisions." What is an average citizen? For respondents who dissociate themselves from the average citizenry because of political alienation, cynicism or a privileged status, the item measures their perceptions of what the ordinary citizenry might believe, not their belief about how much control they personally can wield. Which government—city, state, federal? What constitutes an influence—rectifying grievances, securing projects and services for one's community, gaining enactment of laws, ensuring enforcement of existing statutes? Decisions about what? Some governmental decisions are easily influenceable, others are responsive only to concerted social pressures, and still others remain highly refractory to change even under strong public clamor. Indefiniteness produces considerable ambiguity and variability in what is being measured. Omnibus procedures create problems of predictive relevance as well as obscurity. Why should beliefs about the influenceability of governmental decisions, however interpreted, have much to say about how people will perform in academic courses, on athletic fields, in salesrooms, in production facilities, on concert stages, or in social relationships?

It is unrealistic to expect personality items cast in generalities to shed much light on the contribution of personal factors to psychosocial functioning in particular contexts and task domains. We saw earlier that trait measures usually yield modest correlations. Tests of this sort may have some practical value in that some predictive gain, however small, is better than sheer guesswork. But major progress in understanding how personal factors operate in causal structures is best advanced through microanalysis of interactive processes. This requires explicit measurement of the particular personal determinants that are germane to given domains of functioning. Particularized indices of personal determinants have greater predictiveness than do omnibus ones (Bandura, 1986, in press). The convenience of general purpose tests of personality characteristics is thus gained at the cost of explanatory and predictive power.

The affinity to global constructs and measures has also fostered an erroneous dichotomy that pervades the literature in the field of personality. This is the disjoined duality of process and structure. Social cognitive conceptions of personality are often depicted as being solely process theories, whereas dispositional approaches are said to give major consideration to personality structures. Social cognitive theory rejects the false separateness of process and structure (Bandura, 1986). Personality structures are created by process operations, and it is difficult to conceive of a personality process that is disembodied from any underlying structure.

Self-regulation of moral conduct is illustrative of this interdependence between process and structure (Bandura, 1990b, 1991a). Social cognitive theory provides a detailed account of how moral rules and standards are constructed through cognitive processing of diverse sources of information conveyed by modeled moral commitments, tuition and evaluative social reactions to one's conduct. The nature and pattern of the acquired moral rules represent an enduring cognitive structure for judging the moral status of conduct in situations containing many morally relevant decisional ingredients. One does not have a full set of moral standards on Monday, none on Tuesday and a new set on Wednesday. The standards of conduct are enduring unless they happen to be altered by powerful subsequent experiences. It is through the cognitive rule structure that the self-regulatory constituent processes of self-monitoring, self-evaluation, and self-sanctions operate anticipatorily on conduct. In short, processes do not operate in a vacuum without structural properties that provide the substance and direction for those processes. People do not run around mindlessly engaging in structure-free processing of experiences.

A social cognitive theory combining moral rule structures and self-regulative processes operating through them is no less a structural theory of personality than, for example, the psychoanalytic approach in which a superego controls conduct. The major differences between these two theories is in their globality, explicitness of acquisition and regulative mechanisms, and predictive power, not in whether one theory postulates a cognitive structure and the other does not (Bandura, 1973, 1991a).

The nature and regulative function of self-conceptions provides a further illustration in which relinquishment of omnibus measures is sometimes misconstrued as abandonment of structure. Self-appraisal has traditionally been conceptualized in personality theory in terms of the self-concept (Rogers, 1959; Wylie, 1974). Such self theories are concerned, for the most part, with global self-images. A global self-conception does not do justice to the complexity of self-belief systems that can vary substantially across different task domains, different levels of activity within the same domain, and different situational circumstances. Thus, people's self-conceptions as parents may differ from their vocational self-conception and, even in the vocational realm, their self-appraisal is likely to differ for different facets of occupational competency. Composite self-images are not equal to the task of predicting with any degree of accuracy such intraindividual variability. Social cognitive theory approaches the structure of self-belief systems in more refined, domain-linked ways that have greater explanatory and predictive power (Bandura, 1986). This is not to say that there is no generality to self-conceptions. For any given individual, one can determine degree of generality from multidomain measures, but one cannot extract the pattern of self-conceptions for different aspects of life from a conglomerate omnibus measure. In any event, the social cognitive view of self-conception is no less a structural theory than is the Rogerian approach.

A major current movement in psychology is away from vague, omnibus cognitive structures to more domain-linked competencies. Even in the field of cognitive development, the bulwark of global structuralism (Piaget, 1950) is being abandoned for more specialized cognitive competencies (Feldman, 1980). My learned colleague at Stanford, John Flavell (1978), summarized this change well when he wrote: "However much we may wish it to believe otherwise, human cognitive growth may simply be too contingent, multiform, and hetero-geneous—too variegated in developmental mechanisms, routes, and rates—to be accurately categorized by any stage theory of the Piagetian kind" (p. 187).

COMPUTER MODEL

The advent of the computer transformed the nature of the psychological franchise and radically altered its research agenda. The phenomenon of learning had al-ways occupied a central position in psychology. The mind as computational program became the conceptual model for the times. Because of its association with behaviorism, learning became a heretical topic. Interest shifted from the acquisition of performance competencies to the processing, storage, and retrieval of information. Fundamental issues of how behavioral competencies are con-structed and adaptively actualized were either trivialized or simply ignored. The mechanisms governing the translation of cognition into proficient action has been a continuing major problem in psychology. The behavioral amputation in the computer model of cognition only aggravated the problem of disconnection.

Issues relating to the performance processes governing the translation of cognition into adaptive competencies could not be ignored indefinitely. Barbara Tversky (1982) has traced the decline and current resurrection of learning in psychology. Learning was originally supplanted by memory for discrete bits of information, sentences, and prose passages. Memory, in turn, was recast as a problem of comprehension. Growth of understanding then became a problem of acquiring declarative knowledge and procedural knowledge which provides the production systems. The requiem for learning was clearly premature. Langley and Simon (1981) have recently argued for the centrality of learning in cognition and have called for a revival of research on learning processes.

Explanation of acquisition of competence in terms of factual and procedural knowledge is well suited for cognitive problem solving where solutions are cognitively generated and no performance skills are involved or they are trivially simple acts used mainly to signify one's judgments. One must distinguish be-tween knowledge and performance competencies. A novice given complete factual information on how to ski, a set of procedural rules, and then launched from a mountain top would most likely end up in an orthopedic ward with multiple fractures. Additional mechanisms are required to get from knowledge structures to proficient action.

In social cognitive theory (Bandura, 1986), the construction of complex performance skills operates through a conception-matching process. Conceptions of adaptive actions guide the production of appropriate behavior and provide the internal standards for corrective adjustments in the development of behavioral proficiency (Carroll & Bandura, 1990). These conceptions are formed on the basis of knowledge gained through observational learning, inferences from exploratory experiences, information conveyed by verbal instruction, and innovative cognitive syntheses of preexisting knowledge. The mechanism for transforming cognition into action involves both transformational and generative operations. Execution of a skill must be constantly varied to suit changing circumstances. Adaptive performance, therefore, requires a generative conception rather than a one-to-one mapping between representation and action. To take a simple example, after young children grasp the conception of a triangle they can draw large or small ones with either hand or foot, and create triangular paths and enclosures with materials, even though they have never produced some of these triangular constructions in this particular way before. By applying an abstract specification of the activity, people can produce many variations on the skill. Conceptions are rarely transformed into masterful performance on the first attempt. Monitored enactments serve as the vehicle for transforming knowledge into skilled action. Performances are perfected by corrective adjustments during behavior production until a close match is eventually achieved between conception and action (Carroll & Bandura, 1985, 1987).

Human action is, of course, regulated by multilevel systems of control. Cognitive guidance is critical during the acquisition of competences (Carroll & Bandura, 1990). But after skills have been perfected, they no longer require cognitive control. Their execution is largely regulated by lower level sensorimotor systems (Carroll & Bandura, 1987). Partial disengagement of thought from proficient action frees cognitive resources for other purposes. If routinized behavior fails to produce expected results, the cognitive control system again comes into play. New courses of action are constructed and tested. Control reverts to the lower control system after an adequate means is found and becomes the habitual way of doing things.

The common image is that the cognitivists pulled into town with their blazing conceptual pistols and promptly vanquished the peripheralistic learning theorists. Actually, peripheralistic theories of learning were falling into disrepute before the computational model of cognition began its ascendancy. Most learning theories had already become cognitivized. Neal Miller interpreted reinforcement in terms of its informative properties (Egger & Miller, 1963). Lawrence (1963) conceptualized external influences on perception and learning as operating through a set of rules or coding operations. Mowrer (1960) adopted imagery as an explanatory mechanism in learning, and hopeful and apprehensive expectations as regulators of action. Psychological modeling was construed in terms of the transmission of information and representational guidance of action (Bandura, 1962). The information-processing paradigm greatly accelerated conferral of a central role to cognition in human functioning.

Both personality and social psychology placed increasing emphasis on cognitive determinism. Human motivation, action, and dysfunction were the product of self-referent thought, cognitive schemata, judgmental heuristics, and causal attributions (Bandura, 1986; Mischel, 1973; Nisbett & Ross, 1980; Weiner, 1972). The impelling impulses proclaimed by psychodynamic theories as the sources of human conduct were supplanted by cognitive motivators in the form of action-outcome expectancies, causal attributions, and cognized goals. Human problems and distresses were viewed as arising largely from faulty thinking (Beck, 1976; Ellis & Grieger, 1978; Meichenbaum, 1977). It is not people's unconscious mental life, but their conscious mental life that is the major source of their problems and miseries. To alter how they feel and behave, they must clean up their conscious cognitive ecology.

Some theorists pushed cognitive determinism to the extreme with born-again fervor, as if thought has no basis in social reality. The words of the stoic philosopher Epictetus were widely quoted as testimony for the power of thought over social reality: "Men are disturbed not by things but by the views which they take of them." To contend that people are distressed, not by what happens to them, but solely by their views of it, is to ignore that environmental factors partly determine what people perceive and think. Nor does thought completely override other determinants of affect and action. There is a marked difference between acknowledging that the impact of happenings is often mediated through cognition and claiming that the happenings themselves are of little consequence. The human condition is better improved by changing deleterious conditions as well as perceptions than it is by focusing solely on perceptions while ignoring the very conditions that nourish them.

The insulated cognitivism of the 1970s is undergoing needed moderation. Behavior is not solely the product of thought. Social factors are being recognized as playing an influential role in the determination of human thought and action. For example, the course of self-development has often been depicted as driven by gender conception in cognitive-developmental theory (Kohlberg, 1966). Once children achieve gender constancy as unchangeably boys and girls, their gender concept then presumably shapes the course of their development. There is little evidence that gender conception wields the kind of controlling power conferred upon it (Bandura, 1986). In centering their theory on gender conception, cognitive theorists neglected the social realities of gender-role functioning. It is not as though the environment provides the grist for ascertaining one's gender, but after the self-categorization as a boy or girl occurs the development of educational, occupational, avocational, and social competencies is motivated intrapsychically by a drive to match one's gender conception. Social realities bear hard through the lifespan on the kinds of lives men and women pursue in a given society. Over the years, women have had to emancipate themselves from inequitable and constraining social systems rather than from their concept of gender. A comprehensive view of how roles get linked to gender must extend beyond gender conception to a social analysis of how institutional systems and social sanctions shape gender roles. Janet Spence (1985) provided such a comprehensive theory.

In addition to resurrecting social factors in the interactive causation, theorists are inserting affect between the informational input and action. In the current conceptual models, the information-processing machine is being invested with some passion and motivational capabilities. In due time, it will have to take on other properties that are distinctively human—self-motivation, self-awareness, self-reflection, affective self-reaction, and creativeness. These characteristics have bearing on the changes that computer models of human thought are currently undergoing. Until recently, the reigning computer model of human thinking was a linear system in which information is fed through a single central processor that cranks out a succession of computational operations according to preordained rules. These linear models are being supplanted by more dynamically organized computer models that perform multiple operations simultaneously and interactively to mimic better how human brains function.

If computer models are to be fully instructive for understanding human cognitive functioning, they must include capabilities to learn and create one's own competencies, to organize and categorize knowledge, to make sense of imprecise and incomplete information by enlisting a frame of reference, to imagine and originate things, and to appraise one's own knowledge and capabilities. It should also have consciousness of its own states and sense of self. A machinelike existence without any consciousness of one's thoughts, feelings and what is happening around one, and with no sense of selfhood would be devoid of meaning or excitement. Moreover, a comprehensive psychological theory must explain not only how the mind works, but also how people construct, motivate, and regulate their actions.

The cybernetic analogues that have guided thinking about human self-regulative capabilities are also being examined more critically. Many theories of motivation and self-regulation are founded on a negative feedback control model. This type of system functions as a motivator and regulator of action through a discrepancy reduction mechanism. Perceived discrepancy between performance and an internal standard triggers action to reduce the incongruity. In negative feedback control, if performance matches the standard the person does nothing. A regulatory process in which matching a standard produces inertness does not characterize human self-motivation. Such a feedback control system would produce circular action that leads nowhere. Nor could people be stirred to action until they receive feedback of a shortcoming. Negative feedback may help to keep people on a preset course, but from time to time they must transcend the feedback loop to initiate new challenges for themselves. Different self-regulative systems operate in the initiation and continued regulation of motivation.

Human self-motivation relies on *discrepancy production* as well as on *discrepancy reduction*. It requires both *proactive control* and *reactive control*. People initially motivate themselves through proactive control by setting themselves valued standards that create a state of disequilibrium and then mobilizing their effort on the basis of anticipatory estimation of what it would take to accomplish what they seek (Bandura, 1988a, 1991b). Reactive feedback control comes into play in subsequent adjustments of effort to achieve desired results. After people attain the standard they have been pursuing, those who are assured of their efficacy set a higher standard for themselves. The adoption of further challenges creates new motivating discrepancies to be mastered. Self-motivation thus involves a dual control mechanism operating through discrepancy production followed by discrepancy reduction.

Cognitive motivation based on a self-regulative model is mediated by three types of self-reactive influences. These include affective self-evaluation of one's performances, perceived self-efficacy for goal attainment, and ongoing readjustment of internal standards. These self-referent influences operating in concert account for the major share of variation in motivation through goal systems (Bandura & Cervone, 1986). A system of self-regulation combining *proactive guidance* with *reactive adjustments* is best suited for adaptive functioning. Human adaptation and survival depend increasingly on the power of forethought to override immediate feedback control of actions that are currently rewarding but detrimental in the long run.

SELF-PROCESSES

The recent years have witnessed a resurgence of interest in the self-referent processes. One can point to several reasons why self-processes have come to pervade many domains of psychology. Self-generated activities lie at the very heart of causal processes. They not only contribute to the meaning and valence of most external influences, but they function as important proximal determinants of motivation, affect and action. Because judgments and actions are partly self-determined, people can effect change in themselves and their situations.

Much of my current research is concerned with mechanisms of personal agency—how people make causal contributions to their own motivation and action. Among the mechanisms of personal agency, none is more central or pervasive than people's beliefs about their capabilities to exercise control over events that affect their lives. Self-beliefs of efficacy function as important proximal determinants of motivation, affect and action. They operate on action through motivational, cognitive, and affective intervening processes.

EXERCISE OF AGENCY THROUGH PERCEIVED SELF-EFFICACY

Self-beliefs of efficacy affect thought patterns that may be self-aiding or self-hindering. These cognitive effects take various forms. Much human behavior is regulated by forethought in the form of cognized goals. Personal goal setting is influenced by self-appraisal of capabilities. The stronger the perceived self-efficacy the higher the goals people set for themselves and the stronger is their commitment to them (Bandura & Wood, 1989; Locke & Latham, 1990).

Many activities involve analytic judgments that enable people to predict and control events that affect their lives. Discovery of conditional relations between actions and outcomes requires cognitive processing of multidimensional information that contains many ambiguities and uncertainties. In ferreting out predictive rules people must draw on their state of knowledge to generate hypotheses about predictive factors, to weight and integrate them into composite rules, to test their judgments against outcome information, and to remember which notions they had tested and how well they had worked. It requires a strong sense of efficacy to remain task oriented in the face of situational demands and judgmental failures. People who believe strongly in their problem-solving capabilities remain highly efficient and task-focused in their analytic thinking in complex decision-making situations (Wood & Bandura, 1989a). Those who are plagued by self-doubts become erratic in their analytic thinking. Quality of analytic thinking, in turn, affects performance accomplishments.

People's perceptions of their efficacy influence the types of anticipatory cognitive scenarios they construct and rehearse. The highly efficacious visualize success scenarios that provide positive guides for performance. Those who judge themselves as inefficacious, are more inclined to visualize failure scenarios, which undermine performance by dwelling on how things will go wrong. Such cognitive simulations affect performance level (Bandura, 1990a; Kazdin, 1978; Markus, Cross, & Wurf, 1990).

People's self-beliefs of efficacy determine their level of motivation as well as thinking patterns. The stronger the belief in their capabilities, the greater and more persistent are their efforts (Bandura, 1988a; Locke & Latham, 1990). When faced with difficulties, people who are beset by self-doubts abort their attempts prematurely and quickly settle for mediocre solutions. Those who have a strong belief in their capabilities exert greater effort to master the challenge. Strong perseverance usually pays off in performance accomplishments.

There is a growing body of evidence that human attainments and positive well-being require an optimistic sense of personal efficacy (Bandura, 1986, 1989). This is because the normative social realities are rather lousy. They are full of impediments, failures, adversities, setbacks, frustrations, and inequities. People must have a robust sense of personal efficacy to sustain the perseverant effort needed to succeed. It is resiliency of self-belief that counts. When people err in their appraisal they tend to overestimate their capabilities. This is a benefit, rather than a cognitive failing to be eradicated. If efficacy beliefs always reflected only what people could do routinely, they would rarely fail, but they would not exert the extra effort needed to surpass their ordinary performances.

Evidence indicates that it is often the so-called normals who are distorters of reality. But they exhibit self-enhancing biases that distort their judgment of their capabilities in the positive direction. The successful, the innovative, the sociable, the nonanxious, the nondespondent, and the social reformers take an optimistic view of their personal efficacy to exercise influence over events that affect their lives. If not unrealistically exaggerated, such self-beliefs foster the perseverant effort needed for personal and social accomplishments.

People's beliefs in their capabilities also affect how much stress and depression they experience in threatening or taxing situations. Threat is not a fixed property of situational events, nor does appraisal of the likelihood of aversive happenings rely solely on reading external signs of danger or safety. Rather, threat is a relational property concerning the match between perceived coping capabilities and potentially aversive aspects of the environment. That perceived coping efficacy operates as a cognitive mediator of anxiety arousal has been tested by raising perceived coping efficacy to different levels and relating self-efficacy beliefs at a microlevel to different manifestations of anxiety (Bandura, Reese, & Adams, 1982; Bandura, Taylor, Williams, Mefford, & Barchas, 1985). The variation in perceived coping efficacy was achieved by modeling coping strategies for phobics until the desired levels of efficacy were attained. People display little anxiety arousal while coping with potential threats they regard with high efficacy. But as they cope with threats for which they distrust their coping efficacy, their subjective distress mounts, their heart rate accelerates, their blood pressure rises, and they display increased catecholamine secretion. After perceived coping efficacy is strengthened to the maximal level, coping with the previously intimidating tasks is no longer psychologically or physiologically stressful.

Anxiety arousal in situations involving some risks is affected not only by perceived coping efficacy but also by perceived efficacy to control aversive cognitions. The exercise of control over one's own consciousness is summed up well in the proverb: "You cannot prevent the birds of worry and care from flying over your head. But you can stop them from building a nest in your head." Perceived thought-control efficacy is a key factor in the regulation of cognitively generated arousal. It is not the sheer frequency of aversive cognitions but the perceived inability to turn them off that is the major source of distress (Kent & Gibbons, 1987; Salkovskis & Harrison, 1984).

Perceived coping efficacy regulates avoidance behavior in risky situations, as well as anxiety arousal. The stronger the perceived coping efficacy the more venturesome the behavior, regardless of whether self-beliefs of efficacy are strengthened by mastery experiences, modeling influences, or cognitive simulations (Bandura, 1988b). Williams and his colleagues have analyzed the causal structure of avoidant behavior in studies in which perceived coping efficacy, anticipated anxiety, and phobic behavior were measured after different forms of treatment. Perceived self-efficacy predicts phobic behavior when anticipated anxiety is partialed out, whereas the relationship between anticipated anxiety and phobic behavior essentially disappears when perceived self-efficacy is partialed out (Williams, Dooseman, & Kleifield, 1984; Williams, Kinney, & Falbo, 1989; Williams, Turner, & Peer, 1985). In short, people avoid potentially threatening situations and activities, not because they experience anxiety arousal, but because they believe they will be unable to cope with situations they regard as risky. They take self-protective action regardless of whether or not they happen to be anxious at the moment.

The dual control of anxiety arousal and avoidant behavior by perceived coping efficacy and thought control efficacy is revealed in analyses of the mechanisms governing personal empowerment over pervasive social threats (Ozer & Bandura, 1990). Women participated in a mastery modeling program in which they perfected physical skills to defend themselves against sexual assault. Mastery modeling enhanced perceived coping efficacy and cognitive control efficacy, decreased perceived vulnerability, and reduced the incidence of intrusive aversive thoughts and anxiety arousal. These changes were accompanied by increased freedom of action and decreased avoidant social behavior. Path analysis of the causal structure revealed a dual path of regulation of behavior by perceived self-efficacy: One path of influence was mediated through the effects of perceived coping self-efficacy on perceived vulnerability and risk discernment, and the other through the impact of perceived cognitive control self-efficacy on intrusive aversive thoughts.

Perceived self-inefficacy to fulfill desired goals that affect evaluation of self-worth and to secure things that bring satisfaction to one's life can give rise to bouts of depression (Bandura, 1988a; Cutrona & Troutman, 1986; Holahan & Holahan, 1987a, 1987b; Kanfer & Zeiss, 1983; Olioff & Aboud, in press). Much human depression is also cognitively generated by dejecting ruminative thoughts (Nolen-Hoeksema, 1987). Therefore, perceived self-inefficacy to exercise control over ruminative thought figures prominently in the occurrence, duration, and recurrence of depressive episodes (Kavanagh & Wilson, 1989).

Other efficacy-activated processes in the affective domain concern the impact of perceived coping efficacy on basic biological systems that mediate health functioning. Stress has been implicated as an important contributing factor to many physical dysfunctions. Controllability appears to be a key organizing principle regarding the nature of these stress effects. Exposure to stressors when one processes controlling efficacy has no adverse physiological effects. But exposure to the same stressors without controlling efficacy impairs cellular components of the immune system. Biological systems are highly interdependent. The types of biochemical reactions that have been shown to accompany weak coping efficacy are involved in the regulation of immune systems. For example, weak perceived self-efficacy in exercising control over stressors activates endogenous opioid systems (Bandura, Cioffi, Taylor, & Brouillard, 1988). There is evidence that some of the immunosuppressive effects of inefficacy in controlling stressors are mediated by release of endogenous opioids. When opioid mechanisms are blocked by opiate antagonists, the stress of weak coping efficacy loses its immunosuppressive power (Shavit & Martin, 1987).

In the laboratory research demonstrating immunosuppression through stress mediation, controllability is studied as a fixed dichotomous property in which animals either exercise complete control over physical stressors or they have no control, whatsoever. In contrast, most human stress is activated in the process of learning how to exercise control over recurring cognitive and social stressors. It would not be evolutionarily advantageous if acute stressors invariably impaired immune function because of their prevalence in everyday life. If this were the case, people would be chronically ill and easily done in by infective invaders. There are evolutionary benefits to experiencing a boost in immune function while one is acquiring coping mastery. Indeed, we found this to be the case in a study examining the impact of enhanced perceived self-efficacy in exercising control over phobic stressor on components of the immune system (Wiedenfeld et al., 1990). Development of strong perceived coping efficacy had an immunoenhancing effect. The more rapid the gains achieved in perceived self-efficacy, the greater the enhancement of the immunologic system. However, intense and prolonged stress of coping inefficacy takes its toll on the immune system.

People can exert some influence over their life course by the environments they select, and environments they create. So far I have discussed efficacy-activated processes that enable people to create beneficial environments and to exercise control over them. Judgments of personal efficacy affect choice of activities and environments. People avoid activities and situations they believe exceed their coping capabilities, but they undertake challenging activities and select social environments they judge themselves capable of managing. Any factor that influences choice behavior can profoundly affect the direction of personal development. This is because the social influences operating in the environments that are selected continue to promote certain competencies, values, and interests long after the decisional determinant has rendered its inaugurating effect. Thus, seemingly inconsequential determinants can initiate selective interpersonal associations that produce major and enduring personal changes (Bandura, 1986; Snyder, 1986).

The power of self-efficacy beliefs to affect the course of life paths through selection processes is revealed in studies of career decision making and career development (Betz & Hackett, 1986; Lent & Hackett, 1987). The more efficacious people judge themselves to be, the more career options they consider appropriate and the better they prepare themselves educationally for different pursuits. Self-limitation of career development arises more from perceived self-inefficacy than from actual inability. Self-disbeliefs create their own validation by restricting choices that can build interests and competencies.

The sociocognitive benefits of a sense of personal efficacy do not arise simply from the incantation of capability. Saying something should not be confused with believing it to be so. Simply saying that one is capable is not necessarily self-convincing, especially when it contradicts preexisting firm beliefs. No amount of reiteration that I can fly will persuade me that I have the efficacy to get myself airborne. Efficacy beliefs are the product of a complex process of self-persuasion that relies on cognitive processing of diverse sources of efficacy information conveyed enactively, vicariously, socially, and physiologically (Bandura, 1986). Self-efficacy beliefs that are firmly established remain resilient to adversity. In contrast, weakly held self-beliefs are highly vulnerable to change and negative experiences readily reinstate disbelief in one's capabilities.

Development of resilient efficacy requires some experience in mastering difficulties through perseverant effort. Some setbacks and difficulties in human pursuits serve a useful purpose in teaching that success usually requires sustained effort. After people become convinced they have what it takes to succeed they persevere in the face of adversity and quickly rebound from setbacks. By sticking it out through tough times they emerge from adversity with a stronger sense of efficacy. Our mentors at Iowa made sure that we did not leave this place with only easy successes. We have not only survived and thrived in our efforts to colonize the various domains of psychology. We have returned from our various expeditions unbowed by years of academic servitude to express our debt of gratitude to you.

REFERENCES

Ader, R. (Ed.). (1981). *Psychoneuroimmunology.* New York: Academic Press.

Bandura, A. (1962). Social learning through imitation. In M. R. Jones (Ed.), *Nebraska symposium on motivation* (Vol. 10, pp. 211–274). Lincoln: University of Nebraska Press.

Bandura, A. (1973). *Aggression: A social learning analysis.* Englewood Cliffs, NJ: Prentice–Hall.

Bandura, A. (1986). *Social foundations of thought and action: A social cognitive theory.* Englewood Cliffs, NJ: Prentice–Hall.

Bandura, A. (1988a). Self-regulation of motivation and action through goal systems. In V. Hamilton, G. H. Bower, & N. H. Frijda (Eds.), *Cognitive perspectives on emotion and motivation* (pp. 37–61). Dordrecht: Kluwer Academic Publishers.

Bandura, A. (1988b). Self-efficacy conception of anxiety. *Anxiety Research, 1,* 77–98.

Bandura, A. (1989). Human agency in social cognitive theory. *American Psychologist, 44,* 1175–1184.

Bandura, A. (1990a). Reflections on nonability determinants of competence. In R. J. Sternberg & J. Kolligian, Jr. (Eds.), *Competence considered* (pp. 315–362). New Haven, CT: Yale University Press.

Bandura, A. (1990b). Mechanisms of moral disengagement. In W. Reich (Ed.), *Origins of terrorism: Psychologies, ideologies, theologies, states of mind* (pp. 162–191). Cambridge: Cambridge University Press.

Bandura, A. (1991a). Social cognitive theory of moral thought and action. In W. M. Kurtines & J. L. Gewirtz (Eds.), *Moral behavior and development: Advances in theory, research and applications* (Vol. 1). Hillsdale, NJ: Lawrence Erlbaum Associates.

Bandura, A. (1991b). Self-regulation of motivation through anticipatory and self-regulatory mechanisms. In R. A. Dienstbier (Ed.), *Perspectives on motivation: Nebraska symposium on motivation* (Vol. 38). Lincoln: University of Nebraska Press.

Bandura, A. (in press). Self-efficacy mechanism in physiological activation and health-promoting behavior. In J. Madden, IV, S. Matthysse, & J. Barchas (Eds.), *Adaptation, learning and affect.* New York: Raven Press.

Bandura, A., & Cervone, D. (1986). Differential engagement of self-reactive influences in cognitive motivation. *Organizational Behavior and Human Decision Processes, 38,* 92–113.

Bandura, A., Cioffi, D., Taylor, C. B., & Brouillard, M. E. (1988). Perceived self-efficacy in coping with cognitive stressors and opioid activation. *Journal of Personality and Social Psychology, 55,* 479–488.

Bandura, A., & Jourden, F. J. (in press). Self-regulatory mechanisms governing social-comparison effects on complex decision making. *Journal of Personality and Social Psychology.*

Bandura, A., Reese, L., & Adams, N. E. (1982). Microanalysis of action and fear arousal as a function of differential levels of perceived self-efficacy. *Journal of Personality and Social Psychology, 43,* 5–21.

Bandura, A., Taylor, C. B., Williams, S. L., Mefford, I. N., & Barchas, J. D. (1985). Catecholamine secretion as a function of perceived coping self-efficacy. *Journal of Consulting and Clinical Psychology, 53,* 406–414.

Bandura, A., & Walters, R. H. (1959). *Adolescent aggression.* New York: Ronald Press.

Bandura, A., & Wood, R. E. (1989). Effect of perceived controllability and performance standards on self-regulation of complex decision-making. *Journal of Personality and Social Psychology, 56,* 805–814.

Beck, A. T. (1976). *Cognitive therapy and the emotional disorders.* New York: International Universities Press.

Bem, D. J., & Allen, A. (1974). On predicting some of the people some of the time: The search for cross-situational consistencies in behavior. *Psychological Review, 81,* 506–520.

Bem, D. J., & Funder, D. C. (1978). Predicting more of the people more of the time: Assessing the personality of situations. *Psychological Review, 85,* 485–501.

Betz, N. E., & Hackett, G. (1986). Applications of self-efficacy theory to understanding career choice behavior. *Journal of Social and Clinical Psychology, 4,* 279–289.

Bower, G. H. (1983). Affect and cognition. *Philosophical Transactions of the Royal Society of London* (Series B), *302,* 387–402.

Cantor, N., & Kihlstrom, J. F. (1987). *Personality and social intelligence.* Englewood Cliffs, NJ: Prentice–Hall.

Carroll, W. R., & Bandura, A. (1985). Role of timing of visual monitoring and motor rehearsal in observational learning of action patterns. *Journal of Motor Behavior, 17,* 269–281.

Carroll, W. R., & Bandura, A. (1987). Translating cognition into action: The role of visual guidance in observational learning. *Journal of Motor Behavior, 19,* 385–398.

Carroll, W. R., & Bandura, A. (1990). Representational guidance of action production in observational learning: A causal analysis. *Journal of Motor Behavior, 22,* 85–97.

Cutrona, C. E., & Troutman, B. R. (1986). Social support, infant temperament, and parenting self-efficacy: A mediational model of postpartum depression. *Child Development, 57,* 1507–1518.

Egger, M. D., & Miller, N. E. (1963). When is reward reinforcing? An experimental study of the information hypothesis. *Journal of Comparative and Physiological Psychology, 56,* 132–137.

Ellis, A., & Grieger, R. (Eds.). (1978). *Handbook of rational-emotive therapy.* New York: Springer.

Epstein, S. (1983). The stability of behavior across time and situations. In R. Zucker, J. Aronoff, & A. I. Rabin (Eds.), *Personality and the prediction of behavior* (pp. 209–268). San Diego, CA: Academic Press.

Feldman, D. H. (1980). *Beyond universals in cognitive development.* Norwood, NJ: Ablex.

Flavell, J. H. (1978). Developmental stage: Explanans or explanadum? *The Behavioral and Brain Sciences, 2,* 187–188.

Hamilton, V., Bower, G. H., & Frijda, N. H. (Eds.). (1988). *Cognitive perspectives on emotion and motivation.* Dordrecht: Kluwer Academic Publishers.

Holahan, C. K., & Holahan, C. J. (1987a). Self-efficacy, social support, and depression in aging: A longitudinal analysis. *Journal of Gerontology, 42,* 65–68.

Holahan, C. K., & Holahan, C. J. (1987b). Life stress, hassles, and self-efficacy in aging: A replication and extension. *Journal of Applied Social Psychology, 17,* 574–592.

Holroyd, K. A., & Creer, T. L. (1986). *Self-management of chronic disease.* New York: Academic Press.

Jones, E. E. (1976). How do people perceive the cause of behavior? *American Scientist, 64,* 300–305.

Kanfer, R., & Zeiss, A. M. (1983). Depression, interpersonal standard-setting, and judgments of self-efficacy. *Journal of Abnormal Psychology, 92,* 319–329.

Kavanagh, D. J., & Wilson, P. H. (1989). Prediction of outcome with a group version of cognitive therapy for depression. *Behaviour Research and Therapy, 27,* 333–347.

Kazdin, A. E. (1978). Covert modeling—Therapeutic application of imagined rehearsal. In J. L. Singer & K. S. Pope (Eds.) *The power of human imagination: New methods in psychotherapy. Emotions, personality, and psychotherapy* (pp. 255–278). New York: Plenum.

Kent, G., & Gibbons, R. (1987). Self-efficacy and the control of anxious cognitions. *Journal of Behavior Therapy & Experimental Psychiatry, 18,* 33–40.

Kohlberg, L. (1966). A cognitive-developmental analysis of children's sex-role concepts and attitudes. In E. E. Maccoby (Ed.), *The development of sex differences* (pp. 82–173). Stanford, CA: Stanford University Press.

Langley, P., & Simon, H. A. (1981). The central role of learning in cognition. In J. R. Anderson (Ed.), *Cognitive skills and their acquisition* (pp. 361–379). Hillsdale, NJ: Lawrence Erlbaum Associates.

Lawrence, D. H. (1963). The nature of a stimulus: Some relationships between learning and perception. In S. Koch (Ed.), *Psychology: A study of a science* (pp. 179–212). New York: McGraw-Hill.

Lent, R. W., & Hackett, G. (1987). Career self-efficacy: Empirical status and future directions. *Journal of Vocational Behavior, 30,* 347–382.

Locke, E. A., & Latham, G. P. (1990). *A theory of goal setting and task performance.* Englewood Cliffs, NJ: Prentice–Hall.

Lundin, R. W. (1961). *Personality: An experimental approach.* New York: Macmillan.

Markus, H., Cross, S., & Wurf, E. (1990). The role of the self-system in competence. In R. J. Sternberg & J. Kolligian, Jr. (Eds.), *Competence considered:* (pp. 205–225). New Haven, CT: Yale University Press.

Matarazzo, J. D. Weiss, S. M., Herd, J. A., Miller, N. E., & Weiss, S. M. (Eds.). (1984). *Behavioral health: A handbook of health enhancement and disease prevention.* New York: Wiley.

Meichenbaum, D. H. (1977). *Cognitive-behavior modification: An integrative approach.* New York: Plenum Press.

Mischel, W. (1968). *Personality and assessment.* New York: Wiley.

Mischel, W. (1973). Toward a cognitive social learning reconceptualization of personality. *Psychological Review, 80,* 252–283.

Mischel, W., & Peake, P. K. (1982). Beyond deja vu in the search for cross-situational consistency. *Psychological Review, 89,* 730–755.

Mowrer, O. H. (1960). *Learning theory and the symbolic processes.* New York: Wiley.

Nisbett, R., & Ross, L. (1980). *Human inference: Strategies and shortcomings of social judgment.* Englewood Cliffs, NJ: Prentice–Hall.

Nolen-Hoeksema, S. (1987). Sex differences in unipolar depression: Evidence and theory. *Psychological Bulletin, 101,* 259–282.

Olioff, M., & Aboud, F. E. (in press). Predicting postpartum dysphoria in primiparous mothers: Roles of perceived parenting self-efficacy and self-esteem. *Journal of Cognitive Psychotherapy.*

Ozer, E., & Bandura, A. (1990). Mechanisms governing empowerment effects: A self-efficacy analysis. *Journal of Personality and Social Psychology, 58,* 472–486.

Piaget, J. (1950). *The psychology of intelligence.* New York: International Universities Press.

Rogers, C. R. (1959). A theory of therapy, personality, and interpersonal relationships, as developed in the client-centered framework. In S. Koch (Ed.), *Psychology: A study of a science (Vol. III). Formulations of the person and the social context* (pp. 184–256). New York: McGraw–Hill.

Ross, L. (1977). The intuitive psychologist and his shortcomings: Distortions in the attribution process. In L. Berkowitz (Ed.), *Advances in experimental social psychology* (Vol. 10, pp. 174–220). New York: Academic.

Salkovskis, P. M., & Harrison, J. (1984). Abnormal and normal obsessions—a replication. *Behaviour Research and Therapy, 22,* 549–552.

Shavit, Y., & Martin, F. C. (1987). Opiates, stress, and immunity: Animal studies. *Annals of Behavioral Medicine, 9,* 11–20.

Skinner, B. F. (1969). *Contingencies of reinforcement: A theoretical analysis.* New York: Appleton–Century–Crofts.

Snyder, M. (1986). *Public appearances, private realities: The psychology of self-monitoring.* New York: W. H. Freeman.

Sorrentino, R. M., & Higgins, E. T. (1986). *Handbook of motivation and cognition.* New York: Guilford.

Spence, J. T. (1985). Gender identity and its implications for the concepts of masculinity and femininity. In T. B. Sonderegger (Ed.), *Nebraska Symposium on Motivation 1984* (Vol. 32, pp. 59–95). Lincoln: University of Nebraska Press.

Sternberg, R. J. & Kolligian, J. Jr. (Eds.). (1990). *Competence considered.* New Haven, CT: Yale University Press.

Turkle, S. (1988). Artifical intelligence and psychoanalysis: A new alliance. *Daedalus, 117,* 241–268.

Tversky, B. (1982). The rebirth of learning. *Contemporary Psychology, 27,* 679–680.

Weiner, B. (1972). *Theories of motivation.* Chicago: Markham.

Wiedenfeld, S. A., O'Leary, A., Bandura, A., Brown, S., Levine, S., & Raska, K. (1990). Impact of perceived self-efficacy in coping with stressors on components of the immune system. *Journal of Personality and Social Psychology, 59,* 1082–1094.

Williams, S. L., Dooseman, G., & Kleifield, E. (1984). Comparative power of guided mastery and exposure treatments for intractable phobias. *Journal of Consulting and Clinical Psychology, 52,* 505–518.

Williams, S. L., Kinney, P. J., & Falbo, J. (1989). Generalization of therapeutic changes in agoraphobia: The role of perceived self-efficacy. *Journal of Consulting and Clinical Psychology, 57,* 436–442.

Williams, S. L., Turner, S. M., & Peer, D. F. (1985). Guided mastery and performance desensitization treatments for severe acrophobia. *Journal of Consulting and Clinical Psychology, 53,* 237–247.

Wood, R. E., & Bandura, A. (1989a). Social cognitive theory of organizational management. *Academy of Management Review, 14,* 361–384.

Wood, R. E., & Bandura, A. (1989b). Impact of conceptions of ability on self-regulatory mechanisms and complex decision making. *Journal of Personality and Social Psychology, 56,* 407–415.

Wood, R. E., Bandura, A., & Bailey, T. (1990). Mechanisms governing organizational performance in complex decision-making environments. *Organizational Behavior and Human Decision Processes, 46,* 181–201.

Wylie, R. C. (1974). *The self-concept: A review of methodological considerations and measuring instruments* (rev. ed.). Lincoln: University of Nebraska Press.

10 Where's the Action?

Janet T. Spence
University of Texas at Austin

My title, as soon becomes apparent, was intended to have meaning on several levels. Each of them, however, is related to the central theme of these remarks— a concern about recent developments within psychology which, although extremely salutary, carry with them as side effects threats to the integrity of psychology as a recognized discipline whose core characteristics distinguish it from other disciplines. These *centrifugal forces,* as they have been labeled, are most conspicuous in the rift between psychology as a science and as a profession, a widening gulf that I detail later. My initial focus, however, is on the forces of disunity within scientific psychology.

CENTRIFUGAL FORCES WITHIN SCIENTIFIC PSYCHOLOGY

Psychology as the Study of Behavior

Relatively early in the history of American psychology, the mainstream chose to identify their youthful discipline as one of the natural sciences rather than as a branch of the humanities or as a unique mental science with methods and goals difference from the natural sciences. Since that time, the common element that has held psychology together and distinguished it from other neighboring sciences is its interest in *behavior*. Reflecting this emphasis, the standard definition that for many years appeared in introductory texts was that "psychology is the science of the prediction and control of behavior." It was not coincidental that Hull's (1943) seminal book was titled *Principles of Behavior* and that Spence labeled the Hull–Spence system a *behavior* theory (e.g., Spence, 1956).

Iowans of the Spence era will recall in this connection Guthrie's (1935) classic remarks (to which our attention was frequently called) in which he chided Tolman for his purported neglect of what organisms actually do. Guthrie wrote:

> Signs, in Tolman's theory, occasion in the rat *realization,* or *cognition,* or *judgment,* or *hypotheses,* or *abstraction,* but *they do not occasion action.* In his concern with what goes on in the rat's mind, Tolman has neglected to predict what the rat will do. So far as the theory is concerned the rat is left buried in thought; if it gets to the food box at the end that is its concern, not the concern of the theory. (p. 172)

The influence that led to this early emphasis on action had diverse origins, among them the failure of structuralism and other European psychologies aimed at developing a science of mind to produce useful theories that captured the imagination. (Which of you have gone back lately to read Wundt and Tichener for inspiration?) Also crucial was the pragmatic cast to the American temperament and our optimistic belief that solutions not only should but could be found to the problems of society and its members.

Within psychology, the continued focus on behavior and more particularly, the dominant influence that learning theory approaches to behavior exercised for three decades or more, were sustained by additional factors. Most important, these theories aspired to be both comprehensive and explicit, which made them both testable and potentially applicable to a wide range of phenomena. These promising features made them extremely attractive and inspired many psychologists to apply them to complex phenomena far beyond the simple learning paradigms on which the theories were based. At the same time, many of the concepts in these theories were perforce quite primitive in comparison, let us say, to modern theories of learning or cognition. Consequently, attention was focused on the systematic relationships between observable stimuli and responses, with the theoretical constructs postulated to intervene between these two classes of events having more the status of mathematical operators than of processes or entities of interest in their own right. Finally, again in comparison to the present day, the number of academic, research psychologists was small, and technical support for their work was quite meager both in amount and in level of sophistication—facts that limited psychologists' collective output, theoretical and empirical. Certain sets of ideas or types of approach could dominate the field because of the relative dearth of serious competitors. The overall effect was to produce a discipline whose practitioners were relatively homogenous in their interests and orientation and in which it was still possible to be somewhat of a generalist.

But all that changed during the decades of the 1950s and 1960s. Along with other scientific disciplines, academic psychology underwent rapid growth in size as colleges and universities expanded. Research blossomed in all the sciences, fostered by massive federal support as well as by the sheer increase in the number of scientists and research laboratories. Psychologists not only benefitted directly from this expansion but indirectly through the development of new research technologies.

PSYCHOLOGY AS THE STUDY OF MIND

Equally critically, ideas imported *into* psychology from other sources such as the then emerging information theory and computer science provided models and metaphors that stimulated one of the most influential of recent intellectual developments, namely, cognitive psychology. As cognitive psychology has matured, it has become part of a broader cognitive science to which individuals from several conventional disciplines contribute. The contemporary prominence of cognitive science has led some to redefine psychology as the science of cognition (or mind) and behavior. The word "and" in this definition gives cognition, not simply the status of a class of internal processes that are necessary in order to explain and predict behavior, but equal status with behavior. As Amsel (1989) has noted, this view implies that in a return to the stance of the early structuralists, psychology is a study of mind; cognition is a field of inquiry in its own right. Inconveniently, instruments have yet to be invented that will allow us to directly observe the workings of the mind; mental processes must be inferred from observations of behavior. In the words of Dickinson (1979), "behavior is but a spade to disinter thought" (p. 553). According to this perspective, theorists have no obligation to consider the behaviors cognitions produce. Indeed, leaving the human as well as the rat "buried in thought" sometimes seems to be a matter of pride.

Technological advances that put new methodological tools at our disposal have also contributed to an explosive growth of knowledge in the field we now call neuroscience, a field with which a number of psychologists now identify themselves. Here, too, behavior receives relatively little attention. Although some of the work done by psychologists can fairly be described as behavioral neuroscience, the primary emphasis is on the brain and associated neurological structures.

One can only applaud these impressive scientific advancements within psychology and their interdisciplinary thrust. They have brought with them, however, unintended negative consequences.

The Balkanization of Psychology

Until recently, psychology was quite separate from other disciplines. What was then identified as experimental psychology provided the reigning theoretical models and ruling metaphors for all of psychology, and thus served as a unifying force for the discipline. Experimental psychology, however, has been fractionated by the emergence of neuroscience and cognitive science. Further, psychologists identifying with these two areas of inquiry have tended to turn outward toward other disciplines to seek their intellectual home instead of inward toward psychology. At several institutions, in fact, faculty members have moved out of the psychology department en masse into departments or institutes of cognitive science or neuroscience. The specialized bodies of knowledge that are developing in other branches and sub-branches of psychology have also tended to pull us still further apart into separate enclaves.

Some regard this fragmentation as inevitable. Sigmund Koch (1981), for example, has insisted for some time that psychology is in fact a heterogenous collection of relatively independent disciplines and that a search for a unified science of psychology is essentially futile. Whether or not one agrees with this latter position, the grand theories of an earlier era that were expected to lead us to still grander theories that would explain all of behavior were wildly overambitious. Everyone concedes that it is more appropriate today to refer to psychological sciences than to a singular psychological science with a common set of fundamental principles.

If one were to create a doomsday scenario in which the centrifugal tendencies that are operating within contemporary psychology went on unchecked, one could imagine a decimation of institutionalized psychology as we know it. Human experimental psychologists become absorbed by centers or departments of cognitive science, and biopsychologists disappear into neuroscience. Industrial-organizational psychologists find much cushier homes in business schools (as many already have) and psychopathologists are attached to medical schools. Those in so-called health-care provider specialties—clinical, counseling, and school psychology—are trained in separate professional schools or in schools of education, as is already true to a substantial extent. Institutes of child or life-span development claim still others, and so forth. Departments of psychology, if they survive at all, are pale shadows of their former selves, outnumbered and outclassed by the natural sciences on the one hand, and by the humanities on the other.

Is Psychology Worth Preserving?

It seems unlikely that this dissolution will ever come to pass. But would it really matter if it did? Disciplinary and subdisciplinary lines within and among sciences are redrawn from time to time in response to changes in scientific knowledge and theories. Is there any justification, other than attachment to a historical tradition, for trying to preserve psychology as a field of inquiry distinct from neighboring social and natural sciences?

My answer is yes, and I have already hinted at the reason. The common thread that has bound scientific psychology together, I have already suggested, is an interest in behavior. What is—or in my views should be—the central core of psychology as a discipline is a theory of *action:* the how's, why's, and what's of the *behavior* of intact, functioning organisms. It is necessary but not sufficient to have a science of brain and mind (and whatever else goes on under the skin). To be complete, we must also have a science of behavior. Determination of the ties between internal structures and processes and the activities they occasion has historically been the special responsibility of *psychology*. If psychologists collectively allow attention to action to be lost or weakened, other disciplines are unlikely to make up our oversight. Both science and society would be the losers.

ORGANIZATIONAL ISSUES

Up to this point I have been discussing the centrifugal forces that have been operating within scientific psychology and making a plea for preserving the common bonds that, however fragile, have kept us together. I now turn to organizational issues and the divisive role they have played. I consider first the American Psychological Association, and the unfortunate rivalry between professional psychology and academic-research psychology.

When individuals within a university belong to the same department and are housed in propinquity to one another, this departmental membership helps to create and maintain their common sense of purpose and identity. The same is true, although less obviously so, for national organizations. The century-old American Psychological Association (APA) for many decades fulfilled these functions for scientific psychology. Relatively early in the history of the Association, applied psychologists (primarily the forerunners of today's industrial-organizational psychologists) felt less than completely accepted by the dominant group of basic scientists and formed their own organization, the American Association of Applied Psychology. In 1947, however, the two organizations merged. The architects of the reunion could hardly have envisaged the rapid growth of the service professions of clinical, counseling, and school psychology and how the newcomers would swamp the original APA.

To sketch in the basic demographic facts, clinical psychology and other health care specialties developed rapidly in the aftermaths of World War II. Initially, men and women who subsequently entered professional practice received their training in traditional academic departments and in programs based on what came to be known as the scientist-practitioner model. Not only were these scientist-practitioner programs intended to train students in research methodology and the empirical and theoretical foundation of psychology as well as in diagnostic and intervention techniques, their goal was also to educate individuals who would carry on both research and practice in their postdoctoral careers. This latter aspiration is seldom achieved, and the training model itself is becoming less and less popular. Many university-based programs claiming to follow the scientist-practitioner model, in fact, graduate students whose predoctoral and postdoctoral interests are solely professional and whose exposure to research is relatively shallow. Moreover, freestanding professional schools intended only to produce practitioners now rival academic departments as trainers of clinicians and other service providers. The degree to which the results of psychological research continue to inform the activities of many full-time practitioners has also become a matter of some concern.

The number of doctorates awarded annually in research-academic specialties peaked in about 1975 and has steadily decreased since then (although with recent signs of leveling off). Degrees awarded to health service providers, on the other hand, have continued to rise. Since 1970, the annual production of service provider doctorates has increasingly outstripped annual doctorate production in all other specialties, at present by a ratio of more than 2½:1 according to APA figures (Howard et al., 1986). Currently, about 25% of these service provider degrees are awarded by freestanding professional schools, that is, tuition-driven schools without university affiliation. And finally, students in these health-care specialties increasingly go into full time private practice, the bulk of their clients' fees being paid by insurance companies.

Several years ago Gregory Kimble (1984) published an article titled "Psychology's Two Cultures," borrowed from C. P. Snow's image of the cultures of science and humanism. In it he reported the results of a survey assessing psychologists' professional and scientific values and epistemological assumptions. As could have been expected, he essentially found the two cultures of science and humanism existing within psychology, with members of the Psychonomic Society and other similar groups personifying one extreme and psychotherapists the other. With the exception of the behavior modifiers, who have tended to stay close to their scientific roots, many therapists are not only humanistic in their outlook but have also essentially abandoned any attempt to tie practice to scientific psychology's knowledge base.

In addition to having a value system distinguishable from that of research-oriented psychologists, practitioners have different organizational needs. What must be done to promote their professional interests and to uphold their professional standards is not the same as what is needed to promote and uphold the standards of psychological science. Accreditation, licensure, and the inclusion of psychologists as providers of mental health services in health insurance policies are all issues of direct concern to practitioners. Through practitioner-dominated state associations and offices they have set up within the APA, practitioners have become skilled in influencing state legislatures, Congress, federal agencies, and other groups to advance their guild interests. With the possible exception of academically based trainers of clinical students, these issues are rarely of interest to research-academic psychologists, except as they might perceive some practitioner-inspired demands as intruding upon their prerogatives. (Academic researchers, it should be noted in passing, have their own guild interest, although they have been slow to recognize the fact and to work on their own behalf as effectively as the professional community.)

By sheer force of numbers, the APA is gradually becoming transformed into a professional society whose activities are dominated by serving the needs of service providers. The tilt in the composition of the Association is exacerbated by the rising rate of academic, research-oriented psychologists who drop out or never join APA, some 60% of those eligible, according to APA figures. Efforts have been made over the last decade to restructure the Association into semi-autonomous units so that a strong scientific presence could be maintained and strengthened, the most recent being a reorganization plan put before the membership in the Summer of 1988. These efforts have proved to be futile, due in part to the vehement opposition of many within the current professional leadership and in part to the indifference to political issues of its academic members. The current climate within the Association can only be described as schizophrenic, one segment trying (quite genuinely) to do "something for science" in an effort to keep the loyalty of its academic, research-oriented members and another segment, because of motives that are not always clear, acting in ways that are quite effective in destroying that loyalty.

Organizational images are important—sometimes more influential than the actual services the organization provides its members. It seems unlikely that there is anything that the APA could do at this juncture to transform its image into one that already disenchanted experimental and other research oriented psychologists would perceive as representing their values and needs. The American Psychological Society (APS) was founded in 1988 on this assumption, its purpose being to take on the historical role of APA in representing the interests of all of scientific psychology, both tangibly and symbolically.

Paralleling the growing inability of the APA to attract research-oriented psychologists and to serve as the national organization representing scientific psychology as a whole has been the rise of specialized societies, organizations designed the foster the exchange of information among researchers with similar interests. One of the earliest and largest of these is the Psychonomic Society. Founded in 1960 by a group of experimental psychologists (among them Kenneth Spence) disillusioned by the APA, the Psychonomic Society was intended to provide academic (primarily experimental) psychologists with a forum for the exchange of scientific information. Over the years, however, the Society's meetings have come to be dominated by work on human cognition. Other societies, of which there are already a score or more, were deliberately designed to have an even more specific focus than the original Psychonomic Society, for example, Acoustical Society, Society of Experimental Social Psychology, Developmental Psychobiology, Society for Research in Child Development, Society for Neuroscience, and so forth. Most, like Psychonomics, limit their activities almost exclusively to publishing scientific journals and holding scientific conventions.

The appearance of these specialized organizations is an inevitable outcome of the explosion of scientific knowledge, as reflected in the proliferation of psychological journals and books, and have been effective in accomplishing their goals of facilitating communication among researchers with similar interests. But to the extent that they may have encouraged their members to focus solely on their own specialties and to interact intellectually only with their own kind, the creation of such associations may have inadvertantly contributed to the fragmentation of the discipline as well as being a sign of this fragmentation. It is significant that until the formation of the American Psychological Society in 1988, members of specialized societies who were discontented or disinterested in the APA made no move to create a national organization in its stead to advance the common goals of academic psychology.

But the APS has been established and at this writing is flourishing. Other hopeful signs are the concerns that are beginning to be expressed in public forums about the forces pulling psychology apart that mirror those expressed here. Psychology may be healthier and have a brighter future than my remarks suggest.

SUMMING UP

Since my days as a student at Iowa in the late 1940s when we were so excited about the promise of Hull–Spence behavior theory, psychology has grown spectacularly in size, in technical sophistication, and in scientific knowledge. Learning as a phenomenon is but one of many that currently command attention and in every area, once popular theories are continuously being replaced by more useful ones. This is to be expected in an intellectually vigorous discipline. It is a cause for celebration that the kind of intellectual excitement and ferment we experienced as students continues. Even though the specific theory that inspired our youthful enthusiasm did not live up to its initial promise, it helped pave the way to better ones.

The challenge we currently face is to resist the balkanizing tendencies that have come with these advances and to preserve our common heritage. I recall the old aphorism that appeared during the heyday of Watson's radical behaviorism: Psychology has long since lost its soul and is now rapidly losing its mind. The contemporary version might be: Psychology has recovered its mind and is now trying to hold onto its soul.

REFERENCES

Amsel, A. (1989). *Behaviorism, neobehaviorism, and cognitivism in learning theory: Historical and contemporary perspectives.* Hillsdale, NJ: Lawrence Erlbaum Associates.

Dickinson, A. (1979). Review of "Cognitive processes in animal behavior." *Quarterly Journal of Experimental Psychology, 31,* 551–554.

Guthrie, E. R. (1935). *The psychology of learning.* New York: Harper.

Howard, A., Pion, G. M., Gottfreden, G. D., Flattau, P. E., Oskamp, S., Pfafflin, S. M., Bray, D.

M., & Burstein, A. G. (1986). The changing face of American psychology: A report from the Committee on Employment and Human Resources. *American Psychologist, 38,* 1321–1329.

Hull, C. L. (1943). *Principles of behavior.* New York: Harper.

Kimble, G. A. (1984). Psychology's two cultures. *American Psychologist, 39,* 833–839.

Koch, S. (1981). The nature and limits of psychological knowledge: Lessons of a century of "qua" science. *American Psychologist, 36,* 257–269.

Spence, K. W. (1956). *Behavior theory and conditioning.* New Haven, CT: Yale University Press.

11 What I Learned About Frustration at Iowa

Abram Amsel
University of Texas at Austin

I would like to begin this chapter with an adaptation of some remarks I made here at Iowa on another occasion. On this earlier occasion they were made following a cocktail hour, and so, in accord with Overton's principle of state dependency, those of you who were there may not remember them anyway. These are personal vignettes, but they seem appropriate as an introduction to this brief account of what I learned about frustration as a graduate student, and how, in at least two senses, this has carried over and affected me to the present day.

Before I came to Iowa I was a graduate student at McGill University, where one of my professors, Chester Kellogg, had directed Kenneth Spence's work for his master's degree some years earlier. At McGill, I was introduced to research and experimentation, and did my master's degree research, with Bob Malmo at the Allan Memorial Institute of Psychiatry. Like Spence, he had been a graduate student and taken his PhD at Yale. Malmo introduced me to the wonders of Hull's *Principles of Behavior* (1943), and even to draft chapters of what was to become Hull's *A Behavior System* (1952). So it is not too surprising that I ended up at Iowa.

Even before Iowa, it was at the Allan Memorial Institute that I suffered my first serious postgraduate encounter with frustration, and, not incidentally, learned a lesson in statistical inference at the hands of a Viennese psychiatrist. This gentleman had ventured into experimental work, and was examining the effect of age at onset of menopause on depression (or was it the other way around?). With a group of patients and a matched control group, he wanted to show that onset of menopause was earlier in the depressed patients (or was it later?). He had heard about a new thing called statistics, and was told that I knew something about it (from Chester Kellogg's course). He asked me to analyze his data. I went down to my desk, whipped off a *t* for related measures (or was it a Critical Ratio?), and returned a couple of hours later to tell him the outcome. The *t* value, I said, was about 1.0. When he asked what that meant, I said it meant his difference was as much attributable to chance as to his variable. He looked disappointed, then brightened and made a decision: "Oh, well," he said, "then I won't use statistics." In this case, statistics was frustrating for both of us.

From another Viennese, the eminent philosopher and teacher, Gustav Bergmann of Iowa, I learned teaching flair and style, and many of the anticognitive (pro s–R) attitudes and arguments that have sustained me to this day. I also learned how to give and take frustration. In one episode, conveyed to me by my wife, Tess, who was a student in his undergraduate class called "Semantics, Pragmatics, . . . and so on," he was exasperated by a student, an excited, brand-new father, who, during a discussion of the intricacies of the positivistic approach (or some such), kept referring to the cognitive capacity of his 1-day-old son. Bergmann took this as long as he could, then, as the dam of his endurance broke, he exploded in frustration: "Mr. Father," he cried, "Babies don't think, damn you!" And on another occasion, in response to a question from a poor fellow who, a few days from the end of the semester, had finally gotten up the nerve to ask one, and had the misfortune to state it in mentalistic terms, Professor Bergmann, smiling—almost leering—and flicking his cigarette ash over the questioner, who smiled back in anticipation of a coveted reward, said to the student, "Thank you, sir, *thank you, sir,* for just such a *stupid* question I was waiting." You talk about frustration!

From Kenneth Spence I learned many things, and an intense sense of pride in my Iowa education and training was not the least of these. But as many of you here can witness, he could be the source of a reasonable degree of frustration. At the second meeting of the Psychonomic Society—I think in Chicago, in 1961— Kenneth said to me, "I hear you have reviewed Mowrer's book." (The book was *Learning Theory and Behavior* (1960), and Mowrer was one with whom Spence had some theoretical differences. What else is new?) When I admitted I had done such a thing, reviewed Mowrer's book, Spence added accusingly, "And I hear you gave it a favorable review?" I in fact thought the book was important, although I had, naturally, been critical about some things; so feeling trapped and fighting for time, I asked Spence if he had actually read the review. He said he had not, and, breathing relief, I said I would send him a copy. Scene 2 is some months later at a spring meeting, and I asked Kenneth, "Did you read my review of Mowrer's book?" Yes, he had. "And did you think it was a favorable review?" He gave me one of his penetrating looks and said, "No, *I* didn't, but who but an Iowa graduate would have *known* it was not favorable?"

From an anonymous (at this point), but not apocryphal, graduate student in the education department in East Hall, I learned that working on a dissertation was no reason to frustrate one's wife. I actually did not learn it directly from this student; Clete Burke was, as I recall, the messenger. Like my own experience with the Viennese psychiatrist, Clete had been retained by this man to do the statistics on his dissertation for the doctorate in education, and showed Toby Oxtoby and me the acknowledgment this doctor of education had written. After thanking his major advisor, his committee, his subjects, Clete, and his typist, there was the ultimate note of gratitude. It went like this: "And finally, the greatest debt I owe is to my wife, Sally, who, even when my drive was low, persisted." You talk about a case history of frustration and persistence!

I now want to address the more serious side of my intellectual heritage as it relates to frustration. As I said earlier, it has two facets. The first is a brief selective account, with some emphasis on my years at Iowa, of how I came to study frustration, a topic that was the focus of most of my earlier work. The second facet of this heritage, and the one that has caused me great *personal* frustration, had to do with becoming (and stubbornly remaining) a disciple of Hull and Spence and the neobehavioristic tradition, as I am one of the very few left in this age of cognitive psychology. I could talk at some length about either one of these, but I have chosen instead to address both briefly. I deal first with my intellectual debts, and then with the question, "What has happened to learning theory?"

HOW I CAME TO STUDY FRUSTRATION

Let me make a confession here at Iowa, which for me is the St. Peter's Basilica, the Mecca, the Westminster Cathedral, the Western Wall of Learning Theory. I am here to make a clean breast of it. This is difficult to say, but here it is: I was *not* the first to study frustration. Not even the first in psychology. Not even the first in the context of learning theory. I take some pride in the fact, however, that I have *almost* always acknowledged my debt to the past. What I have borrowed I have tried to return with some interest—and this could have been the burden of the second part of this brief address, but I will not bore you with my curriculum vitae: This is not the place for that.

There were references to frustration, even in the literature on learning in animals, in the 1930s. For example, Spence (1936), in the first of his famous discrimination-learning papers, uses the term in relation to the action of the negative stimulus. In the same year, Miller and Stevenson (1936) came close when they referred to "agitated behavior" during extinction in a runway.

In 1939, Dollard, Doob, Miller, Mowrer, and Sears (with other collaborators) published *Frustration and Aggression,* a book that in its own way anticipated much of what came later at Iowa when, under Lewin and then Sears, frustration was studied in children on the top floor of East Hall through the 1940s.

In 1949, John Rohrer, an Iowa PhD, then at the University of Oklahoma, used the term *Frustration Drive* (FD) and was, I think, the first to suggest that Hull's I_R, "the inhibitory drive," as he called it, "[be] conceived as resulting from frustration rather than 'sheer reaction' " (p. 477). His experiment, however, simply showed that extinction was more rapid after massed than after spaced trials; there was no actual evidence for what he called Frustration Drive. In an earlier paper on extinction, which was a report of his dissertation work at Iowa, Rohrer (1947) did not refer to frustration or frustration drive, but favored Pavlovian internal inhibition over Guthrian interference-type theory.

In 1949, N. R. F. Maier wrote a book with the title, *Frustration: The Study of Behavior Without a Goal,* which summarized his work on "experimental neurosis." In a series of experiments, he used shocks and jets of air to force rats faced with an insoluble discrimination to make a choice response from a jumping stand. Maier's rats were obviously frustrated by this insoluble problem; however, the dramatic behaviors he observed were not effects of frustration. They were directly attributable to the high pitch of the air jet, audiogenic seizures studied by C. T. Morgan and others at about the same time (e.g., Morgan & Morgan, 1939).

In 1950, in his famous paper "Are Theories of Learning Necessary?" (of all places), Skinner used "the word": "When we fail to reinforce a response that has previously been reinforced . . . we set up an emotional response—perhaps what is often meant by frustration" (p. 203). And in Hull's last book (1952), there is reference to "frustration of an anticipation"—and, more formally, in Corollary 17: "[T]he abrupt cessation of a customary reinforcement will [result] . . . at first in a slight rise in reaction potential" (p. 134)—clearly a statement about what some of us were beginning to call the Frustration Effect, the result of *primary* frustration.

During my 2 years at Iowa, from 1946 to 1948, there was interest in the experimental study of frustration, both in the Psychology Department and upstairs in Child Welfare, as it was then called. (Where else would John Rohrer and I have gotten ours?) I cannot find it in my notes from those years, but I am sure there were references to frustration in Spence's courses and seminars on learning theory and motivation. As I recall, Spence's use of the term was the same as in his papers in the 1930s, in which, as in Rohrer's use of Frustration Drive, frustration referred to a factor in the inhibitory or extinctive aspects of behavior.

But the other usage, and the one that I found most prevalent at Iowa, was motivational—what Jud Brown, like Rohrer, called Frustration Drive. And in the years just after these, as some of you know, Brown and Farber (1951) were hatching a theory of frustration, in the context of a conceptualization of emotions as intervening variables. Frustration Drive, the energizing or drive property of frustration, was taken by Brown and Farber to emerge out of a number of interactions, including, in the case they worked out in most detail, the operations that define conflict.

In 1951, the year the Brown and Farber article appeared, I made my first foray into Frustration Theory in a paper at the meeting of the Southern Society for Philosophy and Psychology in Roanoke, Virginia. I did this in the context of Hull's theory, and as I look back on it now, I can see some similarity to Rohrer's

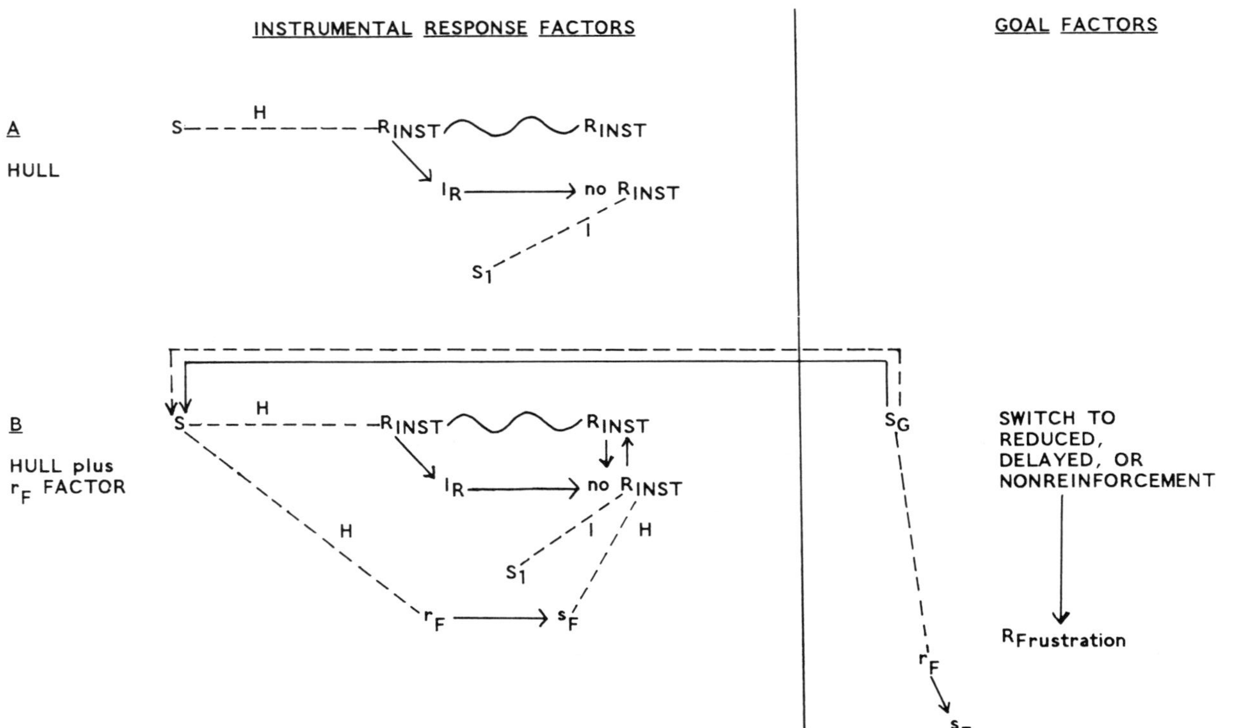

FIG. 11.1. *A*. Diagram of Hull's (1943) two-factor theory of inhibition. *B*. Diagram showing the proposed addition of a third factor, anticipatory frustration (r_F-s_F), to Hull's two-factor theory. Solid lines with arrows = unlearned connections; dashed lines = learned associations; wavy lines = continued responding; solid and dashed return lines from S_G to S = stimulus generalization and higher order conditioning, the mechanisms through which the conditioning of r_F to S_G (the CS) at the goal (on the basis of reduced, delayed, or nonreinforcement as the US, and $R_{Frustration}$ as the UR), moves forward in time so that r_F is evoked by S in the instrumental sequence. S_1 = version of S conditioned to not responding (S_1I_R). From Amsel (1951).

intent in his 1949 paper: Mine also was an attempt to revise Hull's theory of inhibition, not by conceptualizing I_R as FD in simple extinction, but by adding a third factor to Hull's two-factor theory of inhibition. The third factor, conditioned (anticipatory) frustration (r_F-s_F), was added to I_R and $_sI_R$: I called the paper "A Three-Factor Theory of Inhibition: An addition to Hull's Two-Factor Theory" (Amsel, 1951), and used the third factor to account for negative incentive contrast (Fig. 11.1).

After I had defined the conditioned response of frustration, it then seemed necessary to identify a corresponding unconditioned response (primary frustration), and this we began to do in the context of the double-runway *Frustration Effect*, a term, as it turned out, that had been employed by Marzocco (1950) in an unpublished dissertation at Iowa to define the invigorating effects of nonreward in a lever box, and which had been identified earlier by others (e.g., Finch, 1942), but without a specific motivational connotation.

I sent an expanded version of the SSPP paper to Iowa, where it sat around for a couple of years, then submitted it to the *Psychological Review,* where it was promptly rejected because the reviewer said he saw no point in "trying to patch up Hull." This discouraged me for a long time, but finally in the summer of 1957, while Bob Grice and I were at Lowry Air Force Base in Denver trying to find a way to be useful as "Visiting Scientists," I wrote a new version of the paper and submitted it to the *Bulletin.* It was accepted almost by return mail by one of the Associate Editors, Ben Underwood, who apparently had different feelings about "patching up Hull." It was published in 1958.

I promised not to go into what has happened in this work in the 30 years since 1958. Rather, more in the spirit of this occasion, I will end my remarks on the theme of "Learning theory then and now," or "What's frustrating about cognitive psychology?"[1] My text is taken from Robert Frost's "The Black Cottage":

> why abandon a belief
> Merely because it Ceases to be true.
> Cling to it long enough, and not a doubt
> It will turn true again, for so it goes.
> Most of the change we think we see in life
> Is due to truths being in and out of favor.

COGNITION IN HUMANS AND ANIMALS

When, some years ago, the "cognitive revolution" was already well underway, the lines that were drawn by the neo-cognitivists were between investigations

---

[1]Some of this material is adapted from *Behaviorism, Neobehaviorism, and Cognitivism in Learning Theory* (Amsel, 1989).

involving humans and animals as subjects. When the work involved people as laboratory subjects, psychologists were, of course, concerned with processes they regarded as primarily human: remembering and forgetting of verbal material (and later of visual and auditory material), processing of information, perception, imaging, simulation of human problem solving by computers, formation and identification of concepts, reading, and language; it is subjects such as these that still define human cognitive psychology. On the other hand, a number of eminent psychologists had for many years taken the experimental particulars from which they derived their theories from observation of, and experimentation with, non-human animals. Many if not most of these learning theorists were less interested in the cognitive and intellectual abilities of the animals they studied than in the more basic learning processes: Pavlovian conditioning and instrumental (Thorn-dikian) learning, and the motivational or need systems that supported them. In short, they were involved in the scientific investigation of the more primitive processes, ontogenetically as well as phylogenetically, and *in this sense* in the more simple—noncognitive, if you will—kinds of learning that operate *not only in animals but in people as well.* (In recent times, neuropsychologists like Wick-elgren, Weiskrantz, Mishkin, and Squire appear to have appreciated this kind of distinction.) Both Hull and Tolman, two of the leading learning theorists of the 1930s and 1940s, introduced into psychology theoretical systems that were concerned with the identification of the factors that contributed to the formation of habits and goal expectancies, and with the complementary motivational concepts of need, drive, and demand. Hull, for example, was a Darwinian, tremendously preoccupied with the mechanisms of adaptation and survival. Even in his most formal theorizing in *Principles of Behavior* (1943), there are several references to these concepts, and they form a dominant theme in his earlier seminal papers (see Amsel & Rashotte, 1984), and in his last book, *A Behavior System* (1952).

The next generation of learning theorists—H. F. Harlow, N. E. Miller, O. H. Mowrer, B. F. Skinner, K. W. Spence—carried on a tradition of experimental research and theory in which the aim was to understand the basic associative and motivational processes of humans by studying and understanding these same processes in lower animals. Or so, at least, it has seemed to me. True, Skinner's work with pigeons has given us a tremendous increase in our understanding of the ways of the pigeon; but obviously Skinner has been interested in pigeons more abstractly, as an animal model for the experimental analysis of behavior. Harlow's later work was primarily with monkeys, and this work has contributed greatly to the knowledge we have about the effects of rearing practices upon emotional-affectional systems of monkeys. But, clearly, this was not Harlow's only, or even primary, intention; the purpose of Harlow's work was to understand developmental influences on affectional (and other) systems in people.

As I suggested at about the time the cognitive revolution began, in the review of Mowrer's book to which I have referred (Amsel, 1961), one of the characteristics of most of the American learning theorists who had worked with animals in the preceding quarter century (or more) was that they had not been interested in animal behavior (or even animal cognition) in the way a naturalist is (they were in no real sense comparative psychologists); rather, they had been interested in these animals as "preparations" from which it might be possible to develop hypotheses about associative and motivational-emotional processes of mammals in general, and humans in particular. (They were interested in these animals in much the same way, for example, that Kandel and Alkon are interested in *Aplysia and Hermissenda* to study the molecular biology of learning and memory.) It is for this reason that the early applications of the study of anxiety, conflict, and frustration to psychopathology and the behavioral therapies did not come from research in human learning; they were, in fact, S–R analyses in the Hullian tradition, based on the work in animal learning (e.g., Amsel, 1958, 1971; Brown & Farber, 1951; Dollard et al., 1939; Dollard & Miller, 1950; Miller, 1944; Mowrer, 1939).

Up to about the late 1960s, it would have been fair to say that learning theorists who based their ideas on work with animals were at least as interested in the conative and affective aspects of behavior as in the cognitive aspect, *and they were (and are) seldom interested in the pigeon, rat, rabbit, or monkey.* They tended to be functionalist in outlook and to be influenced by Darwin, by Pavlov, and by Freud in their emphasis on adaptiveness, on motivation and reinforcement, and *on the nonintentional nature of an important part of learning and personality.* On the other hand, psychologists who were students of human learning and memory tended to be more fascinated by the associative-cognitive aspects of behavior, and showed little interest in the conative or affective. There seemed then to be within their ranks more of an even split between functionalist and structuralist outlook: The ones who studied *human verbal learning* (e.g., Postman, Underwood) were functionalists; those who studied memory (e.g., my colleagues from Toronto days, Mandler, Tulving) were structuralists and cognitivists, and among the great number and variety of their intellectual ancestors, Darwin, Pavlov, and Freud would not have been dominant figures.

Things have changed, thanks in part to quotes like the following from an eminent psychologist, recently (at that time) turned cognitivist, who has been coauthor with Hilgard of the most influential textbook in learning theory:

> [A] fundamental assumption of cognitive psychology [is] that the unit of behavior is the "purposive action" rather than the "colorless movement" or "glandular squirt" of yesterday's behaviorist. (Bower, 1975, p. 27)

It now seems obvious that the work in animal learning, which has been since Spence's day so much a part of Iowa's contribution to the science, has gone in two directions. One direction—Bower to the contrary notwithstanding—is away from the older conative and affective concerns; and, at the same time, from S–R associationism, behaviorism, and neobehaviorism, and toward what is called *in-*

formation processing, or more popularly, *animal cognition.* The second direction in which the work on animal learning has gone is toward behavioral neuroscience, so much of it based on Dore Gormezano's work with the rabbit conditioning preparation.

The animal cognitivists, particularly the lapsed Skinnerians, find *their* principal animal model in that receptacle for knowledge, the pigeon. I would make the point that, unlike Tolman, these neo-cognitivists now regard behavior simply as a vehicle for understanding thinking in animals. An aphorism I like to quote is from a Pavlovian cognitivist (Dickinson, 1979): "Behavior," he wrote, "is but a spade to disinter thought" (p. 553). Two of the interesting features of this animal cognitive position are that behavior per se is not seen to be important; and that, as in the work in human information processing and computer simulation, emotion and motivation are virtually ignored. The fathers of our troubled science, following more-or-less standard philosophical practice, were comfortable with a definition of psychology that included the cognitive, the affective, and the conative. In recent years it has seemed that, for many if not most psychologists, including the animal cognitivists, the definition includes only the cognitive.

For better or worse, a large part of the difference between the learning theory here at Iowa in my day, and the animal cognitivist approach to it now, was in the emphasis at Iowa on motivational-reinforcement factors in learned performance. And a large part of that was attention to the role of the generalized, activating component in motivation, which became important in the experiments at Iowa (e.g., Amsel, 1950; Kendler, 1945; Webb, 1949) on the combination of relevant and irrelevant need states. An example is that when a rat is running to escape cues that have been paired with shock and is also hungry, it will escape faster than if not hungry (Amsel, 1950), even though hunger is irrelevant in the situation. These effects of what Hull called the "alien" drive properties of need states, for example, seem to have no account in cognitive formulations.

And how can a cognitive psychology—of the animal or human variety— account for the fact that when a person is agitated by anxiety, he or she will eat more (or less)? Or, as in experiments like one Irv Maltzman and I performed here at Iowa, unbeknownst to Spence, the fact that when animals are shocked and in a state of residual emotionality, they will drink more water (Amsel & Maltzman, 1950; see also Siegel & Siegel, 1949) or eat more food (Siegel & Brantley, 1951)?

And, of course, somewhat later the same emphasis on generalized drive was applied to work in human eyeblink conditioning and complex learning, beginning with Janet Spence's dissertation and her Manifest Anxiety Scale (Taylor, 1951, 1953), that was followed by a body of work by Janet, Farber, Spence, and others (summarized in Spence, 1958; Taylor, 1956).

Brown's (1961) book, *The Motivation of Behavior,* is by far the single best treatment of this work, to which he and his students contributed so much. Together with Kimble's (1961) revision of the Hilgard and Marquis book that appeared in the same year, the fields of conditioning and learning, and motivation, were at that time integrated as they have not been since, in my opinion.

DECLINE OF THE CONATIVE AND AFFECTIVE

Five apparently unrelated theoretical influences contributed to the decline of the conative and the affective. The first was Hebb's rejection in 1949 of the drive concept in his book, *The Organization of Behavior,* in which the constantly active Hebbian cell, which is again so much in vogue in the nerve-networking theories, did not require a motivating force to put it into action. (The report, also in 1949, by Morruzi and Magoun of the discovery of the brain-stem reticular formation changed Hebb's thinking, and in 1955 he added a concept of drive [arousal] to what he called his "Conceptual Nervous System.") The second influence in the eclipse of the conative and affective was Skinner's concept of the operant, which required reinforcers, but of emitted rather than evoked behaviors. His paper "Are Theories of Learning Necessary?" (Skinner, 1950) relegated Hullian concepts like drive and need to a category Skinnerians liked to call "spooky."

(The term *frustration,* no matter how well defined, appears to be the spookiest of all, so far as Skinnerians and others are concerned. Fear produced by electric shock is okay [how many neuroses do you think have their origin in an electric shock?], but frustration-producing operations just do not make the scientific grade.)

Nowadays, for many of the newly liberalized Skinnerians, *consciousness* is not a problem, and they can accept that pigeons have *knowledge, metaknowledge,* and even *self-awareness* (e.g., Shimp, 1982)—but they do not like frustration. A recent visitor to my laboratory told me (as if I didn't know) that using the word *frustration* in a grant proposal is extremely hazardous. She also said she was told by a well-known Skinnerian that he never really knew what frustration meant until a grant of his was approved with a very good priority score—and was then not funded. Then he sort of got the idea.

Getting back to the factors that put the conative and affective into eclipse, the third one, again right around mid-century, was the influence of the statistical or stochastic learning theories of Estes (1950) and Bush and Mosteller (1951), which, by their very nature, could provide no accommodation for parameters representing motivation or emotion. Incidentally, the more recent, extremely influential mathematical model of conditioning of Rescorla and Wagner (1972), and even the extension of this model by Daly and Daly (1982) to include assumptions from frustration theory, have no place for these concepts either. It obviously occurred to Estes that this was a shortcoming of the statistical approach, because he later (Estes, 1958) attempted to introduce drive into his stimulus-sampling theory in the form of a separate population of stimulus elements. Unfortunately, so far as I am aware, this attempt remained an elegant exercise in theorizing.

The fourth and fifth factors in the decline of the conative and the affective came a decade later in the forms of the new field of psycholinguistics and the work of Hubel and Wiesel on receptive fields in vision.

Many would date the conception of psycholinguistics to Chomsky's (1959) review of Skinner's (1957) book, *Verbal Behavior,* the birth to G. A. Miller's (1962) paper on the psychological study of grammar, and the confirmation to Neisser's (1967) book, *Cognitive Psychology.* This new field of specialization, which became a powerful force in the new cognitive psychology, was and is no more generous in providing living space for concepts representing drive or affect.

Finally, Hubel and Wiesel's (1962) seminal paper, which characterized the elements of the visual receptive field as bars and edges, was taken as support for a rampaging cognitive structuralism which put further into eclipse the functionalist concepts of motivation and emotion. Here, beginning at mid-century, were five really quite different intellectual developments in psychology, each in its own way a rejection—sometimes active, sometimes passive—of the conative and the affective.

In the meantime, a psycholinguist, a mathematical learning theorist, and a neuropsychologist had combined their efforts to write *Plans and the Structure of Behavior* (Miller, Galanter, & Pribram, 1960), a book and a position that grew in influence from rather modest beginnings: As some of you remember, the joke at the time was, Miller thought of it, Galanter wrote it, and Pribram believed it. Nevertheless, it grew to become a rallying point for the new structuralism, which became the hallmark of the cognitive government of psychology in the following years. Cognitivism found another important ally in the unfeeling and unmotivated but all-knowing computer, and in the emerging field of artificial intelligence. (It may be of some interest, that this latter field, which started off so structural and so cognitive, now has among its adherents a group that calls itself "connectionists," surely a more functionalist, Thorndikian designation.) As was written in a review of a recent book on the cognitive revolution in psychology:

> It has been said that cognitive psychology is a disguised S–R formulation with some fancy talk between the S and R. And should the author believe that the history of psychology is linear I would point out that there is discussion again of connectionism among cognitive psychologists, reminiscent of the associationism of behaviorism. (Levin, 1987, p. 1684)

COGNITIVISTS DISCOVER LEARNING-PERFORMANCE DISTINCTION

Some of the more doctrinaire animal cognitivists have recently rediscovered the distinction between learning and performance that was so prominent in Hull–Spence theory and, of course, in Tolman's theory. (The learning-performance distinction seems most basic in Hull–Spence theory in the fundamental assumption of $E = H \times D$, because reducing drive may lower E, and therefore behavior, below threshold.) One such rediscovery is in Dickinson's (1980) concept of "behavioral silence." It is the position of this spokesman for animal cognitivism (or Pavlovian cognitivism, as I have called it; Amsel, 1989) that only the cognitivist "learning theorists," and not the neobehaviorist "behavior analysts" (he put Hull and Mowrer in this category), accept that there can be learning without its being revealed in performance. I am sure Jud Brown, Ray Denny, the McAllisters, and other possible exemplars in the room of this latter class of theorists, will be surprised to hear that being behavior analysts (rather than learning theorists), they would never refer to the effects of electric shock as producing fear. They would simply, to quote Dickinson, say the animal "freezes." And, presumably when shock is terminated, they would never refer to "relief" or "relaxation." Only learning theorists (a.k.a. animal cognitivists) use words like those.

Getting back to "behavioral silence," I am sure it is obvious to those of us with Iowa backgrounds, if not to the animal cognitivists, that it was a feature some 50 years ago in Spence's (1940) work, and 40 years ago in Grice's (1948) and Ehrenfreund's (1948) work on continuity in discrimination learning, and 25 or 30 years ago in my own work on resistance to discrimination (Amsel, 1962; Amsel & Ward, 1965). The issue in discrimination learning that separated the S–R and cognitive positions of those times was whether there is "behaviorally silent" learning in the "presolution phase," which you cannot hear until you reverse the discrimination. In those days it was the "behavior analysts" who believed in behavioral science, and not the cognitivists.

PARADIGM SHIFT

So, in the words of Frost's poem, "Cling to it long enough . . . [and] it will turn true again." I have taken all of this as an example of my favorite physical metaphor for the evolution of theory in psychology (Amsel, 1989), or in any other not-so-highly advanced science: I have thought of it as a two-dimensional expanding spiral (Fig. 11.2), a point that moves around a fixed center at increasing distance from that center, coming back to the same spatial orientation each time at an added distance from its origin. The distance—the "facts"—accumulate, but the organizing, orienting principles—the *models*, the *paradigms*—are few, and we periodically come back to those we have previously abandoned. Because nobody can say when we will be out of this epistemological spiral, I have suggested that the metaphor could be three-dimensional, a conical helix (Fig. 11.3), and we could at least think of the third dimension as representing progress.

We learning theorists have been influenced too much by Thomas S. Kuhn's (1962) concept of "paradigm shift." As I see it, the paradigm shift psychologists

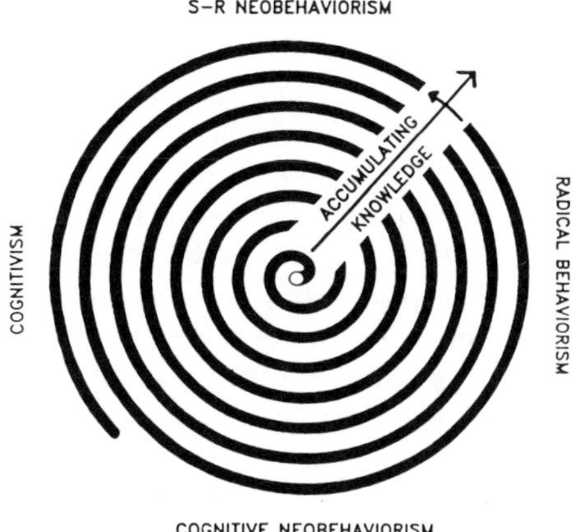

FIG. 11.2.   The expanding spiral. A metaphor for accumulating knowledge and changing meta-theoretical positions. From Amsel (1989).

got involved in was based, not on any specific identifiable theoretical anomaly, but on a kind of redefinition of psychology, stemming from some general dissatisfaction with the existing definition. The new definition of psychology, like a *much* older one, was as the science of the mind; the supplanted definition was as the science of behavior. The animal cognitivists, who recognized a paradigm shift when they saw one, adopted the language and the models of human cognitive psychology and information processing. Consequently, instead of using animals as models for human function, they were interpreting animal behavior in terms of their own introspections and inferring the "animal mind," much as the artificial intelligence people do so elegantly with computers: They were using humans as models for animal cognition. This use of humans as models for animals can happen *only in psychology!*

A couple of years ago, when we were out at the Center for Advanced Study in

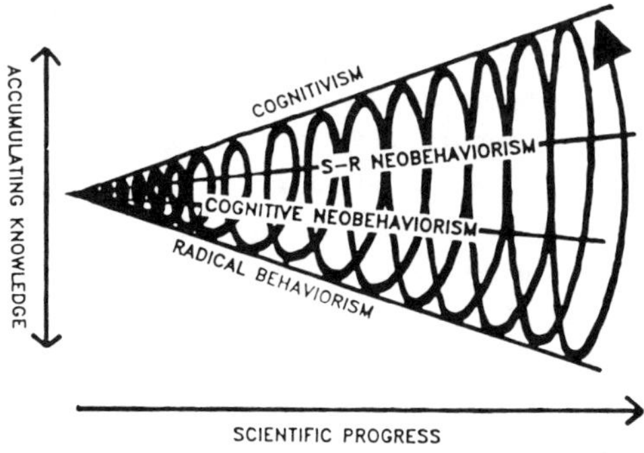

FIG. 11.3.   The conical helix, reflecting the dimension of scientific progress. From Amsel (1989).

the Behavioral Sciences at Stanford, Tess kept hearing the word "paradigm" used a lot by my fellow Fellows in the social and behavioral sciences, and she looked it up in a dictionary. She found that paradigm was preceded in this dictionary by the word "paradiddle," and that paradiddle is defined as the pattern of a drumbeat, whereas paradigm is defined simply as a pattern, and also in most dictionaries, as a model or example. (The words have rather similar meanings, but just imagine having to base a metatheoretical position on the word "paradiddle.") Actually, in most cases of its use in the behavioral sciences, the facile use of "paradigm" does become a drumbeat—a double or even a triple paradiddle, in the words of a song of my youth—to which, happily, we march along thinking we know where we are going. We should be more selective about when, in our march along the expanding spiral or even the conical helix of my metaphor, a perceived change in direction is dignified with the term paradigm, in Kuhn's sense, lest we find ourselves benumbed and bemused by paradiddles. A paradigm shift, if you accept Kuhn's position, based mostly on three or four centuries of the physical sciences, is some major, usually irreversible, change in guiding principles and methods that occurs after a long period of intense accumulation and consolidation of scientific results. There are those who regard the use of the concept of paradigm in psychology, for example to describe the philosophical differences between neobehaviorists and cognitivists, as a bit of an affectation: It's like the story about the man who got rich, bought a yacht, and arrived at his Jewish mother's house for dinner wearing his nautical garb. "Look at me, Ma," he says, "I'm a captain!" To which his doting but worldly wise mother replies, "By you, you're a captain, and by me, you can also be a captain—but by captains, you're no captain."

CONCLUSION

As I pointed out earlier, the "new look" which uses behavior to understand the mind is not in the old Tolmanian style, which was the other way around: He used mentalistic-sounding constructs to try to understand behavior. Tolman's was actually not that different from the style of Hull and the Hullian neobehaviorists. Hull hid any possible "cognitive" proclivities by conceptualizing as *habit* terms such as purpose and anticipation—whereas Tolman's signification and expectation stood as they were. I observed some time ago (Amsel, 1962) that the basic difference between most of Tolman and a large part of Hull (particularly in Hull's theoretical papers, see Amsel and Rashotte, 1984) was a difference between a cognitive-expectancy and a conditioning-expectancy language. But, as you all know, both of these systems, Tolman's and Hull's, were behaviorisms, though one was cognitive and the other S–R. It is a fundamental and almost universal confusion nowadays that behaviorism and S–R are taken to be synonyms. What needs to be understood is that behaviorism (or neobehaviorism) is a definition of psychology; S–R, like Tolman's cognitivism, is an approach to theorizing. It is important to understand, as many of us here do, that a theory is an S–R theory, not because, as some cognitivists insist, it relates the antecedent observable S to the consequent palpable R (even the "muscular twitches" and "glandular squirts"): Everyone, even cognitivists, uses the terms *stimulus* and *response* in this way. A theory is an S–R theory because, just as cognitive theorists choose to use mental-sounding explanatory constructs, S–R theorists choose more physio-logical-sounding terms and use Ss and Rs to represent the afferent and efferent— and even the central—mediating machinery. A psychology defined as the science of the mind, rather than as a science of behavior, could in principle be developed on the basis of mind represented by Ss and Rs, in the same way that Tolman's behaviorism was developed on the basis of mentalistic constructs, such as cognitions, demands, and sign-Gestalt-expectations.

Well, now that I have unburdened myself to an audience I suppose is as sympathetic as one could find nowadays, I feel a great relief from the frustrations I attribute to what I learned at Iowa—I sure hope it lasts.

REFERENCES

Amsel, A. (1950). The combination of a primary appetitional need with primary and secondary emotionally derived needs. *Journal of Experimental Psychology, 40,* 1–14.

Amsel, A. (1951). *A three-factor theory of inhibition: An addition to Hulls two-factor theory.* Paper delivered at Southern Society for Philosophy and Psychology Meetings, Roanoke, VA.

Amsel, A. (1958). The role of frustrative nonreward in noncontinuous reward situations. *Psychological Bulletin, 55,* 102–119.

Amsel, A. (1961). Hope comes to learning theory [Review of O. H. Mowrer's *Learning theory and behavior*]. *Contemporary Psychology, 6,* 33–36.

Amsel, A. (1962). Frustrative nonreward in partial reinforcement and discrimination learning: Some recent history and a theoretical extension. *Psychological Review, 69,* 306–328.

Amsel, A. (1971). Frustration, persistence, and regression. In H. D. Kimmel (Ed.), *Experimental psychopathology: Recent research and theory* (pp. 51–69). New York: Academic Press.

Amsel, A. (1989). *Behaviorism, neobehaviorism, and cognitivism in learning theory: Historical and contemporary perspectives.* Hillsdale, NJ: Lawrence Erlbaum Associates.

Amsel, A., & Maltzman, I. (1950). The effect upon generalized drive strength of emotionality as inferred from the level of consummatory response. *Journal of Experimental Psychology, 40,* 563–569.

Amsel, A., & Rashotte, M. E. (1984). *Mechanisms of adaptive behavior: Clark L. Hull's theoretical papers, with commentary.* New York: Columbia University Press.

Amsel, A., & Ward, J. S. (1965). Frustration and persistence: Resistance to discrimination following prior experience with the discriminanda. *Psychological Monographs, 79*(4, Whole No. 597).

Bower, G. H. (1975). Cognitive psychology: An introduction. In W. K. Estes (Ed.), *Handbook of learning and cognitive processes: Volume 1. Introduction to concepts and issues* (pp. 25–80). Hillsdale, New Jersey: Lawrence Erlbaum Associates.

Brown, J. S. (1961). *The motivation of behavior.* New York: McGraw-Hill.

Brown, J. S., & Farber, I. E. (1951). Emotions conceptualized as intervening variables–with suggestions toward a theory of frustration. *Psychological Bulletin, 48,* 465–495.

Bush, R. R., & Mosteller, F. (1951). A mathematical model for simple learning. *Psychological Review, 58,* 313–323.

Chomsky, N. (1959). A review of B. F. Skinner's *Verbal Behavior. Language, 35,* 26–58.

Daly, H. B., & Daly, J. T. (1982). A mathematical model of reward and aversive nonreward: Its application in over 30 appetitive learning situations. *Journal of Experimental Psychology: General, 111,* 441–480.

Dickinson, A. (1979). Review of S. H. Hulse, H. Fowler, & W. K. Honig (Eds.), "Cognitive processes in animal behavior." *Quarterly Journal of Experimental Psychology, 31,* 551–554.

Dickinson, A. (1980). *Contemporary animal learning theory.* Cambridge: Cambridge University Press.

Dollard, J., Doob, L. W., Miller, N. E., Mowrer, O. H., & Sears, R. R. (1939). *Frustration and aggression.* New York: Yale University Press.

Dollard, J., & Miller, N. E. (1950). *Personality and psychotherapy.* New York: McGraw-Hill.

Ehrenfreund, D. (1948). An experimental test of the continuity theory of discrimination learning with pattern vision. *Journal of Comparative and Physiological Psychology, 41,* 408–422.

Estes, W. K. (1950). Toward a statistical theory of learning. *Psychological Review, 57,* 94–107.

Estes, W. K. (1958). Stimulus-response theory of drive. In M. R. Jones (Ed.), *Nebraska symposium on motivation* (Vol. 6; pp. 35–69). Lincoln: University of Nebraska Press.

Finch, G. (1942). Chimpanzee frustration responses. *Psychosomatic Medicine, 4,* 233–251.

Grice, G. R. (1948). The acquisition of a visual discrimination habit following response to a single stimulus. *Journal of Experimental Psychology, 38,* 633–642.

Hebb, D. O. (1949). *The organization of behavior.* New York: Wiley.

Hebb, D. O. (1955). Drives and the CNS (conceptual nervous system). *Psychological Review, 62,* 243–254.

Hubel, D. H., & Wiesel, T. N. (1962). Receptive fields, binocular interaction and functional architecture in the cat's visual cortex. *Journal of Physiology, 160,* 106–154.

Hull, C. L. (1943). *Principles of behavior.* New York: Appleton–Century–Crofts.

Hull, C. L. (1952). *A behavior system.* New Haven: Yale University Press.

Kendler, H. H. (1945). Drive interaction: I. Learning as a function of the simultaneous presence of the hunger and thirst drives. *Journal of Experimental Psychology, 35,* 96–109.

Kimble, G. A. (1961). *Hilgard and Marquis' conditioning and learning.* New York: Appleton–Century–Crofts.

Kuhn, T. S. (1962). *The structure of scientific revolutions.* Chicago: University of Chicago Press.

Levin, H. (1987). Successions in psychology. [A review of B. J. Baars, *The Cognitive Revolution in Psychology*]. *Science, 236,* 1683–1684.

Maier, N. R. F. (1949). *Frustration: The study of behavior without a goal.* New York: McGraw–Hill.

Marzocco, F. N. (1950). *Frustration effect as a function of drive level, habit strength and distribution of trials during extinction.* Unpublished doctoral dissertation, University of Iowa, Iowa City, IA.

Miller, G. A. (1962). Some psychological studies of grammar. *American Psychologist, 17,* 748–762.

Miller, G. A., Galanter, E., & Pribram, K. H. (1960). *Plans and the structure of behavior.* New York: Holt.

Miller, N. E. (1944). Experimental studies of conflict. In J. McV. Hunt (Ed.), *Personality and the behavior disorders* (Vol. 1, pp. 431–465). New York: Ronald.

Miller, N. E., & Stevenson, S. S. (1936). Agitated behavior of rats during experimental extinction and a curve of spontaneous recovery. *Journal of Comparative Psychology, 21,* 205–231.

Morgan, C. T., & Morgan, J. D. (1939). Auditory induction of an abnormal pattern of behavior in rats. *Journal of Comparative Psychology, 27,* 505–508.

Morruzi, G., & Magoun, H. W. (1949). Brain stem reticular formation and activation of the EEG. *Electroencephalography and Clinical Neurophysiology, 1,* 455–473.

Mowrer, O. H. (1939). A stimulus-response analysis of anxiety and its role as a reinforcing agent. *Psychological Review, 46,* 553–565.

Mowrer, O. H. (1960). *Learning theory and behavior.* New York: Wiley.

Neisser, U. (1967). *Cognitive psychology.* New York: Appleton–Century–Crofts.

Rescorla, R. A., & Wagner, A. R. (1972). A theory of Pavlovian conditioning: Variations in the effectiveness of reinforcement and nonreinforcement. In A. H. Black & W. F. Prokasy (Eds.), *Classical conditioning II: Current theory and research* (pp. 64–99). New York: Appleton–Century–Crofts.

Rohrer, J. H. (1947). Experimental extinction as a function of the distribution of extinction trials and response strength. *Journal of Experimental Psychology, 37,* 473–493.

Rohrer, J. H. (1949). A motivational state resulting from nonreward. *Journal of Comparative and Physiological Psychology, 42,* 476–485.

Shimp, C. P. (1982). Metaknowledge in the pigeon: An organism's knowledge about its own adaptive behavior. *Animal Learning & Behavior, 10,* 358–364.

Siegel, P. S., & Brantley, J. J. (1951). The relationship of emotionality to the consummatory response of eating. *Journal of Experimental Psychology, 42,* 304–306.

Siegel, P. S., & Siegel, H. S. (1949). The effect of emotionality on the water intake of the rat. *Journal of Comparative and Physiological Psychology, 42,* 12–16.

Skinner, B. F. (1950). Are theories of learning necessary? *Psychological Review, 57,* 193–216.

Skinner, B. F. (1957). *Verbal behavior.* New York: Appleton–Century–Crofts.

Spence, K. W. (1936). The nature of discrimination learning in animals. *Psychological Review, 43,* 427–449.

Spence, K. W. (1940). Continuous versus non-continuous interpretations of discrimination learning. *Psychological Review, 47,* 271–288.

Spence, K. W. (1958). A theory of emotionally based drive (D) and its relation to performance in simple learning situations. *American Psychologist, 13,* 131–141.

Taylor, J. A. (1951). The relationship of anxiety to the conditioned eyelid response. *Journal of Experimental Psychology, 41,* 81–92.

Taylor, J. A. (1953). A personality scale of manifest anxiety. *Journal of Abnormal and Social Psychology, 48,* 285–290.

Taylor, J. A. (1956). Drive theory and manifest anxiety. *Psychological Bulletin, 53,* 303–320.

Webb, W. B. (1949). The motivational aspect of an irrelevant drive in the behavior of the white rat. *Journal of Experimental Psychology, 39,* 1–14.

Subject Index